High Level Synthesis of Digital Systems

For Data Path and Control dominated systems

SAMARY BARANOV

ISBN-13: 978-1-7750917-1-4

DEDICATION

I dedicate this book to the bright memory of my parents

ACKNOWLEDGMENTS

Many of my students have made a great contribution to the programming of algorithms presented in this book. First, I want to thank Yury Dorfman and Roman Boguslavsky, as well as Yury Maramzin and Sergei Sheviakov whom I taught and studied with them.

Introduction

The tremendous achievements in chip technology allow to produce chips with hundreds million gates. At the same time, the design technology of such circuits only slightly improved in the last ten years, especially at the highest system level. The traditional digital system design flow contains the manual creation of system description at the Register Transfer Level (hereafter RTL) with Verilog or VHDL code. As a result, the time-to-market has increased three to four times for such complex digital chips. The only possibility to reduce a gap between future technological capability and the lagging designer productivity is to raise the design from the current RTL to the algorithmic or behavior level i.e. to High Level Synthesis (HLS). For that it is necessary to solve several problems:

1. Develop models for describing systems at the high level;
2. Develop tools based on these models;
3. Develop a design methodology based on these models and tools.

These three components should form a technology for designing complex systems on chips, including

a. Description of the behavior of digital systems at a high level;
b. Verification of systems at the high level;
c. Automatic transition from the high level to the low level (RTL).

For several years I looked carefully at the papers about HLS. Here you will find some remarks from these papers. They are not my own remarks. Maybe designers of HLS tools or some specialists using HLS will confirm or disclaim these remarks with corresponding examples.

1. The existing HLS tools are useful only for special types of design systems, mainly for data path dominated systems.
2. The handwork is necessary at the transition from the high level to RTL;
3. If there are some problems with timing, then a designer should fix them by hand;
4. Connections between elements of Data path (buses or direct connections) should be defined at the high level;
5. Splitting of registers should be defined at the high level;
6. Design of FSM (Control unit) requires manual rework at RTL;
7. Difficult to use IP cores automatically at the high level and RTL;
8. Test benches, used for simulation at the high level, cannot be used at RTL without manual rework;
9. Specifications at RTL needs handwork;
10. If a designer must change something after simulation at RTL (even if the design is correct but there are problems with speed, area or power), it is difficult to come back to the high level to improve the design;
11. In the case of problems mentioned in point 10, a designer can fix them only at RTL;
12. It is difficult to master a design methodology of HLS for hardware designers;
13. A designer makes better designs beginning from RTL;
14. It is difficult to understand a design at RTL constructed automatically from the high level.

In my opinion, the problems of existing HLS tools were best revealed in the Braian Beiley's article "ESL Flow Is Dead" (http://semiengineering.com/esl-flow-is-dead/).

My book is about HLS. However, the models and methods presented in this book are fundamentally different from those used in the known industrial and academic instruments. My models and methods do not use the descriptions of digital systems in C-similar languages. In this book I use Algorithmic State Machines (hereafter ASMs) at all stages of high level and RTL designs.

Most ideas from this book were realized in HLS tool Synthagate – the product of Synthezza Company. I used it to construct all examples in this book. *Synthagate* is a tool for design of Control and Data Path Intensive Systems with very complex Control Units containing numerous inputs and outputs. Synthagate performs full automatic synthesis of digital systems from behavior specification to description in HDL at RTL and allows the user to quickly implement, check and estimate multiple design versions, to find an optimized solution for the design problems, to produce automatically the design documentation and to simplify the digital system verification problems.

The design flow in Synthagate is presented in Fig. 1. This flow contains two large automatic stages – High Level Synthesis (HLS) and Register Transfer Level (RTL).

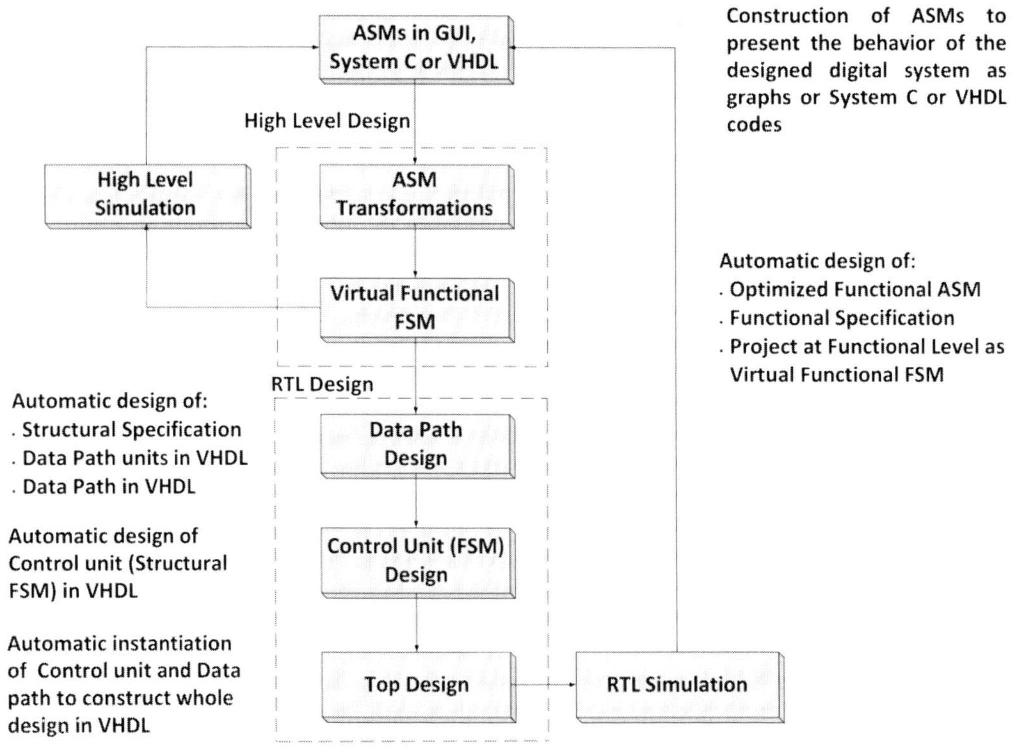

Figure 1. Design Flow in Synthagate

Algorithmic state machines are used in Synthagate as an input to describe the behavior of digital systems. ASMs can be presented as:

- A graph, drawn with GUI (ASM Creator) – the special Synthagate graphical editor;
- A text in pseudo codes of System C or VHDL.

ASM transformations. ASM models and their transformations are used in Synthagate at all stages of behavioral (HLS) and structural (RTL) synthesis. Synthagate is the only tool that implements various transformations of initial behaviors:

- *ASM minimization.* A designer shouldn't think about minimization of an initial description – Synthagate automatically minimizes the number of vertices in the ASM graph.
- *ASM combining.* If a digital system behavior is rather complex but contains several modes (instructions), Synthagate will combine them into one ASM with minimization of operator and conditional vertices. There are no constraints on the number of separate ASMs to combine.
- *Sub ASM insertion.* At the last step of ASM transformations Synthagate inserts all component ASMs (generalized operators) and constructs one combined and minimized Functional ASM without generalized operators. This ASM presents a whole behavior of the design system. The same steps take place when a designer initially presents ASMs in System C or VHDL.

Functional Specifications. To design the behavior description of a digital system the designer should not define each port or signal. Synthagate creates an XML code of the functional specification and the designer should only insert the length of several ports and signals (not all, only a very small part of them) in the dialog mode.

Behavior description of the design system. With Functional ASM and functional specification as an input, Synthagate automatically constructs the behavior (High Level) description of the whole design system in *VHDL* or in *System C.* After preparing the test bench at the behavior level the designer can simulate the functional project with any simulation tool. The same test bench can be used later at the last stage of design – after top design at the structural (RTL) level. For simulation at the High Level the designer can use design of the system in *VHDL* or in *System C.*

Data path design. In Data path design Synthagate uses external specification in XML constructed automatically.

Automatic generation of components. Synthagate automatically generates VHDL codes for components of Data Path. If a designer would like to use some predesigned IP cores, he must put their RTL codes in the special folder before the design at the High level. Later these components will be included in the library of automatically generated units.

Generation VHDL code for Data Path. At the last step of Data Path design Synthagate automatically instantiates components in the Data Path.

Control Unit design. Synthagate automatically creates the RTL code of Control unit. Its input signals are feedbacks from the Data path and some input signals of the digital system, its outputs are micro operations implemented in the Data path and some output signals of the digital system.

Top design. At the last stage, Synthagate creates the code for the top level automatically by instantiating Control Unit and Data Path into the top of the project.

What makes Synthagate different

- *Synthagate* does not require learning a new design language. In two to three days, a designer can begin to use Synthagate to describe system behaviors at the high level.
- *Synthagate* is the only HLS tool to design Control Intensive and Data Path Systems with very complex Control Units containing numerous inputs and outputs. It works with hierarchical designs at the functional and structural levels.
- *Synthagate* is the only tool to implement various transformations of initial behavior – Algorithmic State Machines (ASMs):
    - ASM minimization,
    - ASM combining,
    - ASM inclusion etc.
- *Synthagate* automatically minimizes the number of vertices in initial ASMs, which reduces chip area. The designer does not need to think about the minimization of the initial behaviors.
- Using different generalized operators (subASMs), a designer can quickly design and check different architectures by time and/or area.
- *Synthagate* automatically creates direct and indirect connections (buses) between units using procedures that optimize not only the Data path (its area and speed), but also the Control unit constructed at the following design stages.
- In most Systems-on-Chip (SoCs), a Control unit is an irregular multi-level and multi-output circuit in which delay of connectors between gates may be a lot more than a delay of gates themselves. *Synthagate* can construct optimized multi-matrix regular FSM's circuits while minimizing the area and increasing the speed. This is especially important for SoCs.
- *Synthagate* allows the immediate use any IP cores designed by other companies.
- In the process of design *Synthagate* creates a lot of documents corresponding to each design stage. These documents can be used to prepare the project documentation. In the case of some designer's mistakes at the initial stages of the project, these documents allow to return quickly to the previous design stages and fix possible problems.

I'm sure that my approach to design systems may be rejected by various specialists. Moreover, I am ready for fierce criticism. Nevertheless, my goal in this book is to show that the design methodology, described here and the tool built on the basis of this methodology, will allow the design of very complex Data Path and Control dominated systems with tens and hundreds of input and output signals.

Before you start, go to www.synthezza.com/hls-figures-and-tables to download the PDF file (HLS-Figures-and-Tables.pdf) with all the examples, figures and tables used in this book.

While you're there, you can find the ASMCreator Short Manual: www.synthezza.com/asm-creator-short-manual and download the free *ASMCreator* tool. ASM Creator is a part of the EDA tool Synthagate for High level and Logic synthesis of digital systems, with which it is possible to draw the Algorithmic State Machine (ASM) and build its internal representation for HLS and RTL tool *Synthagate*.

Tables of Contents

Table of Figures

Chapter 4. CASE STUDY. EXAMPLES FROM THE BOOK OF ENOCH HWANG

Chapter 5. CASE STUDY. DESIGN of CODEC

Chapter 6. CASE STUDY. DESIGN of ROBOT

Table of Table

1 ALGORITHMIC STATE MACHINES

In this Chapter, I define Algorithmic State Machines (ASMs), give examples of ASMs and describe how to present sequential processes with ASMs. Then I discuss how to use ASMs to design Finite State Machines with hardly any constrains on their size – namely the number of inputs, outputs and states. To present FSM I use special FSM transition tables, which allow us to define FSM with a very large number of input and output variables. For more information about FSM synthesis I advise to apply to my book "Finite State Machines and Algorithmic State Machines".

1.1 Introduction to Algorithmic state machines

1.1.1 Example of ASM

An Algorithmic state machine is the directed connected graph containing an initial vertex (Begin), a final vertex (End) and a finite set of operator and conditional vertices (Fig. 1). The final, operator and conditional vertices have only one input, the initial vertex has no input. Initial and operator vertices have only one output, a conditional vertex has two outputs marked by "1" and "0". A final vertex has no outputs.

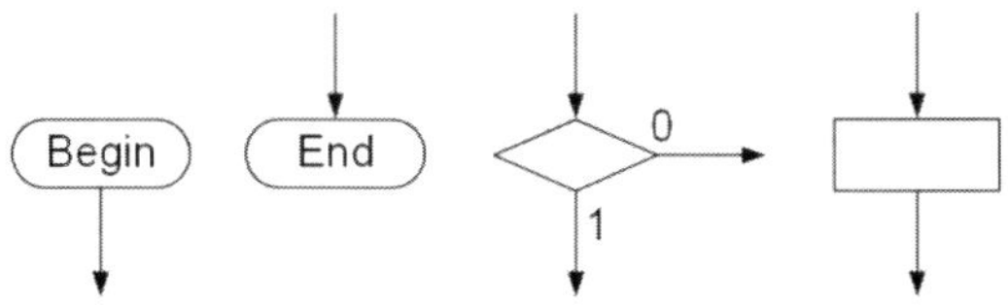

Figure 1. Vertices of Algorithmic state machine

As the first example, let us consider one mode Escape of a mobile robot (Fig. 2). Logical condition Start is used as a turn-on button. Move := 1 is a signal to turn-on a motor to move.

This ASM can be used for different robots with different time for turn and move back. The external signals (t_turn and t_back) should be saved in two registers – Rt_turn and Rt_back. If robot hits obstacle by right bumper, it should turn left during time written in register Rt_turn. The same, if the robot hits obstacle by left bumper it should turn right. If the robot hits obstacle by front bumper it should move back during the time written in register Rt_back and turn right. After that it continues its driving.

In ASM, a logical condition is written in each conditional vertex. It is possible to write the same logical condition in different conditional vertices. A microinstruction (an operator), containing one, two, three or more microoperations, is written in each operator vertex of ASM. It is possible to write the same operator in different operator vertices.

Sometimes we use ASM in which logical conditions and microoperations are replaced by x_1, x_2, ... and y_1, y_2, ... and their operators are replaced by operators Y_1, Y_2,... . Such ASM for ASM in Fig. 2 is shown in Fig. 3.

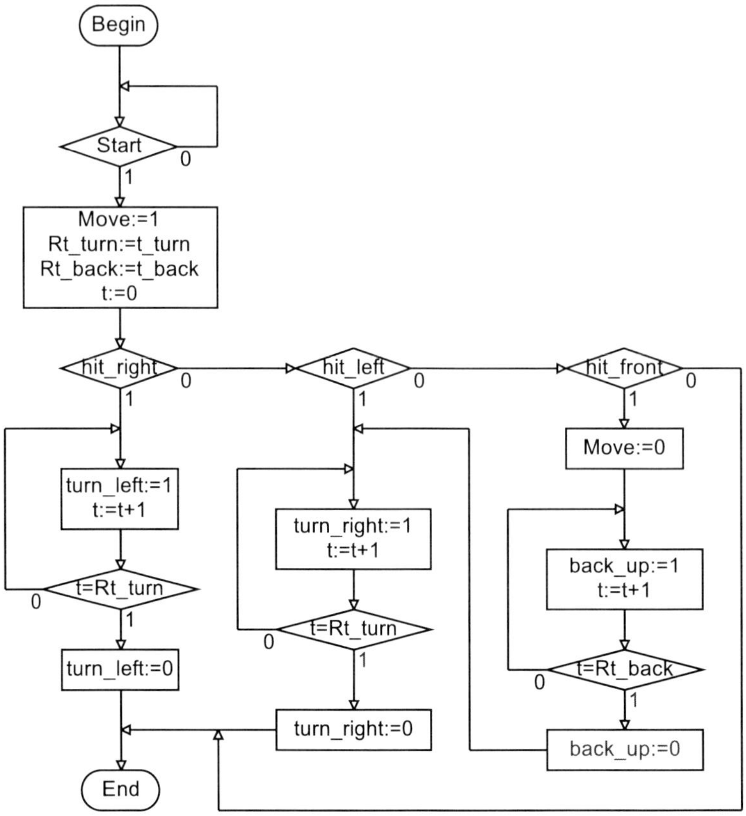

Figure 2. A mode Escape of a mobile robot

ASM vertices are connected in such a way that:

- Inputs and outputs of the vertices are connected by arcs directed from an output to an input, each output is connected to only one input;
- Each input is connected to at least one output;
- Each vertex is located on at least one of the paths from vertex "*Begin*" to vertex "*End*".
- One of the outputs of a conditional vertex can be connected to its input. I will call such conditional vertices the "*waiting vertices*", since they simulate the waiting process in the system behavior description.

1.1.2 Transition functions

In this section, we will look at the paths between operator vertices passing only through conditional vertices. In such a path, we use x_i if the path proceeds from the conditional vertex with x_i via output *'1'*, and $\sim x_i$, if the path proceeds from the conditional vertex with x_i via output *'0'*. In this book I use x_i' and $\sim x_i$ for the negation of x_i. For example, we have the following paths from *Y1* in ASM in Fig. 3:

Y1x6Y8;
Y1~x6x4Y6;
Y1~x6~x4x3Y3;
Y1~x6~x4~x3Ye.

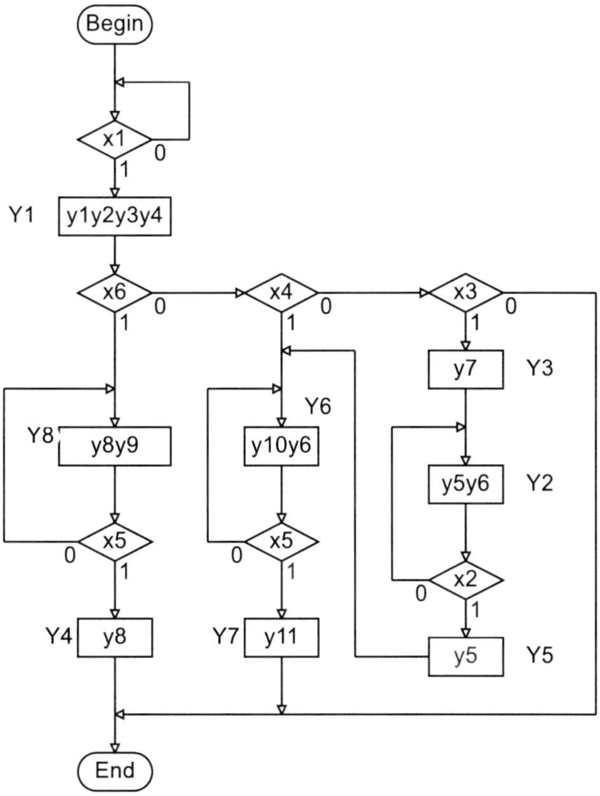

Figure 3. The same ASM with replaced operators and logical conditions

Let *p(Yi,Yj)* be a product of variables in such a path from operator vertex Y_i to operator vertex Y_j. Then, in our example

p(Y1,Y8) = *x6;*

p(Y1,Y6) = *~x6x4;*

p(Y1,Y3) = *~x6~x4x3;*

p(Y1,Ye) = *~x6~x4~x3.*

If there exist several paths between *Yi* and *Yj* through the conditional vertices, then we use the sum of products corresponding to each such a path. Note that for the path *Y3Y2* (operator *Y2* follows operator *Y3* immediately without conditional vertices), *p(Y3,Y2)* = *1*, as the product of an empty set of variables is equal to one. We call *p(Yi,Yj)* a *transition function between operators Yi* and *Yj*.

1.1.3 Time in Algorithmic State Machines

To describe time in ASM let's look at ASM in Fig. 3. Each operator can contain one, two, three etc. microoperations written in the same operator vertex. These microoperations are implemented simultaneously at the same clock.

Two sequential operators, as *Y3* and *Y2* in Fig. 3, are implemented at two sequential clocks. Two operators with any number of conditional vertices between them, as *Y1* and *Y3* in Fig. 3, are implemented at two sequential clocks.

I would like to remind you that ASM, as a Finite State Machine, is a sequential model. To describe parallel processes, we must draw several ASMs. At Fig. 4, I have shown three fragments of parallel working ASMs, dots there present some sequences of vertices.

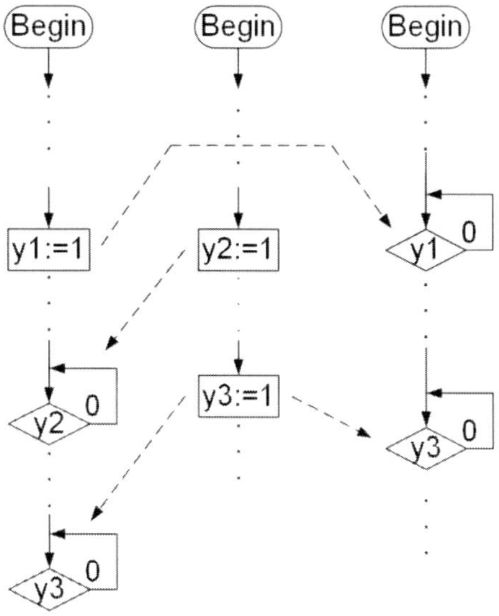

Figure 4. Three pipeline processes

The interaction between these processes is implemented by signals (microoperation). In this example, three processes begin to work simultaneously but at some time the right one stops and waits signal *y1=1* from the left process. Only then it will continue to work. In the same manner, at some stage the left process stops and waits signal *y2=1* from the center one. Three processes continue to work but at some time the left and the right processes are waiting signal *y3=1* from the center process etc.

1.1.4 Value of ASM at the sequence of vectors

One more example of ASM is shown on Fig. 5. This ASM *G1* has seven logical conditions *x1, ..., x7* and ten microoperations *y1, ..., y10*. Thus, it describes the digital system with seven input variables and ten output variables. Each input of this system is a 7-component vector, each its output is 10-component vector (Fig. 6).

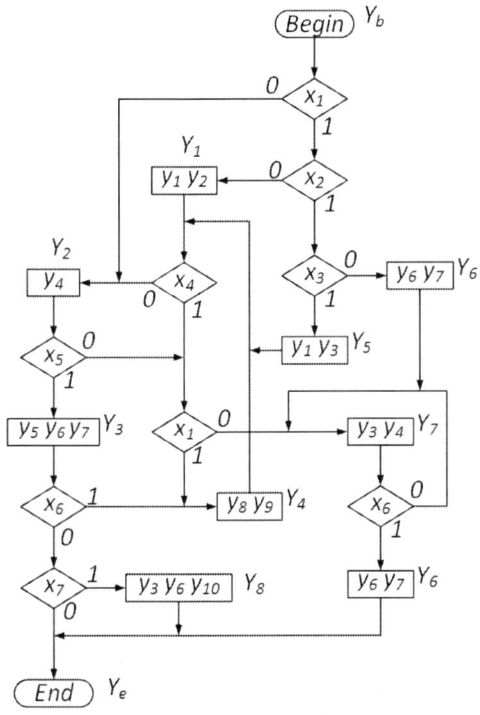

Figure 5. ASM *G1*

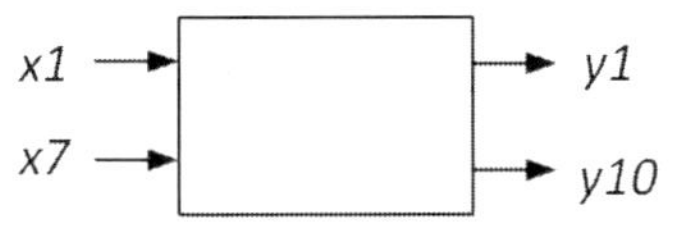

Figure 6. System with 7 inputs and 10 outputs

To explain how such system works I will demonstrate some procedure by travelling in ASM in Fig. 5 with the sequence of vectors *v1, ..., v8* from Table 1. The goal of this travelling – to find the sequence of operators which would be implemented, if we consecutively, beginning from Y_b, give the values from these vectors to logic conditions of ASM in Fig. 5.

Let's define the execution of ASM on any given sequence of vectors *v1, v2, ...* beginning from the initial operator *Yb*. This operator corresponds to vertex *Begin*.

Step 1. Write the initial operator, corresponding to vertex *Begin*:

Yb.

Now I begin travelling from initial vertex *Begin* with the first vector *v1*. The first vertex on my travel is the conditional vertex with variable *x1*. Now I must check the value of component *x1* in vector *v1*. The value of this component tells me via which output I must come out from the conditional vertex. Since *x1=1* in *v1,* I come out from this vertex via output "*1*" and reach the conditional vertex with variable *x2*. *x2=0* in *v1,* then I leave this vertex via output "*0*". Immediately after that I reached operator vertex with operator *Y1*. Each time when I meet operator vertex, I must write this operator on the right from the previous one:

$$YbY1$$

and change the vector.

Table 1. Sequence of vectors for travelling

		x_1	x_2	x_3	x_4	x_5	x_6	x_7
v_1	=	1	0	1	0	1	1	1
v_2	=	0	1	1	0	1	0	0
v_3	=	1	0	1	0	0	1	0
v_4	=	0	1	0	0	0	0	1
v_5	=	1	1	0	1	1	1	0
v_6	=	1	1	0	0	1	0	1
v_7	=	0	1	1	1	0	0	0
v_8	=	0	1	0	1	0	0	1

Step 2. Now I continue my travel with vector *v2*. Since *x4=0* in *v2*, I leave the first conditional vertex via output "0" and meet operator vertex with operator *Y2*. I add *Y2* to my line of operators

$$YbY1Y2$$

and must change vector once again.

The travelling process for the given sequence of vectors may reach its end in two cases:

1. The final vertex "*End*" is reached. In this case, the last operator is *Ye corresponding to vertex "End"*. The number of operators in the operator row (without *Yb*) is less or equal to the number of vectors if we reached the final vertex with the last vector;
2. The vectors are exhausted but we have not yet reached the final vertex. In this case, the number of operators in the operator row is equal to the number of vectors.

In our example, we reached the final vertex "*End*" at the eighth vector

$$v7 = 0\ 1\ 1\ 1\ 0\ 0\ 0$$

and we get the row

$$Y_b\, Y_1\, Y_2\, Y_4\, Y_2\, Y_3\, Y_8\, Y_e. \qquad (1)$$

The operator row thus obtained is *the value of ASM G1 in Fig. 5 for the given sequence of vectors from Table 1.*

1.2 Synthesis of Mealy FSM

1.2.1 Construction of a marked ASM

As an example, I will use ASM *G1* in Fig. 5. I have repeated it in Fig. 7. A Mealy FSM implementing given ASM may be constructed in two stages:

Stage1. Construction of a marked ASM;

Stage 2. Construction of a state diagram (FSM graph).

At the first stage, the inputs of vertices following *operator vertices* are marked by symbols $a_1, a_2, ..., a_M$ as follows:

1. Symbol a_1 marks the input of the vertex, following the initial vertex *"Begin"*, and the input of the final vertex *"End"*;
2. Symbols $a_2, ..., a_M$ mark the inputs of all vertices following operator vertices;
3. Vertex inputs are marked only once;
4. Inputs of different vertices, except the final one, are marked by different symbols.

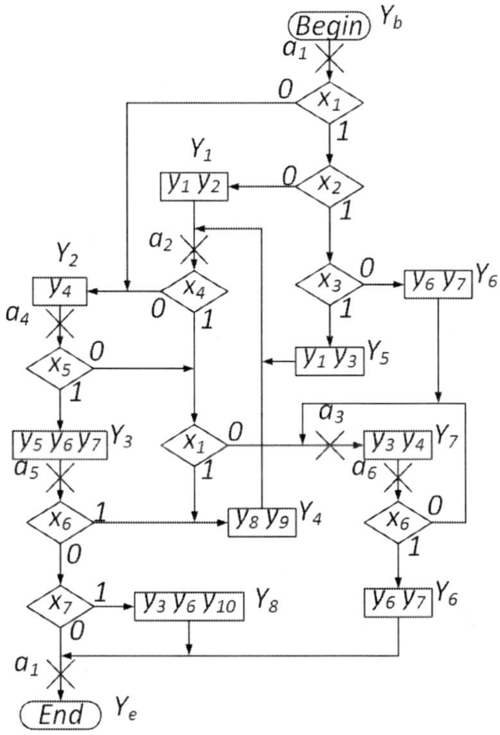

Figure 7. ASM *G1* marked for Mealy FSM synthesis

Marked ASM G_1 in Fig. 7 is a result of the first step. Symbols $a_1, \ldots, a_6$ are used to mark this ASM. Note, that we mark not only the inputs of conditional vertices but of operator vertices as well (see mark a_3 at the input of the vertex with operator Y_7). It is important that each marked vertex follows an operator vertex.

1.2.2 Transition Paths

At the second stage, we will consider the following paths in the marked ASM:

$$a_m \tilde{x}_{m1} \ldots \tilde{x}_{mR_m} Y_g a_s \qquad (P1)$$

$$a_m \tilde{x}_{m1} \ldots \tilde{x}_{mR_m} a_1 \qquad (P2)$$

We call these paths *transition paths*. Thus, the path *P1* proceeds from a_m to a_s ($a_m = a_s$ is also allowed) and contains only one operator vertex at the end of this path. The path *P2* proceeds from a_m *only to* a_1 without operator vertex. Here, $\tilde{x}_{mr} = x_{mr}$ if, on the transition path, we leave the conditional vertex with x_{mr} via output '1' and $\tilde{x}_{mr} = x'_{mr}$ if we leave it via output '0'. If $R_m = 0$ on the path *P1*, two operator vertices follow one after another and this path turns into

$$a_m Y_g a_s.$$

There are sixteen transition paths in the marked ASM G_1 (Fig. 8):

$a_1\ x_1x_2x_3\ Y_5\ a_2$	$a_2\ x_4x_1\ Y_4\ a_2$	$a_4\ x_5\ Y_3\ a_5$	$a_5\ x'_6x_7\ Y_8\ a_1$
$a_1\ x_1x_2x'_3\ Y_6\ a_3$	$a_2\ x_4x'_1\ Y_7\ a_6$	$a_4\ x'_5x_1\ Y_4\ a_2$	$a_5\ x'_6x'_7\ a_1$
$a_1\ x_1x'_2\ Y_1\ a_2$	$a_2\ x'_4\ Y_2\ a_4$	$a_4\ x'_5x'_1\ Y_7\ a_6$	$a_6\ x_6\ Y_6\ a_1$
$a_1\ x'_1\ Y_2\ a_4$	$a_3\ Y_7\ a_6$	$a_5\ x_6\ Y_4\ a_2$	$a_6\ x'_6\ Y_7\ a_6$

Figure 8. Transition paths in the marked ASM G_1

Note, that the path $a_2\ x_4x'_1\ a_3$ doesn't correspond to the transition path *P1* (the operator vertex is absent on the path) and to transition path *P2* (it isn't a path to a_1). Thus, it isn't a transition path and we should go on to get the path $a_2\ x_4x'_1\ Y_7\ a_6$. For the same reason, paths $a_4\ x'_5x'_1\ a_3$ and $a_6\ x'_6\ a_3$ are not the transition paths either.

1.2.3 Graph of FSM

Next, we construct a graph (state diagram) of FSM Mealy with states (marks) $a_1, \ldots, a_M$, obtained at the first stage. We have six such states $a_1, \ldots, a_6$ in our example. Thus, the FSM graph contains as many states as the number of marks we get at the previous stage. Now we should define transitions between these states.

FSM has a transition from state a_m to state a_s with input $X(a_m, a_s)$ and output Y_g (see the upper subgraph in Fig. 9) if, in ASM, there is a transition path *P1*

$$a_m \widetilde{x}_{m1} .. \widetilde{x}_{mR_m} Y_g a_s \, .$$

Here $X(a_m, a_s)$ is the product of logical conditions written in this path:

$$X(a_m, a_s) = \widetilde{x}_{m1} ... \widetilde{x}_{mRm} \, .$$

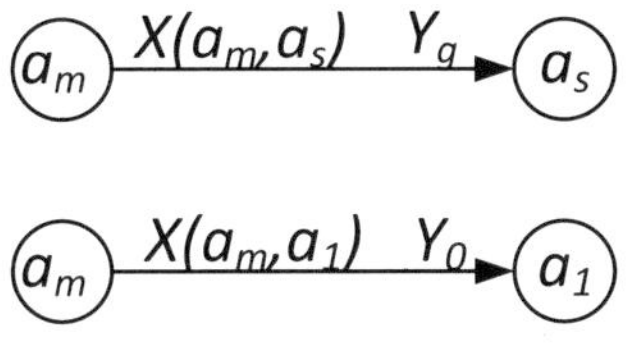

Figure 9. Subgraphs for transition paths *P1* and *P2*

In exactly the same way, for the path $a_m Y_g a_s$ we have a transition from state a_m to state a_s with input $X(a_m, a_s) = 1$ and output Y_g, as the product of an empty set of variables is equal to one. If, for a certain r $(r = 1, ..., R_m)$, symbol x_{mr} (or x'_{mr}) occurs several times on the transition path, all symbols x_{mr} (x'_{mr}) but one should be deleted. If for a certain r $(r = 1, ..., R_m)$, both symbols x_{mr} and x'_{mr} occur on the transition path, this path is removed. In such a case $X(a_m, a_s) = 0$.

For the second transition path $P2$, FSM transits from state a_m to the initial state a_1 with input $X(a_m, a_1)$ and output Y_0 (see the lower subgraph in Fig. 9). Y_0 is the operator containing an empty set of microoperations.

As a result, we obtain a Mealy FSM with as many states as the number of marks we used to mark the ASM in Fig. 7. The state diagram of the Mealy FSM is shown in Fig. 10.

1.2.4 How not to lose transitions paths

Sometimes, if ASM contains many conditional vertices, it is easy to lose one or several transition paths. Here we give a very simple algorithm to resolve this problem. As an example, we use a fragment ASM in Fig. 11. This algorithm has only two steps.

1. Find the first transition path leaving each conditional vertex through output '*1*'. For subgraph of ASM in Fig. 11 we will get the following first path from state a_2:

   $$a_2 \, x_1 \, x_2 \, x_5 \, Y_6 \, a_3.$$

2. Invert the *last non-inverted* variable in the previous path, return to ASM and continue the path (if it is possible) leaving each conditional vertex through output '*1*'. To construct the second path, we should invert variable x_5. We cannot continue because we reached an operator vertex:

$$a_2\, x_1 x_2 x'_5\, Y_2\, a_3.$$

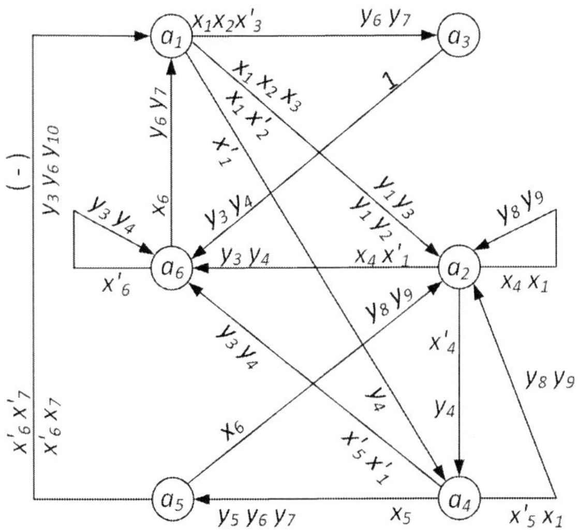

Figure 10. The state diagram (graph) of the Mealy FSM

In this path, we must invert variable x_2 and continue the path leaving each conditional vertex through output '*1*'. As a result, we will get the path

$$a_2\, x_1 x'_2 x_5 x_6\, Y_3\, a_4.$$

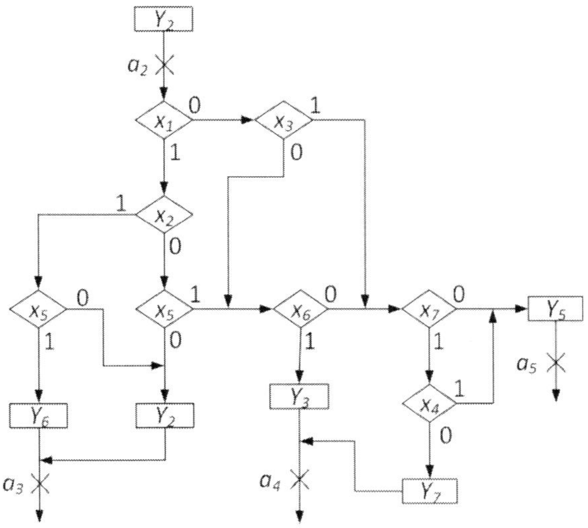

Figure 11. Subgraph of ASM

We should construct paths in the same manner until all variables in the transition path will be inverted. For our example, we will get the paths in Fig. 12.

$a_2 x_1 x'_2 x_5 x_6 Y_3 a_4;$	$a_2 x_1 x'_2 x'_5 Y_2 a_3;$	$a_2 x'_1 x'_3 x_6 Y_3 a_4;$
$a_2 x_1 x'_2 x_5 x'_6 x_7 x_4 Y_5 a_5;$	$a_2 x'_1 x_3 x_7 x_4 Y_5 a_5;$	$a_2 x'_1 x'_3 x'_6 x_7 x_4 Y_5 a_5;$
$a_2 x_1 x'_2 x_5 x'_6 x_7 x'_4 Y_7 a_4;$	$a_2 x'_1 x_3 x_7 x'_4 Y_7 a_4;$	$a_2 x'_1 x'_3 x'_6 x_7 x'_4 Y_7 a_4;$
$a_2 x_1 x'_2 x_5 x'_6 x'_7 Y_5 a_5;$	$a_2 x'_1 x_3 x'_7 Y_5 a_5;$	$a_2 x'_1 x'_3 x'_6 x'_7 Y_5 a_5.$

Figure 12. Transition paths from state a_2

1.2.5 Transition tables of Mealy FSM

The graph of Mealy FSM in Fig. 10 has only 6 states and 16 arcs. Practically, however, we must construct FSMs with tens of states and more than one-two hundreds of transitions. In such a case, it is difficult to use a graph, so we will present it as a table.

Table 2 for the same Mealy FSM has five columns:

- a_m – a current state;
- a_s – a next state;
- $X(a_m, a_s)$ – an input signal;
- $Y(a_m, a_s)$ – an output signal;
- H – a line number.

Table 2. Direct transition table of Mealy FSM S_1

a_m	a_s	$X(a_m,a_s)$	$Y(a_m,a_s)$	H
a_1	a_2	$x_1x_2x_3$	y_1y_3	1
	a_3	$x_1x_2{\sim}x_3$	y_6y_7	2
	a_2	$x_1{\sim}x_2$	y_1y_2	3
	a_4	${\sim}x_1$	y_4	4
a_2	a_2	x_4x_1	y_8y_9	5
	a_6	$x_4{\sim}x_1$	y_3y_4	6
	a_4	${\sim}x_4$	y_4	7
a_3	a_6	1	y_3y_4	8
a_4	a_5	x_5	$y_5y_6y_7$	9
	a_2	${\sim}x_5x_1$	y_8y_9	10
	a_6	${\sim}x_5{\sim}x_1$	y_3y_4	11
a_5	a_2	x_6	y_8y_9	12
	a_1	${\sim}x_6x_7$	$y_3y_6y_{10}$	13
	a_1	${\sim}x_6{\sim}x_7$	-	14
a_6	a_1	x_6	y_6y_7	15
	a_6	${\sim}x_6$	y_3y_4	16

Really, immediately from ASM, we should write transition paths, one after another, into the transition table. In Table 2, $\sim x_t$ is used instead of x'_t for the inversion of x_t.

Now we will discuss what kind of FSM we have received. Our ASM G_1 in Fig. 7 which we used to construct FSM S_1 in Table 2, has seven logical conditions and ten microoperations. FSM S_1 has seven binary inputs in the column $X(a_m,a_s)$ and ten binary outputs in the column $Y(a_m,a_s)$. The input signal of this FSM (Fig. 13) is the 7-component vector, the output signal of this FSM is the 10-component vector.

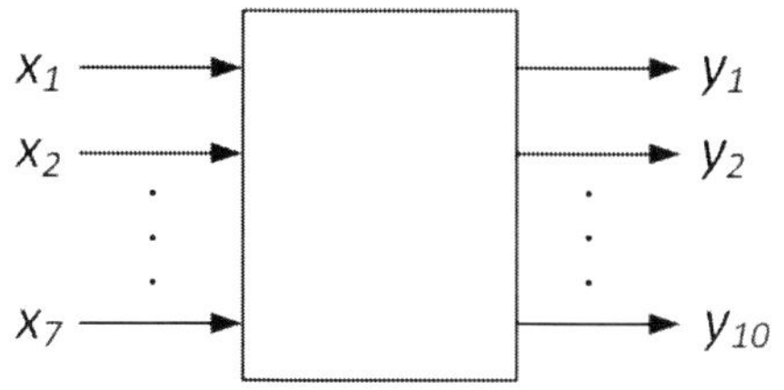

Figure 13. FSM as a black box

Let us look at one of the rows in Table 2, for example row 3, and discuss the behavior of FSM presented in this row. Our FSM transits from state a_1 into state a_2 when the product x_1 $x'_2 = 1$. It is clear, that such a transition takes place for any input vector in which the first component is equal to 1 and the second component is equal to 0. The values of other components are not important. Thus, we can say that the third row of Table 2 presents transitions from a_1 with any vector which is covered by cube *10xxxxx*. In other words, this row presents not one, but $2^5 = 32$ transitions. Similar, the first and the second rows present 16 transitions, the fourth row – 64 transitions and the eighth row – 128 transitions.

Two microoperations y_1, y_2, written in the third row of the output column, mean that two components y_1 and y_2 of the output vector are equal to *1* and others are equal to *0* ($y_1 = y_2 = 1$; $y_3 = y_4 = \dots = y_{10} = 0$). I remind you that if the operator, written in the operator vertex of some ASM, contains microoperations y_m and y_n, only these microoperations are equal to one and other microoperations are equal to zero during implementation of this operator.

The specific feature of such FSM is a large number of inputs in the column $X(a_m,a_s)$, maybe several tens or even hundreds, but each product in one row contains only few variables from the whole set of input variables – as a rule, not more than 8 – 10 variables. It means that each time the values of the output variables depend only on the values of a small number of the input variables. Really, if, for example, FSM has 30 input variables, the total number of input vectors is equal to 2^{30}, and if each time the values of the output variables are depended on the values of all the input variables, no designer could either describe or construct such an FSM.

Let's briefly discuss the correspondence between FSM S_1 (Table 2) and ASM G_1 (Fig. 7) which we used to construct FSM S_1. In Section 1.1.4 we got the value of ASM G_1

$$Y_b\, Y_1\, Y_2\, Y_4\, Y_2\, Y_3\, Y_8\, Y_e$$

for some random sequence of vectors of logical conditions in Table 1 (here I repeated this table in Table 3).

Table 3. Sequence of vectors for FSM *S1*

		x_1	x_2	x_3	x_4	x_5	x_6	x_7
v_1	=	1	0	1	0	1	1	1
v_2	=	0	1	1	0	1	0	0
v_3	=	1	0	1	0	0	1	0
v_4	=	0	1	0	0	0	0	1
v_5	=	1	1	0	1	1	1	0
v_6	=	1	1	0	0	1	0	1
v_7	=	0	1	1	1	0	0	0
v_8	=	0	1	0	1	0	0	1

In Fig. 14 we will find the response of FSM S_1 in the initial state a_1 to the sequence of input vectors from Table 3. Let FSM be in the initial state a_1 with the first vector $v_1 = 1010111$ at its input. To determine the next state and the output we should find such a row in the array of transitions from a_1 (Table 2) that the product $X(a_m,a_s)$, written in this row, be equal to one at input vector v_1. Since $x_1x'_2(v_1) = 1$ (the third row), FSM S_1 produces output signal $y_1y_2 = Y_1$ and transits into state a_2. Similarly, we find that $x'_4(v_2)$ is equal to one at one of transitions from state a_2 and FSM transits to the state a_4 with the output signal $y_4 = Y_2$ (see row 7 in Table 1) etc. As a result, we get the response of FSM S_1 in the initial state a_1 to the input sequence $v_1, \ldots, v_6$ in the fourth row of Fig. 14.

State sequence	a_1	a_2	a_4	a_2	a_4	a_5	a_1
Input sequence	v_1	v_2	v_3	v_4	v_5	v_6	
Response	y_1y_2	y_4	y_8y_9	y_4	$y_5y_6y_7$	$y_3y_6y_{10}$	
Microinstructions	Y_1	Y_2	Y_4	Y_2	Y_3	Y_8	

Figure 14. Response of FSM S_1 in a_1 to the sequence vectors from Table 3

As seen from this row, the FSM response is equal to the value of ASM G_1 for the same input sequence. Note, that we consider here only the FSM response until its return to the initial state a_1 and this response $Y_1\ Y_2\ Y_4\ Y_2\ Y_3\ Y_8$ corresponds to the value of ASM G_1 between the operator Y_b (vertex "Begin") and the operator Y_e (vertex "End").

Let us define *FSM S as implementing ASM G* if the response of this FSM in the state a_1 to any input sequence (until its return to the state a_1) is equal to the value of ASM G for the same input sequence. From the considered method of synthesis of Mealy FSM S_1 from ASM G_1 it follows that this FSM S_1 implements ASM G_1.

1.2.6 ASMs with waiting vertices

In this section, I will show that the algorithm for FSM synthesis does not change if ASM contains waiting vertices. In a waiting vertex, one of its outputs is connected with its input (see the ASM subgraph in Fig. 15,a). Let us find all transition paths from the state a_8. The first two are trivial – see the first two rows in Table 4.

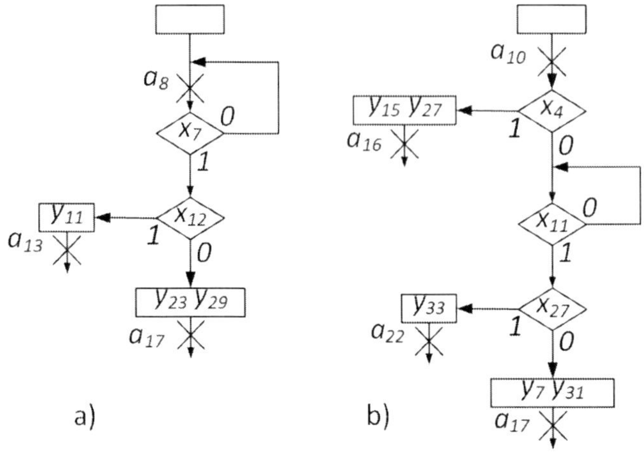

Figure 15. Two subgraphs with waiting vertices

To find the next path we should invert the variable x_7. The output *'0'* for x_7 brings us to the input of this conditional vertex. So, the next paths will be:

$$a_8 \sim x_7\, x_7 x_{12}\, (y_{11})\, a_{13};$$
$$a_8 \sim x_7\, x_7 \sim x_{12}\, (y_{23},\, y_{29})\, a_{17}.$$

The products of input variables for both these paths are equal to zero ($\sim x_7\, x_7 = 0$), so FSM cannot transit from the state $a8$ to any other state when $x_7 = 0$. If FSM cannot transit into any other state, it remains in the same state a_8 or, we can say, it transits from a_8 to a_8 with $X(a_8, a_8) = \sim x_7$. No output variables are equal to *'1'* at this transition, so we have dash in the column $Y(a_m, a_s)$ in the third row.

The next example (Fig. 15,b) presents a general case. The only difference from the previous example – the waiting vertex is in the middle of the path. After the third path in Table 5 we should invert variable x_{11} and again return to the input of the conditional vertex with x_{11}. We can construct the following transitions paths:

$$a_{10} \sim x_4 \sim x_{11}\, x_{11}\, x_{27}\, (y_{33})\, a_{22} \text{ and } a_{10} \sim x_4 \sim x_{11}\, x_{11} \sim x_{27}\, (y_7,\, y_{31})\, a_{17}.$$

Table 4. Transition table for subgraph in Fig. 15,a

a_m	a_s	$X(a_m,a_s)$	$Y(a_m,a_s)$	H
		. . .		
a_8	a_{13}	x_7x_{12}	y_{11}	
	a_{17}	x_7~x_{12}	$y_{23}y_{29}$	
	a_8	~x_7	–	

The products for both these paths are equal to zero. So, when $x_4 = 0$, we reached a waiting vertex with condition x_{11}. If $x_{11} = 0$ (return to the input), FSM transits from state a_{10} to state a_{10} (remains in this state) with input ~x_4~x_{11} and each output variable is equal to zero (the forth row in Table 5).

Table 5. Transition table for subgraph in Fig. 12,b

a_m	a_s	$X(a_m,a_s)$	$Y(a_m,a_s)$	H
		. . .		
a_{10}	a_{16}	x_4	$y_{15}y_{27}$	
	a_{22}	~$x_4x_{11}x_{27}$	y_{33}	
	a_{17}	~x_4x_{11}~x_{27}	y_7y_{31}	
	a_{10}	~x_4~x_{11}	–	

Thus, to construct transitions between states a_m and a_s we must use algorithm presented in section ***1.2.4*** "How not to lose transition paths". But when we have reached the return output, we shouldn't continue and write this path into transition from am to as without the output signals. We don't write the outputs into column Y(am,as). It means that all y-s are equal to zero at this transition.

The example of FSM synthesis from ASM with waiting vertices, constructed by our tool Synthagate, is presented in Fig. 16 and Tables 6.

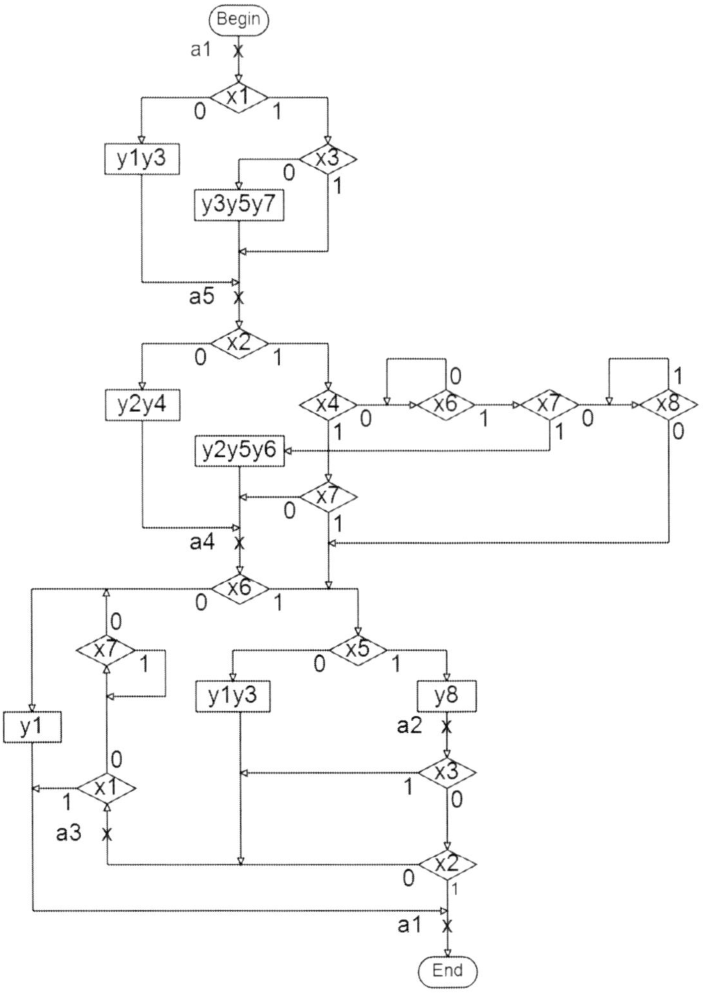

Figure 16. ASM B2 with waiting vertices

Table 6. Transition table of FSM Mealy constructed from ASM in Fig. 16

a_m	a_s	$X(a_m,a_s)$	$Y(a_m,a_s)$	H
a1	a1	x1*x3*x2*x4*~x7*~x6	y1	1
a1	a1	x1*x3*x2*~x4*x6*~x7*x8	--	2
a1	a1	x1*x3*x2*~x4*~x6	--	3
a2	a1	x3*x1	--	4
a2	a1	x3*~x1*~x7	y1	5
a2	a1	~x3*x2	--	6
a2	a1	~x3*~x2*x1	--	7
a2	a1	~x3*~x2*~x1*~x7	y1	8
a3	a1	x1	--	9
a3	a1	~x1*~x7	y1	10
a4	a1	~x6	y1	11
a5	a1	x2*x4*~x7*~x6	y1	12

a2	a2	x3*~x1*x7	--	13
a1	a2	x1*x3*x2*~x4*x6*~x7*~x8*x5	y8	14
a1	a2	x1*x3*x2*x4*x7*x5	y8	15
a4	a2	x6*x5	y8	16
a1	a2	x1*x3*x2*x4*~x7*x6*x5	y8	17
a5	a2	x2*x4*x7*x5	y8	18
a5	a2	x2*x4*~x7*x6*x5	y8	19
a2	a2	~x3*~x2*~x1*x7	--	20
a5	a2	x2*~x4*x6*~x7*~x8*x5	y8	21
a1	a3	x1*x3*x2*~x4*x6*~x7*~x8*~x5	y1y3	22
a3	a3	~x1*x7	--	23
a5	a3	x2*x4*x7*~x5	y1y3	24
a1	a3	x1*x3*x2*x4*~x7*x6*~x5	y1y3	25
a5	a3	x2*x4*~x7*x6*~x5	y1y3	26
a1	a3	x1*x3*x2*x4*x7*~x5	y1y3	27
a4	a3	x6*~x5	y1y3	28
a5	a3	x2*~x4*x6*~x7*~x8*~x5	y1y3	29
a5	a4	x2*~x4*x6*x7	y2y5y6	30
a1	a4	x1*x3*x2*~x4*x6*x7	y2y5y6	31
a1	a4	x1*x3*~x2	y2y4	32
a5	a4	~x2	y2y4	33
a1	a5	~x1	y1y3	34
a1	a5	x1*~x3	y3y5y7	35
a5	a5	x2*~x4*~x6	--	36
a5	a5	x2*~x4*x6*~x7*x8	--	37

1.3 Synthesis of Moore FSM

As an example, we will use ASM G_1 in Fig. 17. A Moore FSM, implementing given ASM, can be constructed in two stages:

Stage 1. Construction of a marked ASM;

Stage 2. Construction of an FSM transition table.

At the first stage, the vertices "*Begin*", "*End*" and operator vertices are marked by symbols a_1, a_2, ..., a_M as follows:

1. Vertices "*Begin*" and "*End*" are marked by the same symbol a_1;
2. Operator vertices are marked by different symbols a_2, ..., a_M;
3. All operator vertices should be marked.

Thus, while synthesizing a Moore FSM, symbols of states do not mark inputs of vertices following the operator vertices (as in the Mealy FSM) but operator vertices themselves. The number of marks is $T+1$, where T is the number of operator vertices in the marked ASM. In our example (Fig. 17), we need marks a_1, ..., a_{10} for ASM G_1.

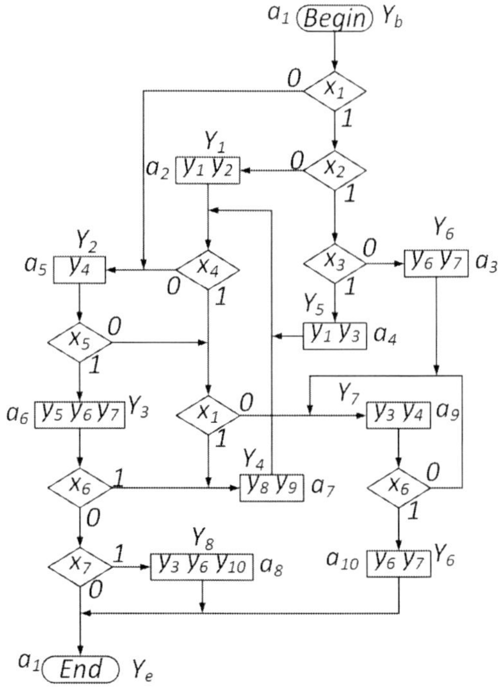

Figure 17. ASM G_1 marked for the Moore FSM synthesis

We will find the following transition paths in the marked ASM:

$$a_m \tilde{x}_{m1} .. \tilde{x}_{mR_m} a_s .$$

Thus, the transition path is the path between two operator vertices, containing R_m conditional vertices. Here, as above in the case of Mealy FSM, $\tilde{x}_{mr} = x_{mr}$, if in the transition path, we leave the conditional vertex with x_{mr} via output '1' and $\tilde{x}_{mr} = x'_{mr}$ if we leave the vertex with x_{mr} via output '0'. If $R_m = 0$ in such a path, there are no conditional vertices between two operator vertices, and this path turns into $a_m a_s$.

At the second stage, we construct a transition table (or the state diagram) of the Moore FSM with states (marks) $a_1, \ldots, a_M$, obtained at the first stage. We have ten such states $a_1, \ldots, a_{10}$ in our example. Thus, the FSM contains as many states as the number of marks we get at the previous stage. Now we should define transitions between these states.

A Moore FSM transits from state a_m to state a_s with input $X(a_m, a_s)$ (see the upper subgraph in Fig. 18) if, in ASM, there is a transition path $a_m \tilde{x}_{m1} .. \tilde{x}_{mR_m} a_s$. Here $X(a_m, a_s)$ is a product of logical conditions written in this path – $X(a_m, a_s) = \tilde{x}_{m1} ... \tilde{x}_{mRm}$. In exactly the same way, for the path $a_m a_s$ (see the lower subgraph in Fig. 18) we have a transition from state a_m to state a_s with input $X(a_m, a_s) = 1$, because the product of an empty set of variables is equal to zero. If a_m marks the operator vertex with operator Y_t, then $\lambda(a_m) = Y_t$, i.e. we identify the operator Y_t written in the operator vertex with this state a_m.

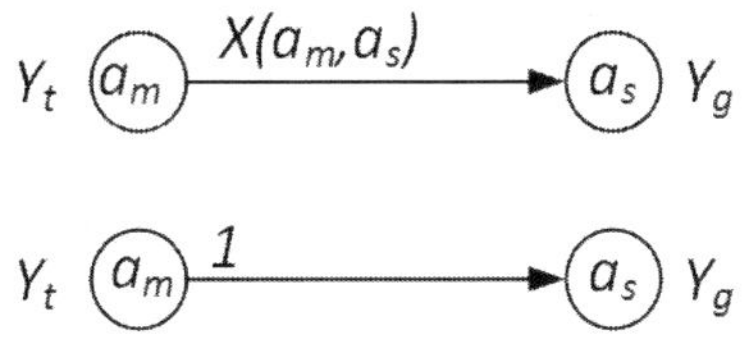

Figure 18. Subgraphs to illustrate transitions in the Moore FSM

The transition table for Moore FSM S_2, thus constructed, is presented in Table 7. The outputs are written in column $Y(a_m)$ immediately after the column with the current states.

Table 7. The transition table of Moore FSM S_2

a_m	$Y(a_m)$	a_s	$X(a_m,a_s)$	H
a1	--	a2	x1*x2*x3	1
a1	--	a3	x1*x2*~x3	2
a1	--	a4	x1*~x2	3
a1	--	a5	~x1	4
a2	y1y3	a8	x4*x1	5
a2	y1y3	a9	x4*~x1	6
a2	y1y3	a5	~x4	7
a3	y6y7	a9	1	8
a4	y1y2	a8	x4*x1	9
a4	y1y2	a9	x4*~x1	10
a4	y1y2	a5	~x4	11
a5	y4	a6	x5	12
a5	y4	a8	~x5*x1	13
a5	y4	a9	~x5*~x1	14
a6	y5y6y7	a8	x6	15
a6	y5y6y7	a7	~x6*x7	16
a6	y5y6y7	a1	~x6*~x7	17
a7	y3y6y10	a1	1	18
a8	y8y9	a8	x4*x1	19
a8	y8y9	a9	x4*~x1	20
a8	y8y9	a5	~x4	21
a9	y3y4	a10	x6	22
a9	y3y4	a9	~x6	23
a10	y6y7	a1	1	24

The example of Moore FSM synthesis from ASM B_2 with waiting vertices is presented in Fig. 19 and Tables 8.

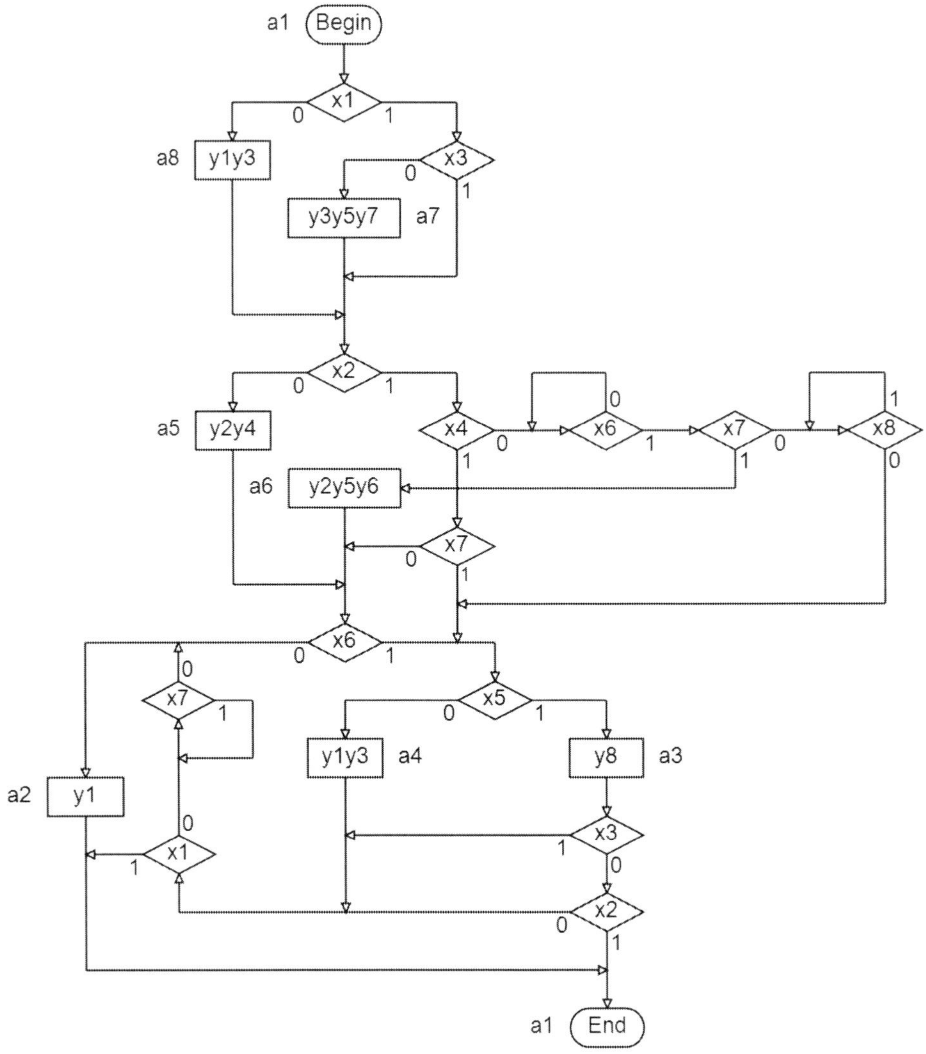

Figure 19. ASM *B2* marked for the Moore FSM synthesis

Table 8. The transition table of Moore FSM *B2*

am	Y(am)	as	X(am,as)	H
a1	--	a3	x1*x3*x2*x4*x7*x5	1
a1	--	a4	x1*x3*x2*x4*x7*~x5	2
a1	--	a3	x1*x3*x2*x4*~x7*x6*x5	3
a1	--	a4	x1*x3*x2*x4*~x7*x6*~x5	4
a1	--	a2	x1*x3*x2*x4*~x7*~x6	5
a1	--	a6	x1*x3*x2*~x4*x6*x7	6
a1	--	a3	x1*x3*x2*~x4*x6*~x7*x8	7
a1	--	a3	x1*x3*x2*~x4*x6*~x7*~x8*x5	8
a1	--	a4	x1*x3*x2*~x4*x6*~x7*~x8*~x5	9

a1	--	a6	x1*x3*x2*~x4*~x6	10
a1	--	a5	x1*x3*~x2	11
a1	--	a7	x1*~x3	12
a1	--	a8	~x1	13
a2	y1	a1	1	14
a3	y8	a1	x3*x1	15
a3	y8	a4	x3*~x1*x7	16
a3	y8	a2	x3*~x1*~x7	17
a3	y8	a1	~x3*x2	18
a3	y8	a1	~x3*~x2*x1	19
a3	y8	a4	~x3*~x2*~x1*x7	20
a3	y8	a2	~x3*~x2*~x1*~x7	21
a4	y1y3	a1	x1	22
a4	y1y3	a4	~x1*x7	23
a4	y1y3	a2	~x1*~x7	24
a5	y2y4	a3	x6*x5	25
a5	y2y4	a4	x6*~x5	26
a5	y2y4	a2	~x6	27
a6	y2y5y6	a3	x6*x5	28
a6	y2y5y6	a4	x6*~x5	29
a6	y2y5y6	a2	~x6	30
a7	y3y5y7	a3	x2*x4*x7*x5	31
a7	y3y5y7	a4	x2*x4*x7*~x5	32
a7	y3y5y7	a3	x2*x4*~x7*x6*x5	33
a7	y3y5y7	a4	x2*x4*~x7*x6*~x5	34
a7	y3y5y7	a2	x2*x4*~x7*~x6	35
a7	y3y5y7	a6	x2*~x4*x6*x7	36
a7	y3y5y7	a3	x2*~x4*x6*~x7*x8	37
a7	y3y5y7	a3	x2*~x4*x6*~x7*~x8*x5	38
a7	y3y5y7	a4	x2*~x4*x6*~x7*~x8*~x5	39
a7	y3y5y7	a6	x2*~x4*~x6	40
a7	y3y5y7	a5	~x2	41
a8	y1y3	a3	x2*x4*x7*x5	42
a8	y1y3	a4	x2*x4*x7*~x5	43
a8	y1y3	a3	x2*x4*~x7*x6*x5	44
a8	y1y3	a4	x2*x4*~x7*x6*~x5	45
a8	y1y3	a2	x2*x4*~x7*~x6	46
a8	y1y3	a6	x2*~x4*x6*x7	47
a8	y1y3	a3	x2*~x4*x6*~x7*x8	48
a8	y1y3	a3	x2*~x4*x6*~x7*~x8*x5	49
a8	y1y3	a4	x2*~x4*x6*~x7*~x8*~x5	50
a8	y1y3	a6	x2*~x4*~x6	51
a8	y1y3	a5	~x2	52

1.4 Synthesis of Combined FSM model

In this book, I use two kinds of transition tables – direct and reverse. In a *direct table* (Table 9), transitions are ordered according to the current state (the first column in this table) – first we write all transitions *from* the state a_1, then *from* the state a_2, etc. In a *reverse table* (Table

10), transitions are ordered according to the next state (the second column in this table) – first we write all transitions *to* the state a_1, then *to* the state a_2, etc.

Table 9. Direct transition table of Mealy FSM S_3

a_m	a_s	$X(a_m,a_s)$	$Y(a_m,a_s)$	H
a1	a2	x6	y8y9	1
a1	a5	~x6*x7	y6	2
a1	a5	~x6*~x7	y3y6y10	3
a2	a2	x4*x1	y1y2	4
a2	a6	x4*~x1	y3y4	5
a2	a4	~x4	y4	6
a3	a6	1	y3y5	7
a4	a1	x5	--	8
a4	a2	~x5*x1	y8y9	9
a4	a6	~x5*~x1	y3y4	10
a5	a2	x1*x2*x3	y1y3	11
a5	a3	x1*x2*~x3	y1y4	12
a5	a2	x1*~x2	y1y2	13
a5	a4	~x1	y4	14
a6	a5	x6	y6y7	15
a6	a6	~x6	y3y5	16

Table 10. Reverse transition table of Mealy FSM S_3

a_m	a_s	$X(a_m,a_s)$	$Y(a_m,a_s)$	H
a4	a1	x5	--	1
a2	a2	x4*x1	y1y2	2
a1	a2	x6	y8y9	3
a4	a2	~x5*x1	y8y9	4
a5	a2	x1*x2*x3	y1y3	5
a5	a2	x1*~x2	y1y2	6
a5	a3	x1*x2*~x3	y1y4	7
a2	a4	~x4	y4	8
a5	a4	~x1	y4	9
a1	a5	~x6*x7	y6	10
a1	a5	~x6*~x7	y3y6y10	11
a6	a5	x6	y6y7	12
a4	a6	~x5*~x1	y3y4	13
a2	a6	x4*~x1	y3y4	14
a3	a6	1	y3y5	15
a6	a6	~x6	y3y5	16

I remind you that Combined FSM has two kinds of output signals:

- Signals depending on the current state and the current input (as in the Mealy model);
- Signals depending only on the current state (as in the Moore model).

Fig. 20,a illustrates all transitions into state a_s of some Mealy FSM. Here we have three transitions with different outputs but all of them contain the same output variable y_r. So, we can identify this output variable y_r with the state a_s as a Moore signal (see Fig. 20,b).

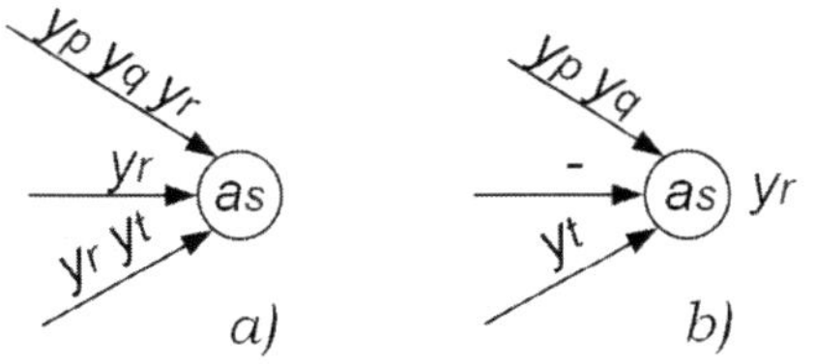

Figure 20. Transformation from Mealy FSM to Combined FSM

After this, the transformation of Mealy FSM into Combined model is trivial. Let us return to the reverse Table 10 and begin to construct the reverse transition table of Combined FSM S_4 (Table 11).

For that, In Table 10, we look at the transitions to each state, beginning from transitions to state a_1. Let Y_S be the set of output variables at the transitions into state a_s ($Ys = \{y_p, y_q, y_r, y_t\}$ in Fig. 20,a) and Y_{sMoore} be the subset of common output variables at all transitions into a_s ($Y_{sMoore} = \{y_r\}$ in Fig. 20). Then, in Table 11, we remove Y_{sMoore} from the column $Y(a_m, a_s)$ at each row with transition to a_s and write Y_{sMoore} next to a_s in the column $Y(a_s)$. In our example Y_{1Moore} and Y_{2Moore} are empty, but:

$$Y_{3Moore} = \{y_1, y_4\};\ Y_{4Moore} = \{y_4\};\ Y_{5Moore} = \{y_6\};\ Y_{6Moore} = \{y_3\}.$$

Table 11. Reverse transition table of Combined FSM S_4

a_m	a_s	$Y(a_s)$	$X(a_m,a_s)$	$Y(a_m,a_s)$	H
a4	a1	--	x5	--	1
a1	a2	--	x6	y8y9	2
a2	a2	--	x4*x1	y1y2	3
a4	a2	--	~x5*x1	y8y9	4
a5	a2	--	x1*x2*x3	y1y3	5
a5	a2	--	x1*~x2	y1y2	6
a5	a3	y1y4	x1*x2*~x3	--	7
a2	a4	y4	~x4	--	8
a5	a4	y4	~x1	--	9
a1	a5	y6	~x6*~x7	y3y10	10
a1	a5	y6	~x6*x7	--	11
a6	a5	y6	x6	y7	12
a2	a6	y3	x4*~x1	y4	13
a3	a6	y3	1	y5	14
a4	a6	y3	~x5*~x1	y4	15
a6	a6	y3	~x6	y5	16

2 HIGH LEVEL SYNTHESIS FOR ALBI

2.1 ALBI

In this Chapter, I will present the most important stage of each design – High Level Synthesis (HLS). To demonstrate the design methodology, I need some examples. As my first example, I will use the design of a very simple processor ALBI containing only four operations:

- Arithmetical (*ao*);
- Load (*lod*);
- Branch unconditional (*bun*);
- Input (*inp*).

I call this processor *ALBI* by the first letters of its operations. In the Chapters "Case Studies" I will give several designs such as Codec, Robot etc.

Our design methodology contains the following steps:

1. Representation of separate sub-behaviors (instructions in my first example) with functional ASMs;
2. Combining of these ASMs into one combined functional ASM and its minimization;
3. Design *ALBI* at the High Level;
4. Synthesis of Data path at the Register Transfer Level (RTL);
5. Transfer from the combined functional ASM to the structural ASM corresponding to Data path;
6. Control unit design at the Register Transfer Level;
7. Composition of Data path and Control unit into top design of ALBI at the Register Transfer Level.

2.1.1 Main units

ALBI has 16-bit word and contains main components common for such a device – memory, arithmetic logic unit, program counter, instruction register etc. The processor has the following components:

- a set of 16 general-purpose software-accessible registers (Block of register – *bor*);
- two instruction registers (*ir1* and *ir2*);
- program counter (*pc*);
- 2 random-access-memories (*ram*) – *m0* (for program) and *m1* (for operands);
- an arithmetic and logic unit (*alu*);
- indexing arithmetic and logic unit (*ialu*);
- 16-bit input register (*inpr*) to load data from external devices.
- In addition, ALBI must provide a direct-memory-access (*dma*) feature. A 16-bit address bus, 16-bit data bus and external read/write and memory selection (*m*) signals are needed to implement it. If *m=0* DMA uses program memory *m0*, if *m=1* – operand memory *m1*.

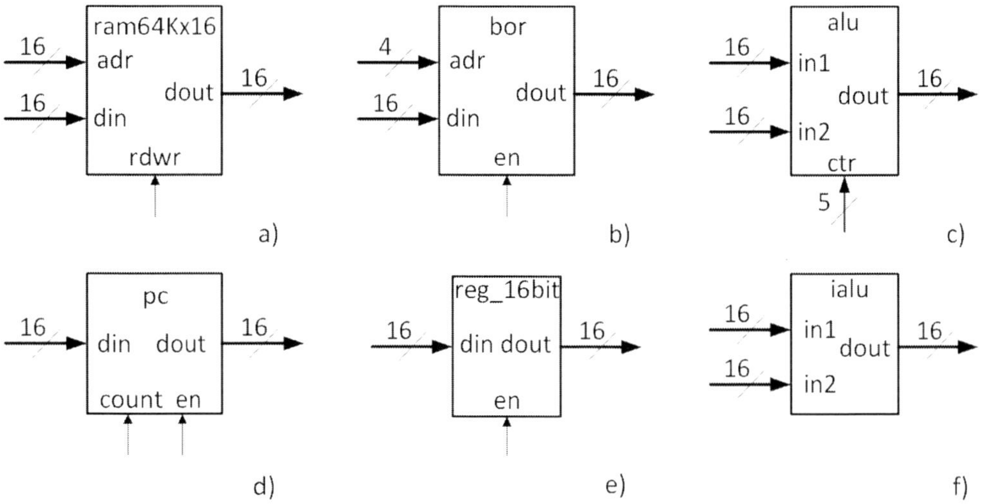

Figure 1. Elements of Data Path

Instruction Memory m0 and *operand memory m1* (Fig. 1,a) have 16-bit address bus (*adr*) and two 16-bit data buses – input (*din*) and output (*dout*). Input *rdwr* (read-write) is the instruction input of the memory. The work with memory at the High level is very simple. Fig. 2,a shows the operator vertex with writing the contents of some register *r2* to the memory *m0* with an address in the register *r1*. Fig 2,b presents the reading from this memory to r4 with the address in r3.

Register memory – *Block of Register (bor)* contains sixteen 16-bit registers (Fig. 1,b). The reading from *m1* or *bor* and writing to *m1* or *bor* at the High Level are the same as with instruction memory *m0*.

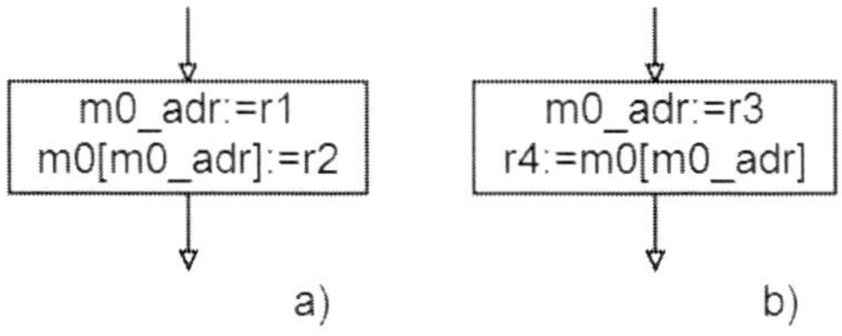

Figure 2. Write to and read from the instruction memory *m0*

Arithmetic logic unit (*alu*) is used for implementation of arithmetic and logic operations (Fig. 1,c). Two 16-bit inputs *in1* and *in2* serve for operands of *alu*, 5-bit input *ctr* serves for instruction codes of *alu* operations. The result of the operation appears at the output *dout*. Our *alu* is a combinational circuit (circuit without memory) so *ALBI* has *ralu* (the register of *alu*) to save the results of arithmetic and logic operations.

Program counter (*pc*) points to the next instruction which should be implemented (Fig. 1,d). It saves the address of such instruction. Input *en* is used to load 16-bit information from *din* to the counter when *en = 1*. When *count=1* the content of the counter are incremented by one. At the High Level, to increment counter *pc* we write *pc:=pc+1* in operator vertex of ASM and we write *pc:=r* to assign the value of register *r* to *pc*.

Instruction register contains the instruction which is being currently implemented. As most of *ALBI* registers, it has the structure shown in Fig. 1,e. Such a register has 16 clocked *D* flip-flops with input *rst* to reset it and input *en* (enable signal), this signal should be equal to one to write information from input *din* into the register. We skipped signals *clk* (clock) and *rst* (reset) in our pictures. At the High Level we write *r3:=r4* to load information from register *r4* to register *r3*.

Index arithmetic logic unit (*ialu* in Fig. 1,f) can implement only one operation – addition. With one operation, it doesn't need input *ctr*. *IALU* is used in the *indexed addressing mode* – see section "Addressing modes" below.

2.1.2 Instruction formats

ALBI has two instruction formats – *short* (one word, 16 bits, Fig. 3) and *long* (two words, 32 bits, Fig. 4). The first twelve bits have the same mission in both formats. Bit 10 points to the *length* of instructions – *short* (bit 10 equal to zero) or *long* (bit 10 equal to one). The next two bits define the *addressing mode*.

15	14	13	12	11	10	9	8	7	6	5	4	3	2	1	0
Instruction code					0	Addressing mode		First operand address				Second operand address			

Figure 3. Short instruction (needs ir1 only)

The short instruction cannot use operands from operand memory *m1*. To access this memory, the 16-bit address should be in the instruction. So, the short instruction uses only operands from *bor* – bits 7-4 define the address of the first operand in *bor* and the address of the result, whereas bits 3-0 define the address of the second operand in *bor*. In the long instruction, we will use the field 3-0 as address of index register, the second operand is in the memory *m1* and its 16 bit address is in the second instruction word. Sometimes, we have operand itself in the second word – see the *immediate* addressing mode below.

15	14	13	12	11	10	9	8	7	6	5	4	3	2	1	0
Instruction code					1	Addressing mode		First operand address				Index for second operand address			

15	14	13	12	11	10	9	8	7	6	5	4	3	2	1	0
Second operand (data or address)															

Figure 4. Long instruction (needs *ir1* and *ir2*)

Our ALBI uses 16-bit words, so 16-bit *Instruction Register* cannot save the long instruction. Therefore, ALBI has two instruction registers – *ir1* and *ir2*, sixteen bits each. In the memory, the short instruction takes one word, the long one – two sequential words. ALBI fetches the short instruction into *ir1* and the long instruction – into *ir1* and *ir2*. The first half of the long instruction, containing its code, length, addressing mode and two short addresses is fetched into *ir1*, the second half – into *ir2*.

Bit distribution in the instruction registers:

Bits 15-11 in any instruction contain the instruction code.

Bit 10 defines the length of the instruction:

0 = short instruction; 1 = long instruction.

Bits 9 and *8* define three addressing modes as follows:

00 = direct; 01 = immediate; 10 = indirect.

Bits 7-4 define addresses of one of the 16 registers in *bor*.

Bits 3-0 have different meaning depending on the instruction length. With a short instruction, this is the address of another register in *bor*. With a long instruction, this is an address of 16-bit offset used for index addressing.

Bits 15-0 in the second instruction word (the second operand address) are only considered for long instructions.

2.1.3 Addressing modes

Addressing mode defines how *ALBI* finds operands using their addresses in the instruction. In both formats – short and long, the address of the first operand and the address of the result are in bits 7-4 of the first instruction word. So, *the different addressing modes will be essential only for the second operand.*

Now we shortly discuss several addressing modes. *Direct addressing* mode is the simplest one. In this mode, addresses of operands are written within the instruction.

In the short format (Fig. 5,a), addresses of the first and the second operands *A1* and *A2* are in bits 7-4 and 3-0, operands themselves are in *bor*. In the long format (Fig. 5,b), address *A1* is in the bits 7-4 and the long address *A3* of the second operand is in the second word of such instruction. The second operand is in the operand memory *m1* in the cell with address *A3*.

In the *immediate mode*, not the address of the operand, but the second operand itself is written in the second word of the instruction (Fig. 5,c). Thus, the immediate mode can be used only in the long instructions.

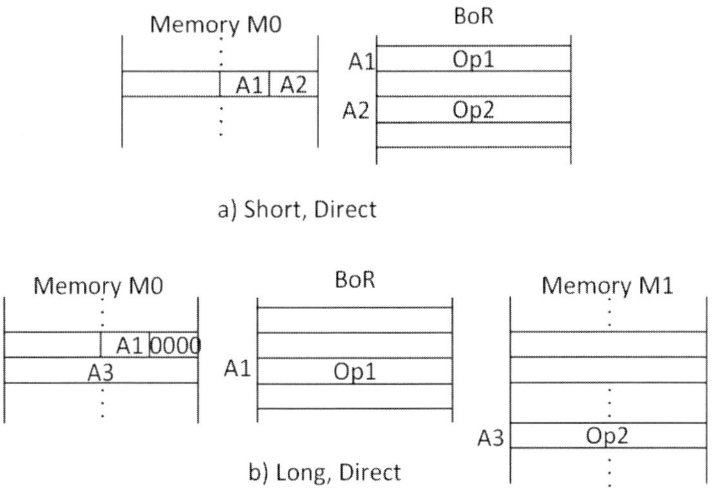

Figure 5a, b. Addressing modes

In *indirect mode*, not the address of the operand, but the address of the address of the operand is written in the instruction. For the short format (Fig. 5,d), *A2* in the field 3-0 points to the register in *bor*, where the memory address *A3* of the second operand is saved.

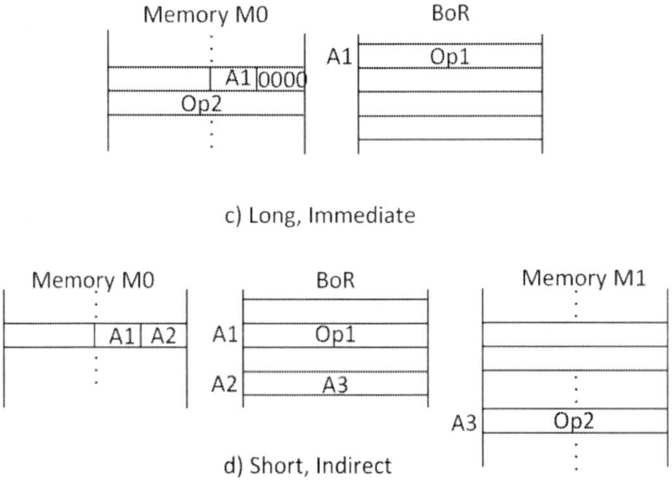

Figure 5c, d. Addressing modes

For the long format (Fig. 5,e), address *A3* in the second word of the instruction points to the cell of the memory *m1* which contains address *A4* of the second operand. Thus, to reach the second operand in the long instruction, *ALBI* should access the memory twice: first time – for its address, second time – for the operand itself.

In the *indexed addressing mode*, *ALBI* uses an index register to find the address of the operand. Any *bor* register except *bor[0]*, can be used as an index register. For the long direct indexed mode (Fig. 5,f) the content *A2* of the second address field (bits 3-0) in the first instruction word points to the index register in *bor*. *ALBI* should add the content of this index register (*offset*) to the long address *A3* (base address) from the second instruction word to find the address of the second operand (*A3 + offset*). Exactly in the similar way, we can define indirect indexed addressing mode.

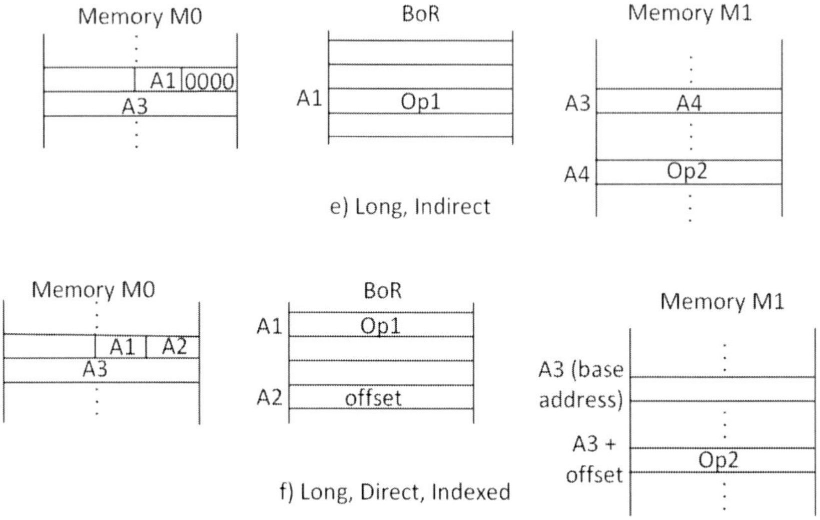

Figure 5e, f. Addressing modes

2.2 Algorithmic State Machines for *ALBI* instructions

Before we present ASMs for each instruction let us discuss how to describe the instruction execution with ASM. As an example, we will use ASM for instruction *lod* in Fig. 6. The goal of this instruction is to send the second operand to the place of the first one. For the long instruction, the second operand is in memory *m1*, for the short instruction it is in *bor* with the second short address (*ir1(3-0)*). The first operand in both cases is in *bor* with the first address (*ir1(7-4)*).

In Fig. 6, I used two kinds of microoperations in ASM:

- *Simple micro operation*, containing assignments ":=".
- *Component micro operation* (I call it a *generalized operator*), not containing an assign operator ":=". In this disclosure, we color them by the silver color, but the color is not important. These operators are subASMs, Synthagate automatically includes them in the mother's (upper) ASM to get the whole behavior of digital system or one of its modes if we would like to present them separately. Each generalized operator should be drawn separately. This file must have the same name as the name of generalized operator in the mother's ASM. The generalized operator can contain

generalized operators as well. *There are no any constraints on the number of generalized operators and the number of levels of their inclusions.*

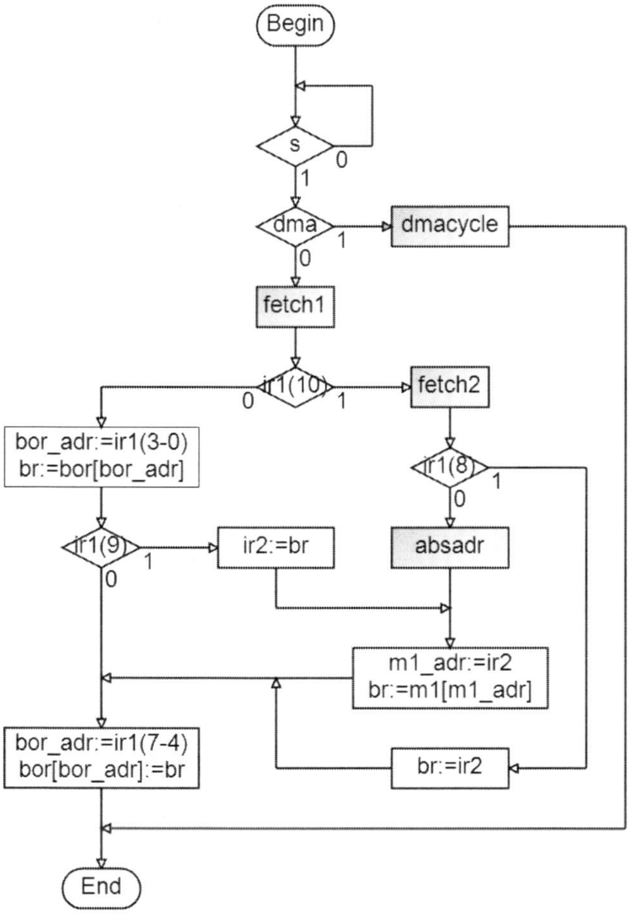

Figure 6. ASM of instruction *lod* with generalized operators

Now let's return to ASM of instruction *lod*. In Fig. 6 the first vertex after *Begin* is a waiting conditional vertex with the logical condition *s*. You can look at "*s*" as a signal from a *Start-Stop* button, so the instruction will be executed only when *s=1*. Such conditional vertex should be at the beginning of ASM for each instruction.

The next condition *dma* (Direct Memory Access – Fig. 7) corresponds to the special mode that doesn't execute an operation but connects the processor memory with the outside storage device to read or write information. *ext_rdwr* is the signal from outside. When *ext_rdwr=1*, external system writes information to memory *m0* or to memory *m1*.

When *ext_rdwr = 0*, external system reads information from memories *m0* or *m1* to its input *ext_in*. When external system is working with instruction memory *m0* the external signal *m* should be equal to zero, with operand memory *m1* – to one.

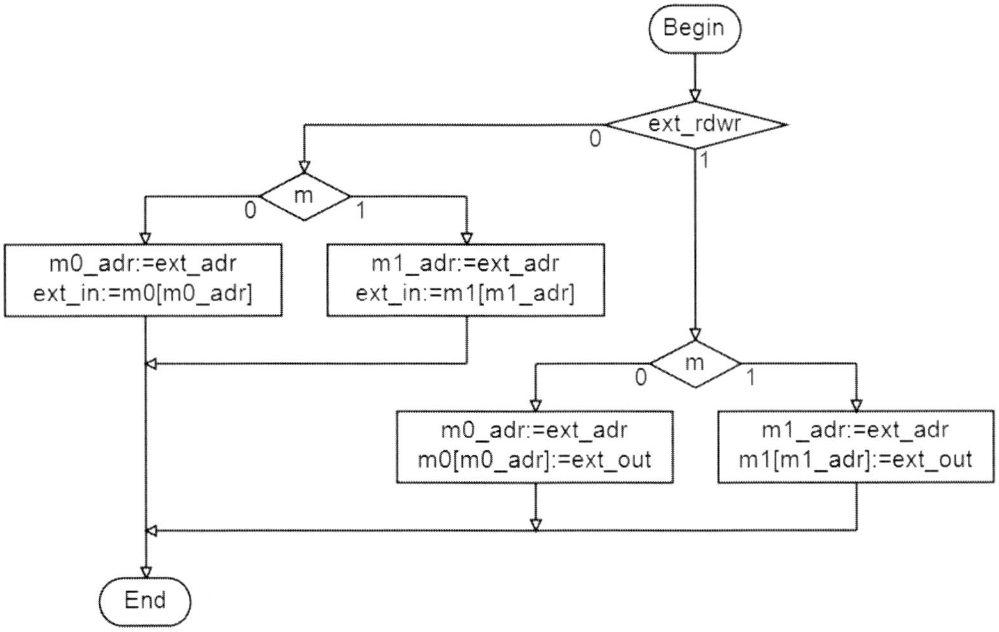

Figure 7. DMA Cycle

To explain the implementation of the instruction *lod*, we will use the sequence of figures beginning with Fig. 8. This figure presents the state of *ALBI* before execution of instruction *lod*. We can see instruction memory *m0, ALU register ralu* and *program counter pc* on the left, operand memory *m1* and *br* on the right and *bor, ir1* and *ir2* in the middle. Really, here we have most of ALBI units, except *alu* and *ialu*, because these units are combinational circuits, and in any case, the result of their operations will appear in registers *ralu* and *rialu*. Going through these steps, follow at the same time ASM *lod* and generalized operators in Fig. 15 and 16. I marked their operators by steps in Fig. 8 – 14.

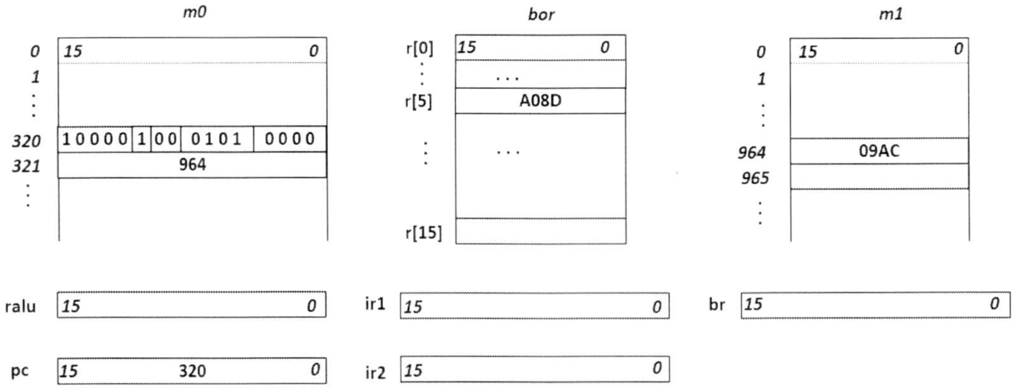

Figure 8. Before implementation of instruction *lod*

The only information important prior to the instruction implementation is the content of *pc*, which contains an address of the instruction in memory *m0*. Therefore, in the first step (Fig.

8 and the first operator vertex in *fetch1* in Fig. 15 and Fig. 16), the output of *pc* should be connected to the address bus of the memory *(m0_adr := pc)* and the content of the memory cell with this address will be sent to the first instruction register *ir1 (ir1:=m0[m0_adr])*. Only when a short instruction, or the first word of the long instruction is in *ir1*, ALBI can analyze the instruction code *(ir1(15-11))*, length *(ir1(10))*, addressing mode *(ir1(9-8))* etc. In our notation, we use square brackets for addresses *(m0[m0_adr])* and parenthesis for the fields of the register. For example, *ir1(15-11)* means bits *15-11* of *ir1*, *ir1(10)* – the tenth bit of *ir1* etc.

Figures 8 – 14 are not the part of High Level Synthesis. I gave them for students or engineers which never designed processors and even don't know how the processor instructions are implementing. My goal here is to show that beginning from ASMs we can present the behavior at the High level and automatically transfer to the Register transfer level.

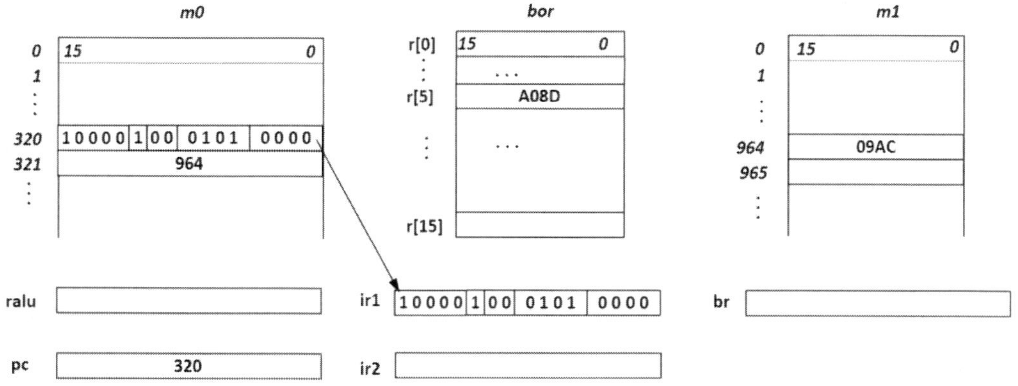

Figure 9. First step: *m0_adr := pc; ir1 := m0[m0_adr]*

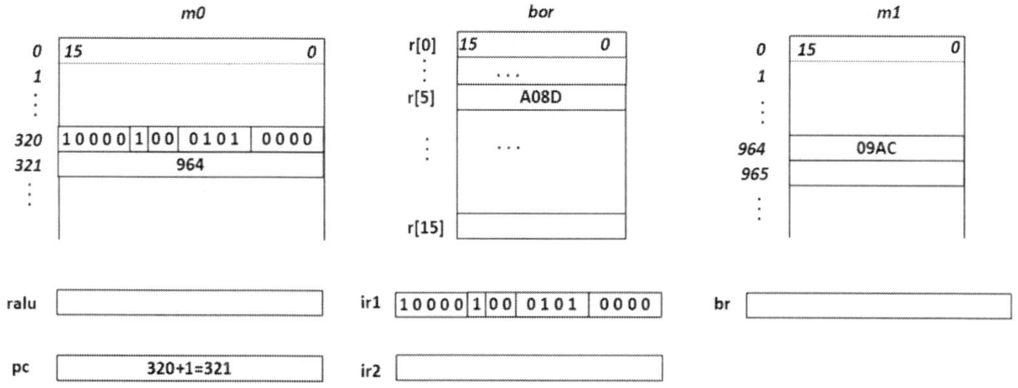

Figure 10. Second step: pc := pc + 1

In the second step (Fig. 10 and the second operator vertex in Fetch1 in Fig. 16), *ALBI* increments *pc (pc := pc + 1)*. It is necessary to get an address of the next instruction in *pc* if the current instruction is short, or to give *pc* the address of the second word of the long instruction. So, if the current instruction is short, the fetch is finished and the instruction is in *ir1*. If the instruction is long, the fetch should be continued. In our example, *ir1(10)* = *1* so we have a long instruction and *ALBI* should access memory *m0* again (Fig. 11 and Fig. 12)) for *fetch2* – see the check of *ir1(10)* and the stage *fetch2* with two steps in Fig. 15 and Fig. 16.

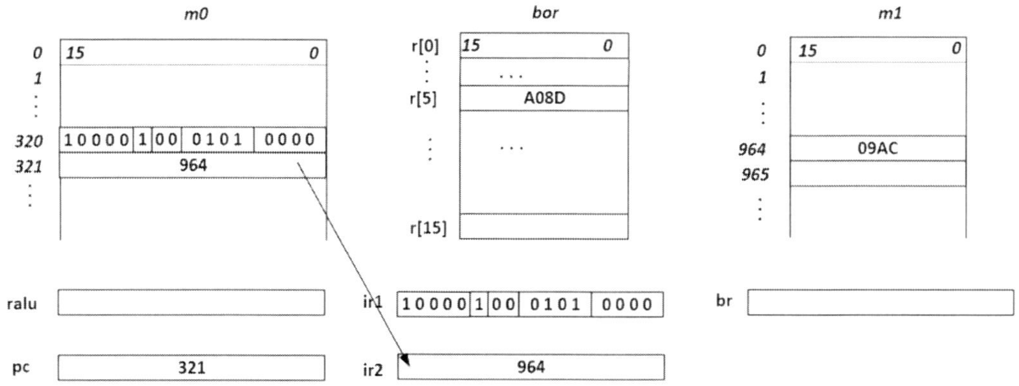

Figure 11. Third step: *m0_adr := pc; ir2 := m0[m0_adr]*

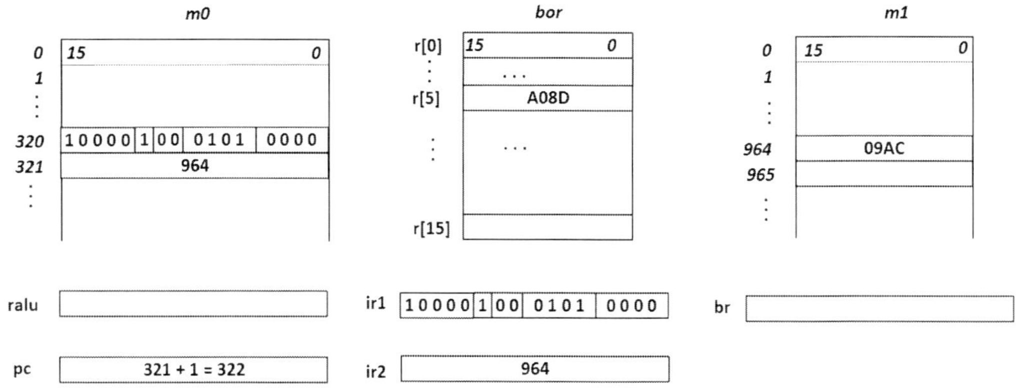

Figure 12. Fourth step: *pc := pc + 1*

After Fetch2, the long instruction is in two instruction registers *ir1* and *ir2*. *ir1* tells us that it is long *(ir1(10) = 1)* with the direct addressing mode *(ir(9-8) = 00)*. *ir2 = 964*, and it means that the second 16-bit operand (*09AC*) is in the memory *m1* in cell *964 (ir2=964)*. According the definition of instruction *lod*, this operand should be loaded into the place of the first operand – into register 5 of *bor* (*ir1(7-4) = 0101*) – steps five and six on Fig. 13 and Fig. 14. We use binary numbers in short fields, decimal numbers for addresses and hexadecimal numbers for operands, although in all cases, the binary radix is used in *ALBI* for the number representation.

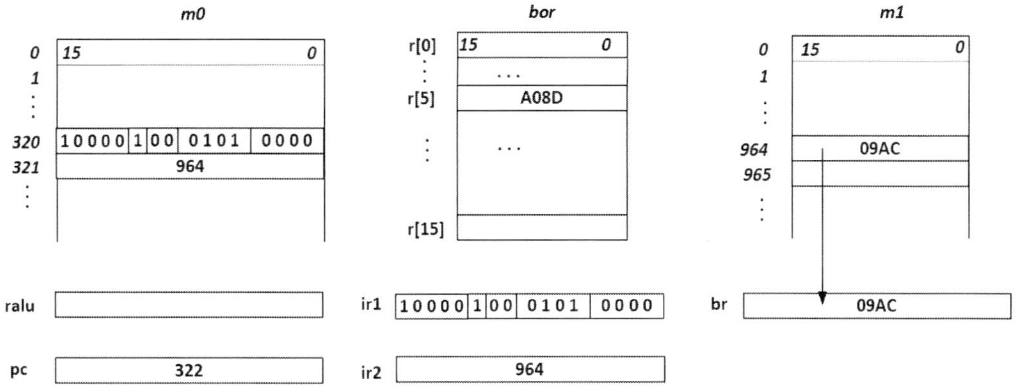

Figure 13. Fifth step: ***m1_adr:=ir2; br:=m1[m1_adr]***

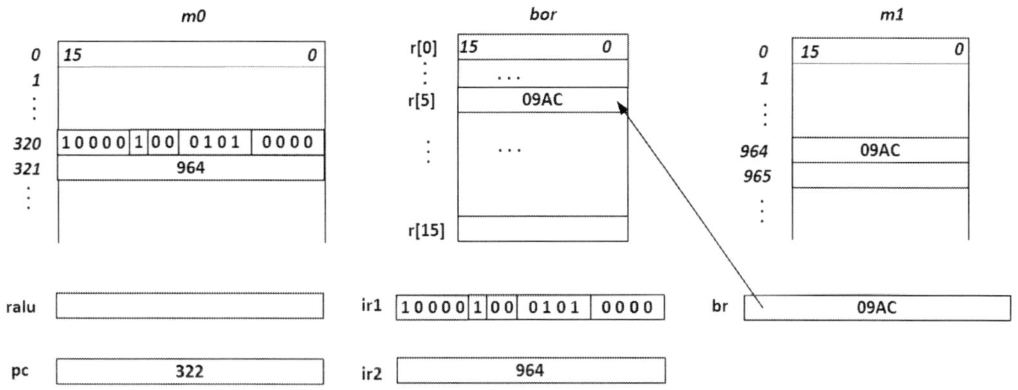

Figure 14. Sixth step: ***bor_adr := ir1(7-4); bor[bor_adr] := br***

I have discussed implementation of *lod long* instruction using two generalized operators in Fig. 16. All generalized operators are in Fig. 17.

For the best understanding of instruction *lod* I will give you one more description of this instruction for different addressing modes:

- Short direct: *bor[ir1(7-4)]:= bor[ir1(3-0)];*
- Short indirect: *bor[ir1(7-4)]:= m1[bor[ir1(3-0)]];*
- Long immediate: *bor[ir1(7-4)]:=ir2;*
- Long direct: *bor[ir1(7-4)]:=m1[ir2];*
- Long indirect: *bor[ir1(7-4)]:=m1[m1[ir2]];*
- Long direct with index: *bor[ir1(7-4)]:=m1[ir2 + bor[ir1(3-0)]];*
- Long indirect with index: *bor[ir1(7-4)]:=m1[m1[ir2] + bor[ir1(3-0)]].*

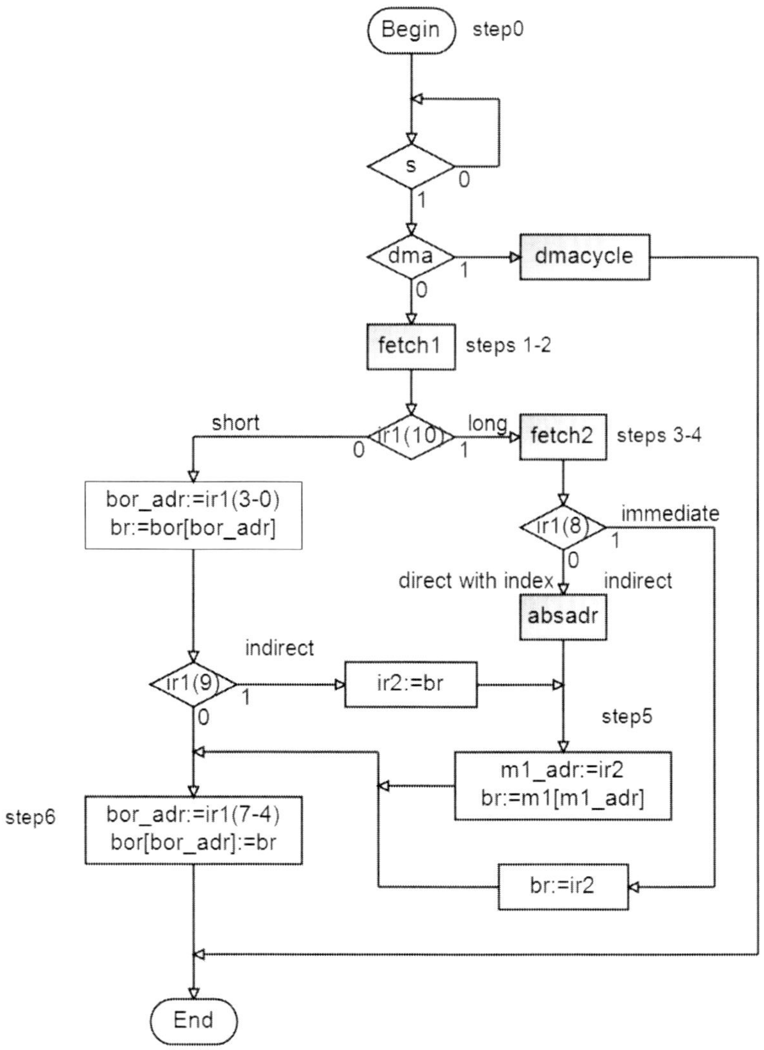

Figure 15. ASM lod marked by steps

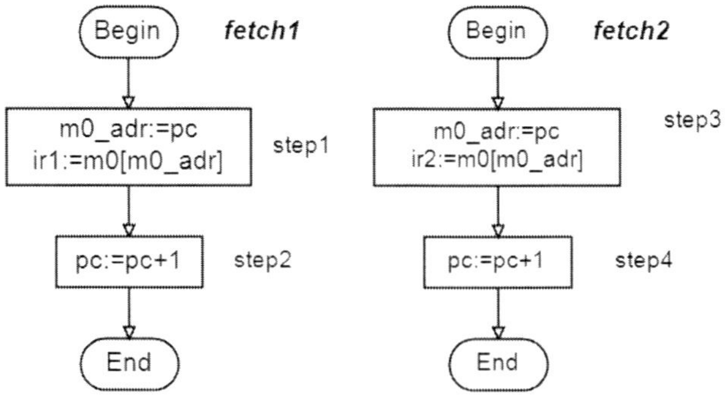

Figure 16. Generalized operators marked by steps for *lod long* instruction

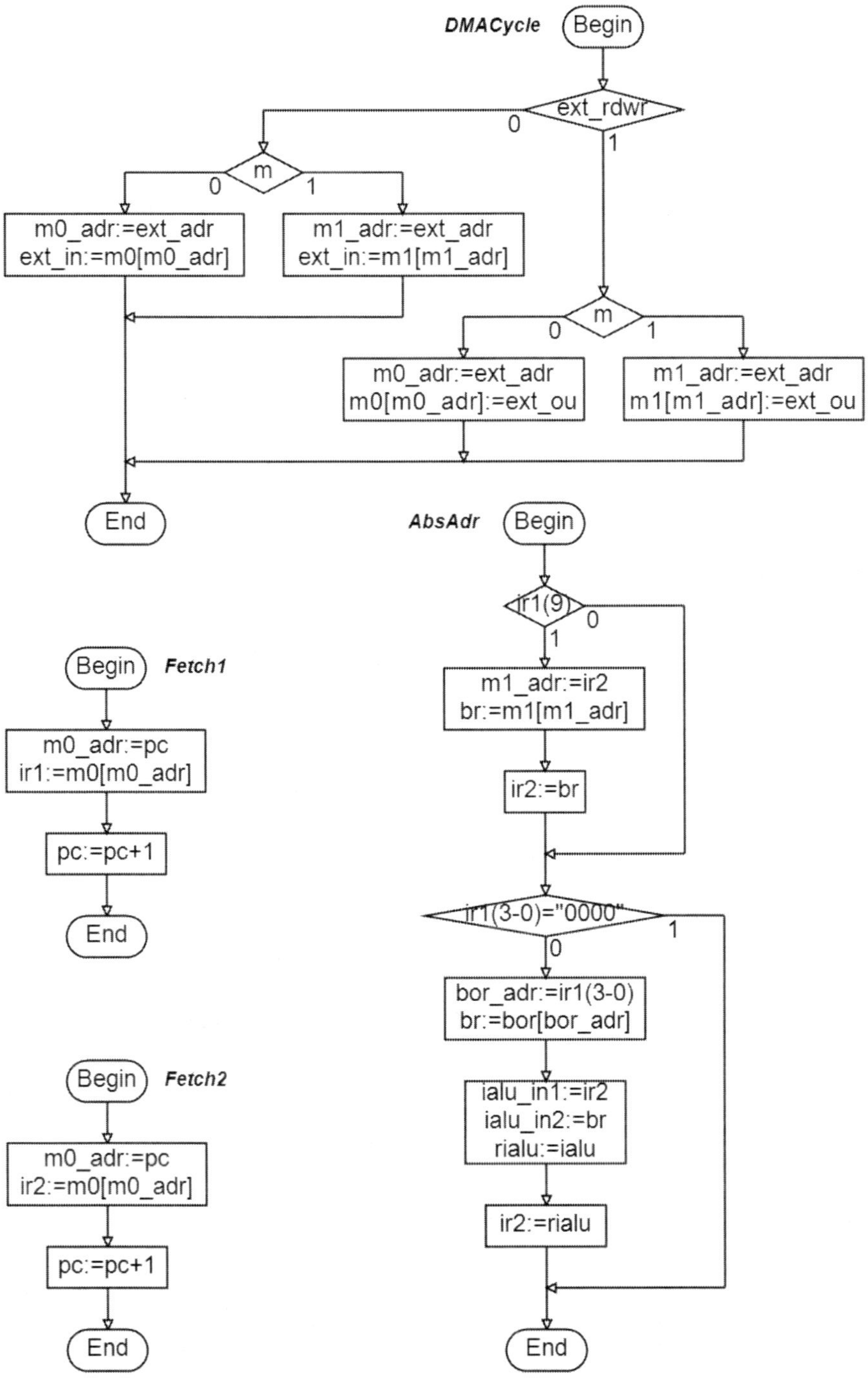

Figure 17. All generalized operators

Let's discuss shortly an implementation of *lod* instruction with other addressing modes (look at Fig. 15 and Fig. 16). If *ir1(10) = 0* we have short direct or short indirect mode. In both cases, *ALBI* must take the word from *bor* with address *in ir1(3-0): bor_adr:=ir1(3-0); br:=bor[bor_adr]*. If *ir1(9) = 0* (direct mode), ALBI writes this second operand into the place of the first one: *bor_adr:=ir1(7-4); bor[bor_adr]:=br*. If *ir1(9) = 1* (indirect mode), *ALBI* uses this word from *bor* with the second address as an address of operand, send it into *ir2* (*ir2:=br*) and applies to the operand memory *m1* for the second operand *(m1_adr:=ir2; br:=m1[m1_adr])*. Then *ALBI* writes this second operand into the place of the first one: *bor_adr:=ir1(7-4); bor[bor_adr]:=br*.

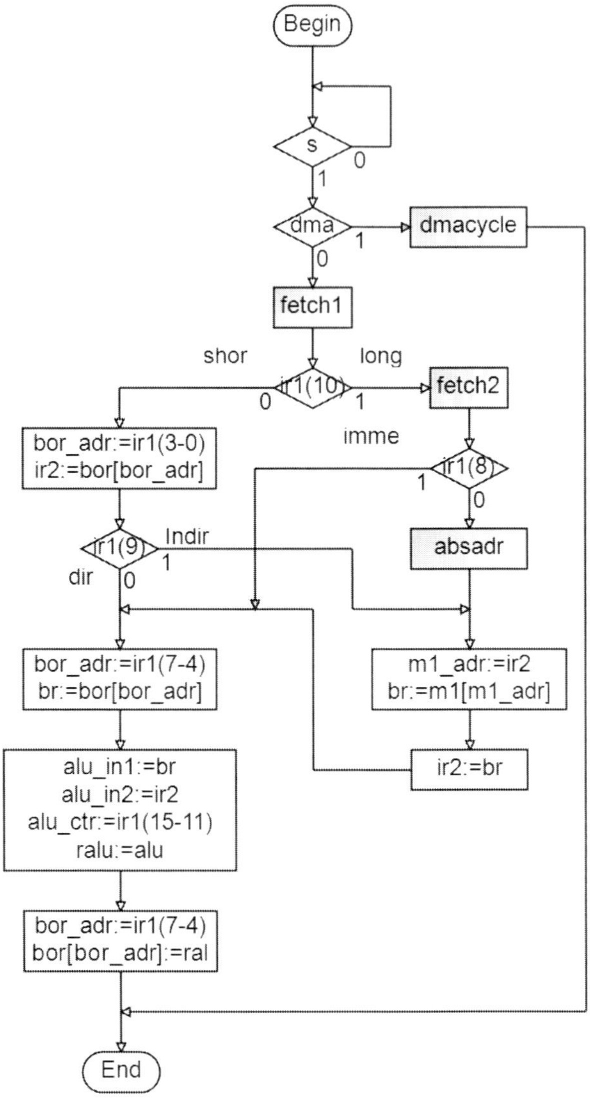

Figure 18. ASM of instruction *ao*

ASMs for three other instructions of *ALBI* – *ao, bun* and *inp* are presented at Fig. 18-20. Instruction *ao* implements arithmetic operation between the first and the second operands and sends the result at the place of the first operand. In *ao*, ALBI uses the same addresses modes as in *lod*. The first operand is always in *bor* with an address in *ir1[7-4]:*

- Short direct: *bor[ir1(7-4)]:=bor[ir1(7-4)] ao bor[ir1(3-0)];*
- Short indirect: *bor[ir1(7-4)]:=bor[ir1(7-4)] ao m1[bor[ir1(3-0)]];*
- Long immediate: *bor[ir1(7-4)]:=bor[ir1(7-4)] ao ir2;*
- Long direct: *bor[ir1(7-4)]:=bor[ir1(7-4)] ao m1[ir2];*
- Long indirect: *bor[ir1(7-4)]:=bor[ir1(7-4)] ao m1[m1[ir2]];*
- Long direct with index: *bor[ir1(7-4)]:=bor[ir1(7-4)] ao m1[ir2 + bor[ir1(3-0)]];*
- Long indirect with index: *bor[ir1(7-4)]:=bor[ir1(7-4)] ao m1[m1[ir2] + bor[ir1(3-0)]].*

Instruction *bun* changes unconditionally the sequential execution of the program. The ASM for unconditional branch *bun* is shown in Fig. 19. It has three modes – direct, immediate long and indirect.

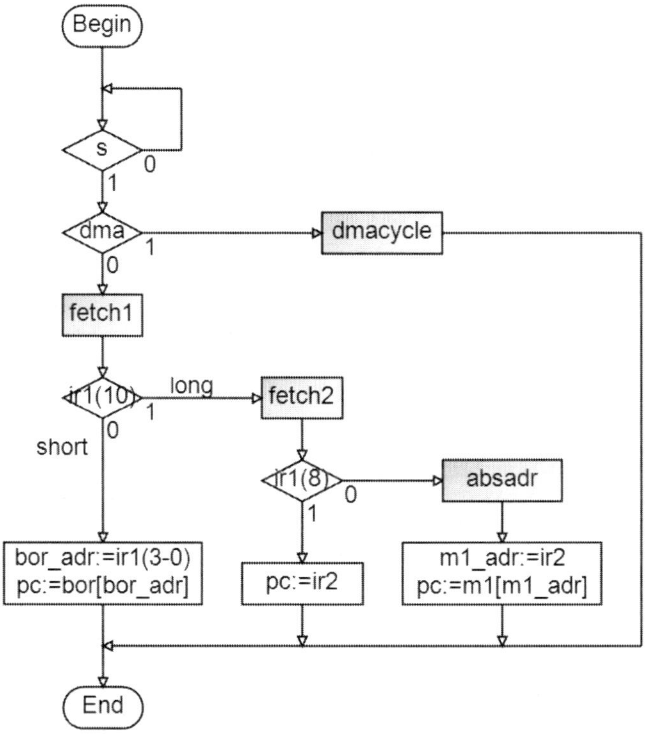

Figure 19. ASM of instruction *bun*

In the short direct mode, ALBI sends the address of the new instruction from *bor* with the second address in *ir1(3-0)* into program counter *pc* which points to the instruction that should be implemented:

bor_adr:=ir1(3-0); pc:=bor[bor_adr].

In the long immediate mode (*ir1(8) = 1*), ALBI sends the address of the new instruction from *ir2* to *pc*:

pc:=ir2.

In the long direct or indirect mode, as in the previous instructions, ALBI finds the second operand according the generalized operator *absadr* and uses it as the address of the next instruction.

The goal of instruction *inp* is to take the word from the input of *ALBI* into input register

inpr:=data_in

and then to send *inpr* into *bor* with an address in *ir1(7-4):*

bor_adr:=ir1(7-4); bor[bor_adr]:=inpr.

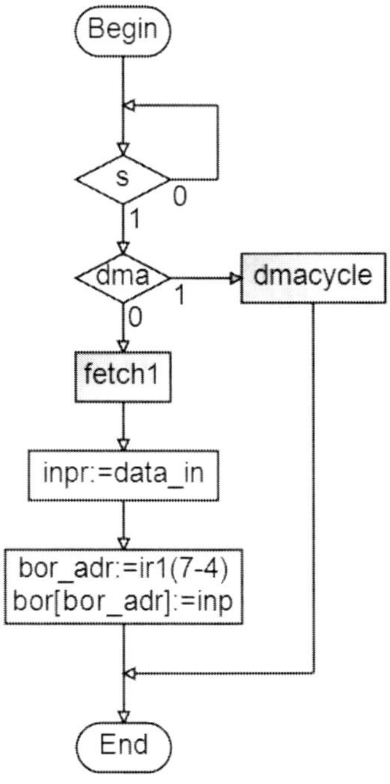

Figure 20. ASM of instructions *inp*

Thus, I finished the detailed explanation of instructions and constructed ASMs for all of them. Now I can turn to design of *ALBI* based on our design methodology with the use of VHDL. But first, I would like to underline here that at the behavior level we don't have an architecture or Data Path of the designed system. If we write

ir2:=br

in the operator vertex, we mean that *ir2* is an input of some unit and *br* is the output of another unit but we don't know yet how these units will be connected later – directly or through buses (multiplexes). Here we use these signals as variables and the connection between them (buses) will be constructed automatically and optimal at the design of Data path.

2.3 High Level Synthesis of ALBI

2.3.1 Internal representation of ASMs in Synthagate

Before I move to ASM combining, I would like to show the internal representation of ASMs in Synthagate. Designer must draw ASM in ASM Creator – the special graphical interface of Synthagate. ASM Creator numbers vertices, operators, microoperations and logical conditions and constructs two files – *name.gsa* and *name.txt*. Here *name* is the name of ASM. After that Synthagate is working not with pictures but with these files (*.gsa* and *.txt*). Such two files for instruction *ao* (Fig. 21) are presented in Fig. 22 and Fig. 23. In Fig. 21 I have numbered vertices to explain Fig. 22 and Fig. 23.

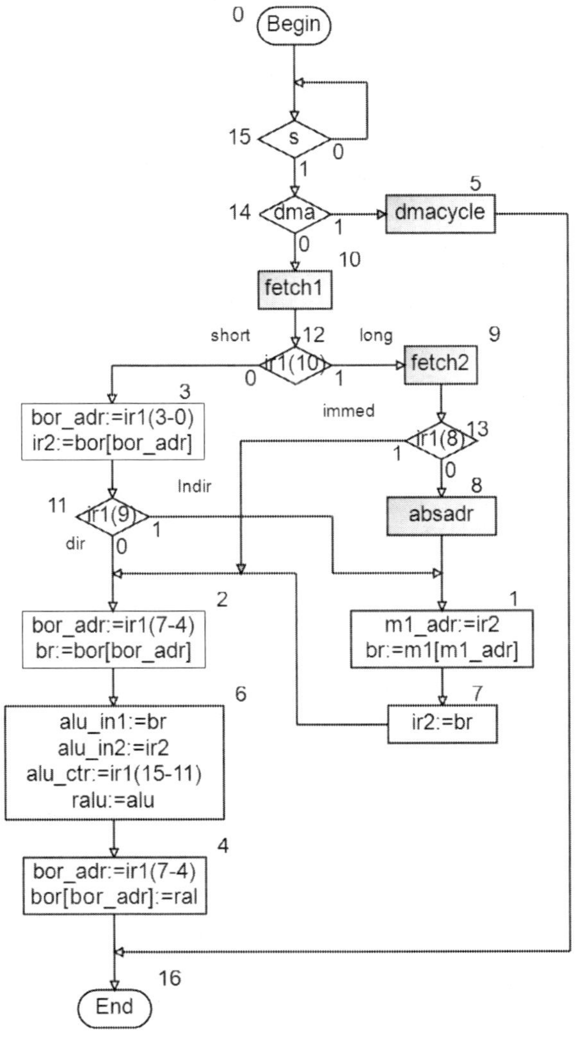

Figure 21. ASM *ao.asd* with numbered vertices

File *name.gsa* is the two-connected list of ASM graph. Each row of this list corresponds to one vertex. Columns in this list:

1. The number of the vertex;
2. The content of the vertex – Y_n for operator and x_m for logical condition;
3. The number of the vertex following the operator vertex, or following output "1" of the conditional vertex;
4. The number of the vertex following output "0" of the conditional vertex.

Vertices *Begin* and *End* are described as operator vertices. File *name.txt* (Fig. 23 for ASM *ao*) contains three sections - Microinstructions (operators), Microoperations and Logical conditions.

```
 0 Begin  15    0
 1 Y1     7     0
 2 Y2     6     0
 3 Y3     11    0
 4 Y4     16    0
 5 Y5     16    0
 6 Y6     4     0
 7 Y7     2     0
 8 Y8     1     0
 9 Y9     13    0
10 Y10    12    0
11 x1     1     2
12 x2     9     3
13 x3     2     8
14 x4     5     10
15 x5     14    15
16 End    0     0
```

Figure 22. ASM ao as two-connected list (file *ao.gsa*)

```
Micro Instructions:     Micro Operations:                 Logical
Y1 = y1 y2              y1  :  m1_adr:=ir2                Conditions:
Y2 = y3 y4              y2  :  br:=m1[m1_adr]             File  Draw
Y3 = y5 y6              y3  :  bor_adr:=ir1(7-4)          x1  : ir1(9)
Y4 = y3 y7              y4  :  br:=bor[bor_adr]           x2  : ir1(10)
Y5 = y8                 y5  :  bor_adr:=ir1(3-0)          x3  : ir1(8)
Y6 = y9 y10 y11 y12     y6  :  ir2:=bor[bor_adr]          x4  : dma
Y7 = y13                y7  :  bor[bor_adr]:=ralu
Y8 = y14                y8  :  dmacycle
Y9 = y15                y9  :  alu_in1:=br
Y10 = y16               y10 :  alu_in2:=ir2
                        y11 :  alu_ctr:=ir1(15-11)
                        y12 :  ralu:=alu
                        y13 :  ir2:=br
                        y14 :  absadr
                        y15 :  fetch2
                        y16 :  fetch1
```

Figure 23. File *ao.txt*

2.3.2 ASM Combining

You can read more about transformation of ASMs – minimization, combining etc. in my previous book "Finite State Machines and Algorithmic State Machines". Synthagate combined four ASMs *ao, lod, bun* and *inp*. Really, the designer should do nothing except presenting ASMs as graphs or as SystemC or VHDL codes. Synthagate will make everything from initial ASMs including constructing VHDL codes at the Register Transfer Level. Thus, several next files will be results obtaining by Synthagate.

Synthagate used two additional variables *bit0* and *bit1* to encode ASMS in ASM combining (Table 1). Such encoding minimizes the number of vertices in combined ASM. Nevertheless, a designer can use his own encoding as well.

Table 1. ASM encoding

ASMs	bit0 bit1
ao	*00*
lod	*01*
bun	*10*
inp	*11*

Initial four ASMs before combining had 54 vertices. Combined ASM *Func* had 47 vertices, but after minimization ASM *Funcm* contains only 35 vertices. I would like to underline that practically there are no constraints at the number of ASMs to combine, at the complexity these ASMs and on the complexity ASM for minimization.

```
0     begin 21    0         18    Y18    16    0
1     Y1    22    0         19    end    0     0
2     Y2    6     0         20    x4     5     10
3     Y3    24    0         21    x5     20    21
4     Y4    19    0         22    x7     16    7
5     Y5    19    0         23    x1     7     16
6     Y6    4     0         24    x1     1     2
7     Y7    25    0         25    x7     1     2
8     Y8    26    0         26    x6     12    1
9     Y9    29    0         27    x7     18    2
10    Y10   34    0         28    x6     11    27
11    Y11   19    0         29    x3     28    8
12    Y12   19    0         30    x2     9     13
13    Y13   19    0         31    x7     14    30
14    Y14   15    0         32    x7     17    3
15    Y15   19    0         33    x2     9     32
16    Y16   19    0         34    x6     31    33
17    Y17   23    0
```

Figure 24. Combined and minimized ASM *Funcm* (file *Funcm.gsa*)

```
Micro Instructions:
Y1 = y1 y2
Y2 = y3 y4
Y3 = y5 y6
Y4 = y3 y7
Y5 = y8
Y6 = y9 y10 y11 y12
Y7 = y13
Y8 = y14
Y9 = y15
Y10 = y16
Y11 = y17
Y12 = y1 y18
Y13 = y5 y19
Y14 = y20
Y15 = y3 y21
Y16 = y3 y22
Y17 = y5 y4
Y18 = y23
```

```
Micro Operations:
y1  : m1_adr:=ir2
y2  : br:=m1[m1_adr]
y3  : bor_adr:=ir1(7-4)
y4  : br:=bor[bor_adr]
y5  : bor_adr:=ir1(3-0)
y6  : ir2:=bor[bor_adr]
y7  : bor[bor_adr]:=ralu
y8  : dmacycle
y9  : alu_in1:=br
y10 : alu_in2:=ir2
y11 : alu_ctr:=ir1(15-11)
y12 : ralu:=alu
y13 : ir2:=br
y14 : absadr
y15 : fetch2
y16 : fetch1
y17 : pc:=ir2
y18 : pc:=m1[m1_adr]
y19 : pc:=bor[bor_adr]
y20 : inpr:=data_in
y21 : bor[bor_adr]:=inpr
y22 : bor[bor_adr]:=br
y23 : br:=ir2
```

```
Logical
Conditions:
File Draw
x1  : ir1(9)
x2  : ir1(10)
x3  : ir1(8)
x4  : dma
x5  : s
x6  : Bit0
x7  : Bit1
```

Figure 25. File *Funcm.txt*

2.3.3 Insert generalized operators

At the last step of ASM transformations Synthagate inserts all component ASMs (generalized operators) and constructs one combined and minimized Functional ASM *Funcmi* without generalized operators. ASM *Funcmi* after inserting generalized operators is presented in Fig. 27 (Funcmi.gsa) and Fig. 28 (Funcmi.txt). As you saw before, designer should draw very small ASMs (average number about 8-10 vertices in initial ASMs), but after combining, minimization and inserting generalized operators, the final functional ASM can contain even several hundred vertices. This ASM presents a whole behavior of the designed system and, in our not complex example, contains 49 vertices. Once again, there are no constraints on the number of generalized operators and the number of levels of their insertion. The same steps take place when a designer initially presents ASMs in SystemC or in VHDL.

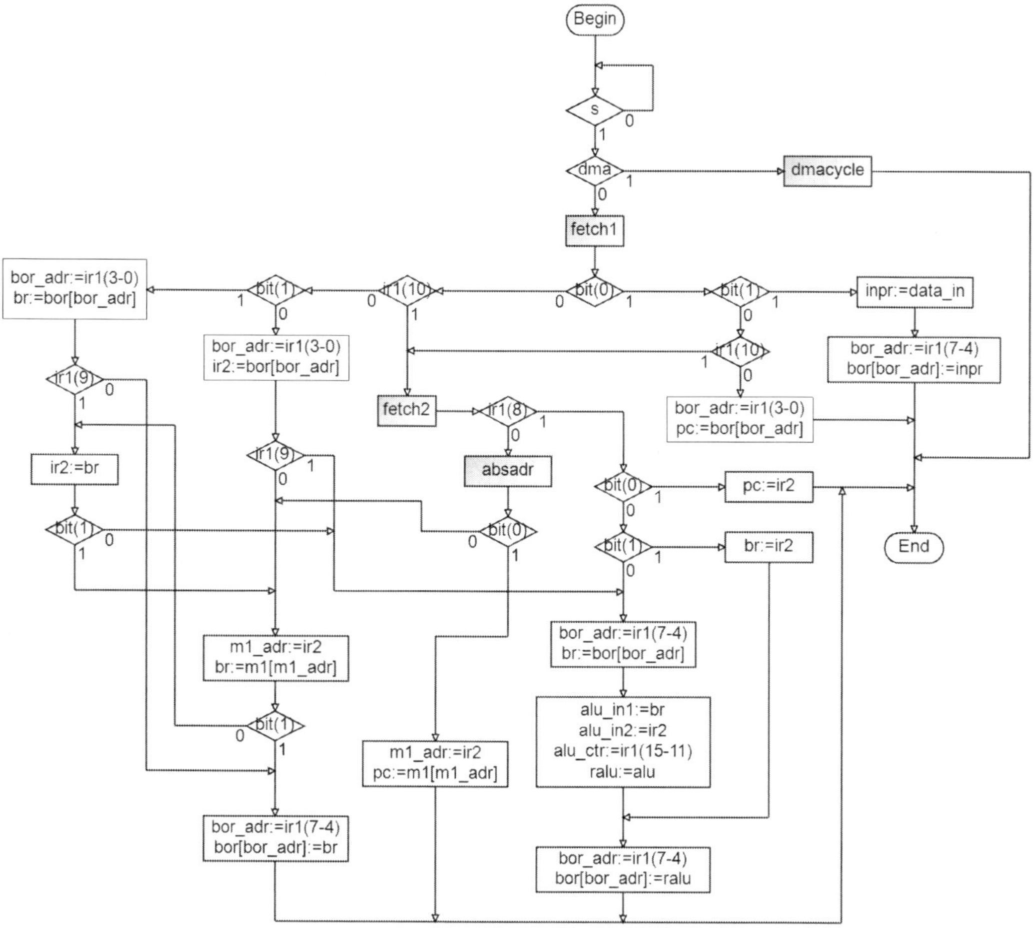

Figure 26. Combined Functional ASM *Funcm*

0	begin	21	0	17	Y13	23	0	33	x2	9	32
1	Y1	22	0	18	Y14	16	0	34	x6	31	33
2	Y2	6	0	19	end	0	0	35	Y15	19	0
3	Y3	24	0	20	x4	5	10	36	Y16	19	0
4	Y4	19	0	21	x5	20	21	37	Y17	19	0
5	x9	40	39	22	x7	16	7	38	Y18	19	0
6	Y5	4	0	23	x1	7	16	39	x8	36	38
7	Y6	25	0	24	x1	1	2	40	x8	35	37
8	x1	42	46	25	x7	1	2	41	Y13	44	0
9	Y22	47	0	26	x6	12	1	42	Y1	45	0
10	Y23	48	0	27	x7	18	2	43	Y19	26	0
11	Y7	19	0	28	x6	11	27	44	Y20	43	0
12	Y8	19	0	29	x3	28	8	45	Y6	46	0
13	Y9	19	0	30	x2	9	13	46	x10	26	41
14	Y10	15	0	31	x7	14	30	47	Y21	29	0
15	Y11	19	0	32	x7	17	3	48	Y21	34	0
16	Y12	19	0								

Figure 27. ASM *Funcmi* with inserted generalized operators

```
Micro Instructions:
Y1 = y1 y2
Y2 = y3 y4
Y3 = y5 y6
Y4 = y3 y7
Y5 = y8 y9 y10 y11
Y6 = y12
Y7 = y13
Y8 = y1 y14
Y9 = y5 y15
Y10 = y16
Y11 = y3 y17
Y12 = y3 y18
```

```
Micro
Instructions:
Y13 = y5 y4
Y14 = y19
Y15 = y20 y21
Y16 = y20 y22
Y17 = y23 y24
Y18 = y23 y25
Y19 = y26
Y20 = y27 y28 y29
Y21 = y30
Y22 = y31 y32
Y23 = y31 y33
```

```
Micro Operations:
y1    : m1_adr:=ir2
y2    : br:=m1[m1_adr]
y3    : bor_adr:=ir1(7-4)
y4    : br:=bor[bor_adr]
y5    : bor_adr:=ir1(3-0)
y6    : ir2:=bor[bor_adr]
y7    : bor[bor_adr]:=ralu
y8    : alu_in1:=br
y9    : alu_in2:=ir2
y10   : alu_ctr:=ir1(15-11)
y11   : ralu:=alu
y12   : ir2:=br
y13   : pc:=ir2
y14   : pc:=m1[m1_adr]
y15   : pc:=bor[bor_adr]
y16   : inpr:=data_in
y17   : bor[bor_adr]:=inpr
y18   : bor[bor_adr]:=br
y19   : br:=ir2
y20   : m1_adr:=ext_adr
y21   : m1[m1_adr]:=ext_out
y22   : ext_in:=m1[m1_adr]
y23   : m0_adr:=ext_adr
y24   : m0[m0_adr]:=ext_out
y25   : ext_in:=m0[m0_adr]
```

```
Micro Operations:
y26   : ir2:=rialu
y27   : ialu_in1:=ir2
y28   : ialu_in2:=br
y29   : rialu:=ialu
y30   : pc:=pc+1
y31   : m0_adr:=pc
y32  : ir2:=m0[m0_adr]
y33  : ir1:=m0[m0_adr]
```

```
Logical Conditions:
File Draw
x1   : ir1(9)
x2   : ir1(10)
x3   : ir1(8)
x4   : dma
x5   : s
x6   : Bit0
x7   : Bit1
x8   : m
x9   : ext_rdwr
x10  :ir1(3-0)="0000"
```

Figure 28. File *Funcmi.txt*

2.3.4 Functional Specifications

To design the behavior description of digital system the designer does not have to define each port and each signal. The special Synthagate program automatically creates an XML code of Functional specifications and the designer should only insert the length of several ports and signals (not all, only a very small part of them) in these specifications in the dialog mode. In Fig. 29 you see 38 specifications for ports, signals and variables, but in dialog I inserted only six of them.

```
<functional_specifications>
    <declarations>
        <port name="bit0" width="1" direction="in" />
        <port name="bit1" width="1" direction="in" />
        <port name="data_in" width="16" direction="in" />
        <port name="s" width="1" direction="in" />
        <port name="ext_in"      width="16" direction="out"    />
        <port name="ext_adr" width="16"     direction="in"     />
        <port name="ext_out" width="16"     direction="in"     />
        <port name="dma" width="1"    direction="in"    />
        <port name="m" width="1" direction="in"   />
        <port name="ext_rdwr" width="1"     direction="in"     />
        <signal name="bor" width="16" size="16" />
        <signal name="m0" width="16" size="65536" />
        <signal name="m1" width="16" size="65536"  />
        <signal name="br" width="16" />
        <signal name="inpr" width="16" />
        <signal name="ir1" width="16" />
        <signal name="ir2" width="16" />
        <signal name="pc" width="16" />
        <signal name="ralu" width="16" />
        <signal name="rialu" width="16" />
        <variable name="bor_adr" width="4" />
        <variable name="m0_adr" width="16" />
        <variable name="m1_adr" width="16" />
    </declarations>
        <functions>
              <func       name="alub" >
                    <param name="alu_in1"   width="16"   />
                    <param name="alu_in2"   width="16"   />
                    <param name="alu_ctr"   width="5"    />
                    <param name="alu"       width="16"   />
              </func>

              <func       name="ialub"      >
                    <param name="ialu_in1"  width="16"   />
                    <param name="ialu_in2"  width="16"   />
                    <param name="ialu"            width="16"   />
              </func>
        </functions>

        <required_libraries>
              <systemc>
                    <library    name="ialu.h"                  />
                    <library    name="alu.h"                   />
              </systemc>

              <vhdl>
                    <library    name="my_package" />
              </vhdl>
    </required_libraries>
</functional_specifications>
```

Figure 29. Functional Specifications *Funcmi.spec*

2.3.5. High level design as a Finite state machine

Synthagate begins this stage by constructing FSM *Funcmi.t1* (Fig. 30) from ASM *Funcmi,* as I presented that in Section 1.2. Signals x_p and y_n here are the same as in Fig. 28.

a_m	a_s	$X(a_m,a_s)$	$Y(a_m,a_s)$	H
a1	a1	x5*x4*x9*x8	y20y21	1
a1	a1	x5*x4*x9*~x8	y23y24	2
a1	a1	x5*x4*~x9*x8	y20y22	3
a1	a1	x5*x4*~x9*~x8	y23y25	4
a1	a8	x5*~x4	y31y33	5
a1	a1	~x5	--	6
a2	a1	x7	y3y18	7
a2	a6	~x7	y12	8
a3	a5	1	y8y9y10y11	9
a4	a2	x1	y1y2	10
a4	a3	~x1	y3y4	11
a5	a1	1	y3y7	12
a6	a2	x7	y1y2	13
a6	a3	~x7	y3y4	14
a7	a17	1	y30	15
a8	a18	1	y30	16
a9	a1	1	y3y17	17
a10	a6	x1	y12	18
a10	a1	~x1	y3y18	19
a11	a1	1	y3y18	20
a12	a15	1	y27y28y29	21
a13	a16	1	y12	22
a14	a1	x6	y1y14	23
a14	a2	~x6	y1y2	24
a15	a14	1	y26	25
a16	a1	x10*x6	y1y14	26
a16	a2	x10*~x6	y1y2	27
a16	a12	~x10	y5y4	28
a17	a1	x3*x6	y13	29
a17	a11	x3*~x6*x7	y19	30
a17	a3	x3*~x6*~x7	y3y4	31
a17	a13	~x3*x1	y1y2	32
a17	a1	~x3*~x1*x10*x6	y1y14	33
a17	a2	~x3*~x1*x10*~x6	y1y2	34
a17	a12	~x3*~x1*~x10	y5y4	35
a18	a9	x6*x7	y16	36
a18	a7	x6*~x7*x2	y31y32	37
a18	a1	x6*~x7*~x2	y5y15	38
a18	a7	~x6*x2	y31y32	39
a18	a10	~x6*~x2*x7	y5y4	40
a18	a4	~x6*~x2*~x7	y5y6	41

Figure 30. FSM Mealy *Funcmi.t1*, implementing ASM *Funcmi*

With Functional FSM *Funcmi.t1* and the functional specification *Funcmi.spec* (Fig. 29) as an input, Synthagate automatically constructs two variants (in VHDL and System C) of the behavior description (High level) of the whole design system in VHDL (*Funcmi.vhd* (Fig. 31), *my_package.vhd* (Fig. 32)) or in System C (*Funcmi.cpp* (Fig. 33), *Funcmi.h* (Fig. 34)).

`Refer to Figure 31 (Chapter 2) in HLS-Figures-and-Tables.pdf`
(www.synthezza.com/hls-figures-and-tables)

Figure 31. VHDL code for High Level Synthesis of *ALBI*

`Refer to Figure 32 (Chapter 2) in HLS-Figures-and-Tables.pdf`

Figure 32. My_package for high level

`Refer to Figure 33 (Chapter 2) in HLS-Figures-and-Tables.pdf`

Figure 33. System C code for High Level Synthesis of *ALBI*

`Refer to Figure 34 (Chapter 2) in HLS-Figures-and-Tables.pdf`

Figure 34. System C code for *Funcmi.h*

After preparing the test bench at the behavior level the designer can simulate the functional project with any simulation tool. A designer should choose what he/she would like to use in simulation at the High level – version in VHDL or version in System C. The same test bench can be used later at the last stage of design – after top design at the structural (RTL) level.

3. FROM HIGH LEVEL TO REGISTER TRASFER LEVEL

3.1 Data Path Design

3.1.1 Functional and Structural approaches

In the previous Chapter I used functional ASM because this ASM represents the functional behavior of *ALBI*. In this ASM, inputs and outputs of *ALBI* units in each assignment were used as variables. We did not have a real structure of *ALBI* yet. For example, in assignments

bor_adr:=ir1(3-0); br:=bor[bor_adr]; m1_adr:=ir2; br:=m1[m1_adr]

we know nothing about how these units are connected – whether direct connections or buses (multiplexers) are used to provide information from the output of one unit to the input of another one. For behavior representation and for understanding of this behavior, functional ASMs are very comprehensible and very compact, especially with the use of generalized operators, such as *Fetch1, Fetch2, DMACycle* and *AbsAdr*.

To explain the difference between functional representation and structural representation (between the function and the structure in our context) I will use a very simple structure in Fig. 1. In this figure, we have sources *s0, ..., s3* and targets (receivers) *t0, ..., t4* (disregard target *t5* for now, we will use it later). For simplicity, you can think about these sources and targets as registers.

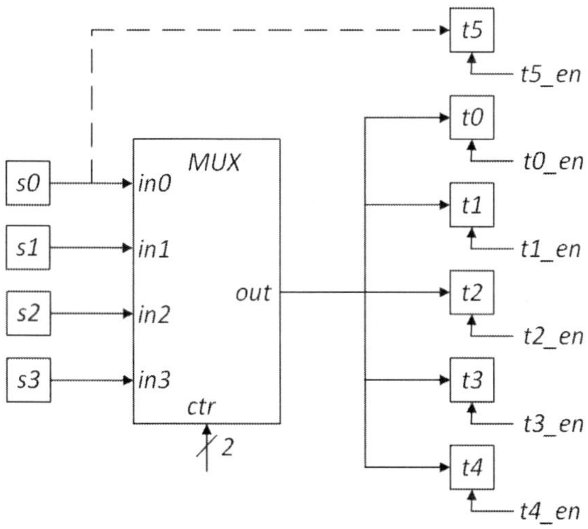

Figure 1. Our first structure

Let us suppose that we should send information from each source to each target except *t5*. Of course, we can connect each source directly to each target, but the cost of such connection is very high. So, we use here a multiplexer (*MUX*) with four inputs. To send information from any input to the output of *MUX* we should supply 2-bit control signal (*ctr_mux*), corresponding to the input. Suppose that the control signal is equal to the number of the input, so for *in0*, the signal at *ctr_mux* is equal to *00*, for *in1* – *01* etc.

We will discuss several examples in Fig. 2. In the first example, source *s2* transfers information to target *t3*. At the functional level, the description is very simple and clear: *t3* := *s2*. At the structural level, to pass information from input *in2* to the output of *MUX*, *ctr_mux* should get control signal *10*. To write information from the output of *MUX* to the target *t3* the signal *enable* of *t3* should be equal to *1*: *t3_en* := '*1*'.

Functional	Structure
1. t3 := s2	ctr_mux := '10' t3_en := '1'
2. t1 := s3 t2 := s3	ctr_mux := '11' t1_en := '1' t2_en := '1'
3. t5 := s0	t5_en := '1'
4. t5 := s0 t4 := s1	t5_en := '1' ctr_mux := '01' t4_en := '1'

Figure 2. Examples of descriptions at the functional and structural levels

In the second example, we send the same information from one source *s3* to two targets *t1* and *t2*. The control signal of *MUX* must be equal to *11* and two *enable* signals, equal to *1*, will write information into *t1* and *t2*. However, if we should like to pass information from several sources to several outputs at the same time, we need several MUXes because one *MUX* transfers only one input to its output. To put it more precisely, we need as many MUXes as the number of sources we wish to pass simultaneously.

One of the targets *t5* in our structure is connected only with one source, i.e. it can get information only from *s0*. We call such a connection a *direct connection*. In example 3 in Fig. 2 to send information from *s0* to *t5* it is sufficient to supply enable signal to this target: *t5_en* := '*1*'.

In the fourth example we have two simultaneous transfers – the first through the direct connection: *t5* := *s0*, and the second – through the indirect connection: *t4* := *s1*. Since only one indirect transfer takes place in this example, we need only one MUX in such a case.

Let us return to our ALBI. Any digital system is usually regarded as a composition of *Control unit* and *Operational unit* (*Data Path*) – see Fig. 3. Data path contains such regular blocks as memory, registers, ALU, counters, coders, encoders, multiplexers, demultiplexers etc. A control unit produces a sequence of control signals that force implementation of microoperations in data path. Sometimes designers include cloud (non-regular) circuits in data path as well. In Fig. 4 we have a fragment of data path with two registers *R1, R2* and a cloud circuit.

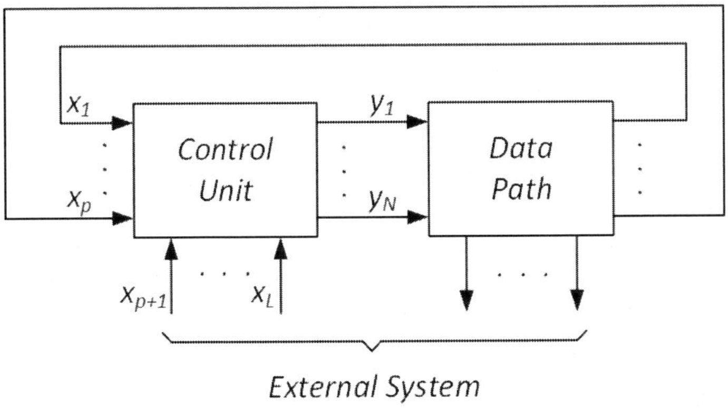

Figure 3. Digital system as a composition of Control unit and Data path

Suppose that in the digital system there are transfers from R1 to R2 at the different time with different conditions. Designers often use a cloud circuit to realize some Boolean function, and the output of this circuit is the signal for the transfer. So, this circuit defines when and under which logic conditions the transfer information from *R1* to *R2* takes place.

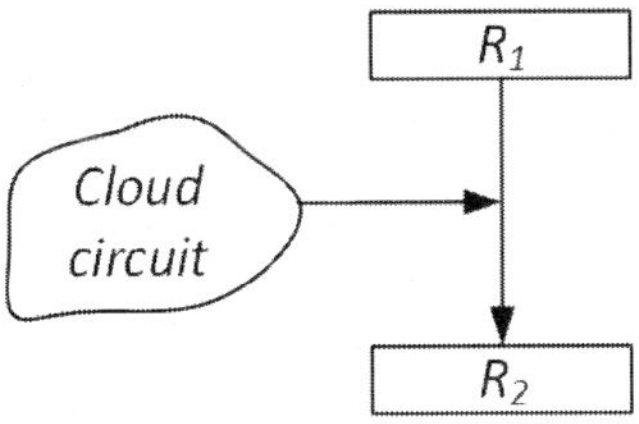

Figure 4. Element of Data path with a cloud circuit

One of the main concepts in our design methodology is the construction of "*naked data path*". Naked data path doesn't contain any cloud circuits, only standard regular units with their inputs and outputs. Such units can be automatically predesigned or even taken from libraries. We leave all check-ups of conditions to control unit. We can afford this because we know how to design very complicated FSM with hardly any constraints on their size, that is, the number of inputs, outputs and states. We will try to show that such design and its verification are very simple. Moreover, we will formalize a design of the digital system with naked data path.

3.1.2 Functional process tables

At the first step of Data Path (DP) design Synthagate constructs the functional process table *Funcmi.tab* (Fig. 5), using file *Funcmi.gsa* (Fig. 2-28) and *Funcmi.txt* (Fig. 2-29).

This file contains four columns:

- Operators (microinstructions) *Yt;*
- Microoperations of operator *Yt*;
- The length of words in the assignment;
- Assignments corresponding to microoperations in column 2.

There are two classes of microoperations in this table. The first one presents the transfer information from the output of one unit to the input of another unit, for example, *br:=m1[m1_adr], bor_adr:=ir1(3-0), pc:=ir2*. Such microoperations contains the length of the assignment. The microoperations from the second class, such as *pc:=pc+1*, are executed in one operational unit. Unfortunately, we have only one such microoperation in this rather simple design. In Chapter 5, I will give more complicated designs and you find many microoperations of the second class. Such microoperations have zero in the third column. For some time, we will continue to work only with microoperations from the first class marked by nonzero numbers in the process table. The microoperations of the second class will not be "our clients" for a while.

```
Y1      y11     16   br:=m1[m1_adr]
        y27     16   m1_adr:=ir2

Y2      y8      4    bor_adr:=ir1(7-4)
        y9      16   br:=bor[bor_adr]

Y3      y7      4    bor_adr:=ir1(3-0)
        y18     16   ir2:=bor[bor_adr]

Y4      y6      16   bor[bor_adr]:=ralu
        y8      4    bor_adr:=ir1(7-4)

Y5      y1      5    alu_ctr:=ir1(15-11)
        y2      16   alu_in1:=br
        y3      16   alu_in2:=ir2
        y32     16   ralu:=alu

Y6      y19     16   ir2:=br

Y7      y29     16   pc:=ir2

Y8      y27     16   m1_adr:=ir2
        y30     16   pc:=m1[m1_adr]

Y9      y7      4    bor_adr:=ir1(3-0)
        y28     16   pc:=bor[bor_adr]

Y10     y16     16   inpr:=data_in

Y11     y5      16   bor[bor_adr]:=inpr
        y8      4    bor_adr:=ir1(7-4)

Y12     y4      16   bor[bor_adr]:=br
```

	y8	4	bor_adr:=ir1(7-4)
Y13	y7	4	bor_adr:=ir1(3-0)
	y9	16	br:=bor[bor_adr]
Y14	y10	16	br:=ir2
Y15	y25	16	m1[m1_adr]:=ext_out
	y26	16	m1_adr:=ext_adr
Y16	y13	16	ext_in:=m1[m1_adr]
	y26	16	m1_adr:=ext_adr
Y17	y22	16	m0[m0_adr]:=ext_out
	y23	16	m0_adr:=ext_adr
Y18	y12	16	ext_in:=m0[m0_adr]
	y23	16	m0_adr:=ext_adr
Y19	y21	16	ir2:=rialu
Y20	y14	16	ialu_in1:=ir2
	y15	16	ialu_in2:=br
	y33	16	rialu:=ialu
Y21	y31	0	pc:=pc+1
Y22	y20	16	ir2:=m0[m0_adr]
	y24	16	m0_adr:=pc
Y23	y17	16	ir1:=m0[m0_adr]
	y24	16	m0_adr:=pc

Figure 5. Functional process table *Funcmi.tab*

The next step of Synthagate – construction of the Functional process table after splitting of registers. We don't have such a case in this design, but a lot in designs in Chapter 5. In this design *Funcmi.mrk* (our next file) has the same microoperations but if splitting of registers takes place, they can be renumbered. You can ask me why?

To answer to this and maybe to other questions I will explain you what Synthagate does at the stage of splitting of registers.

Look, please, at Fig.6 – it is the fragment of another design. Let's some Processor has a *bor* with 4-bit word and it must load a 16-bit operand from *bor* to *br*. In this case, Processor should sequentially take words from *bor* and save them *in br(15-12), br(11-8), br(7-4)* and *br(3-0)*. Thus, *br* must be divided into four registers with their own enables.

Next suppose that in this Processor must be microoperation *br:=ralu* which is written in some operator vertex of ASM at the functional level. At this level we shouldn't think about splitting of registers. Suppose that in *Fucmi.tab* be the line

```
Y1    y22    16    br:=ralu
```

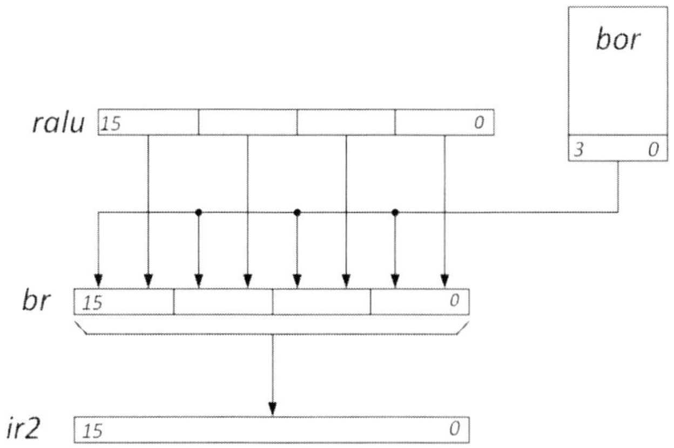

Figure 6. Some structure with splitting of register

Next suppose that in this Processor must be microoperation *br:=ralu* which is written in some operator vertex of ASM at the functional level. At this level we shouldn't think about splitting of registers. Suppose that in *Fucmi.tab* be the line

```
Y1    y22    16    br:=ralu
```

Since *br* was split, the assignment *br:=ralu* must be divided into four assignments which implement in parallel. The file *Funcmi.mrk* has the same operator *Y1* with four microoperations:

```
Y1  y1  4    br(15-12):=ralu(15-12)
    y2  4    br(11-8):=ralu(11-8)
    y3  4    br(7-4):=ralu(7-4)
    y4  4    br(3-0):=ralu(3-0).
```

Thus, after splitting the number of microoperations is increased and Synthagate renumbers microoperations in *Funcmi.mrk*. Nevertheless, even if *br* was split, but *ir2* wasn't split (see the same Fig. 6) the assignment *ir2:=br* should not be divided. In such a case, if in *Funcmi.tab* we have *ir2:=br* then in *Funcmi.mrk* this assignment should be the same: *ir2:=br*.

Our *Funcmi.mrk* which coincides with *Funcmi.tab* is shown in Fig. 7.

```
Y1      y1      16      br:=m1[m1_adr]
        y2      16      m1_adr:=ir2

Y2      y3       4      bor_adr:=ir1(7-4)
        y4      16      br:=bor[bor_adr]

Y3      y5       4      bor_adr:=ir1(3-0)
        y6      16      ir2:=bor[bor_adr]
```

Y4	y7	16	bor[bor_adr]:=ralu
	y3	4	bor_adr:=ir1(7-4)
Y5	y8	5	alu_ctr:=ir1(15-11)
	y9	16	alu_in1:=br
	y10	16	alu_in2:=ir2
	y11	16	ralu:=alu
Y6	y12	16	ir2:=br
Y7	y13	16	pc:=ir2
Y8	y2	16	m1_adr:=ir2
	y14	16	pc:=m1[m1_adr]
Y9	y5	4	bor_adr:=ir1(3-0)
	y15	16	pc:=bor[bor_adr]
Y10	y16	16	inpr:=data_in
Y11	y17	16	bor[bor_adr]:=inpr
	y3	4	bor_adr:=ir1(7-4)
Y12	y18	16	bor[bor_adr]:=br
	y3	4	bor_adr:=ir1(7-4)
Y13	y5	4	bor_adr:=ir1(3-0)
	y4	16	br:=bor[bor_adr]
Y14	y19	16	br:=ir2
Y15	y20	16	m1[m1_adr]:=ext_out
	y21	16	m1_adr:=ext_adr
Y16	y22	16	ext_in:=m1[m1_adr]
	y21	16	m1_adr:=ext_adr
Y17	y23	16	m0[m0_adr]:=ext_out
	y24	16	m0_adr:=ext_adr
Y18	y25	16	ext_in:=m0[m0_adr]
	y24	16	m0_adr:=ext_adr
Y19	y26	16	ir2:=rialu
Y20	y27	16	ialu_in1:=ir2
	y28	16	ialu_in2:=br
	y29	16	rialu:=ialu
Y21	y30	0	pc:=pc+1
Y22	y31	16	ir2:=m0[m0_adr]
	y32	16	m0_adr:=pc

```
Y23     y33       16       ir1:=m0[m0_adr]
        y32       16       m0_adr:=pc
```

Figure 7. Functional process table *Funcmi.mrk*

3.1.3 Connection graph

After constructing Functional table *Funcmi.mrk*, Synthagate designs a Connection graph separately for each length of assignments. In Fig. 7 we have three such lengths – 16, 4 and 5 – see column three in this figure. Let's begin from the length equal to 16.

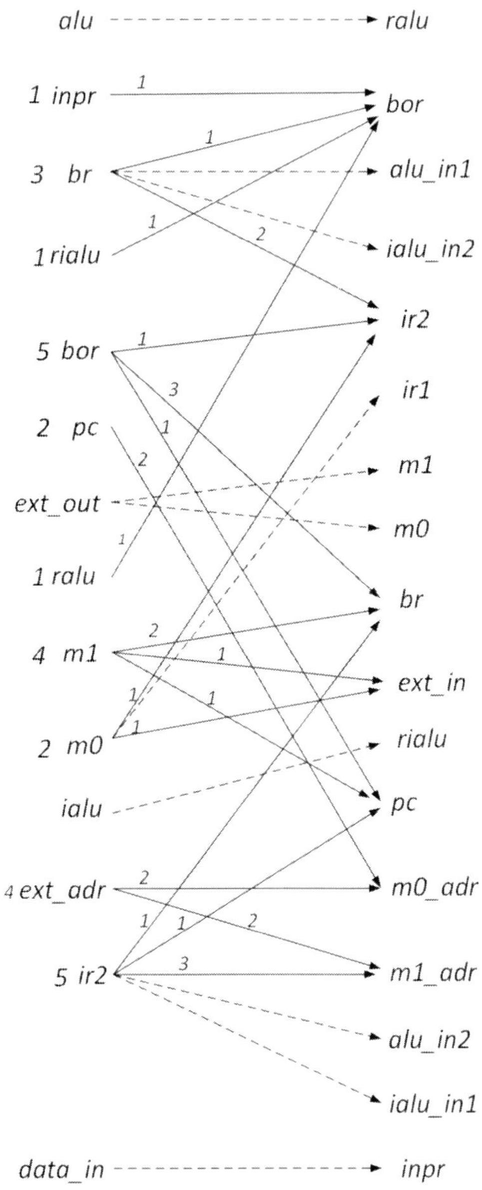

Figure 8. Connection graph for 16-bit assignments

In the connection graph (Fig. 8 for the sixteen bit transfers), source *A,* located on the left, is connected by an arc with target *B* on the right, if there is microoperation *B:=A* in the set of microoperations marked by 16. In this graph, we use a dotted arc if a target has only one source (similarly, target *t5* has only one source *s0* in Fig. 1).

Otherwise, we use a solid arc. Each solid arc has a weight, written over the arc. This weight is equal to the number of appearances of the corresponding microoperation in Fig. 7. For example, the arc with source *ir2* and target *m1_adr* has the weight equal *3*, because *m1_adr :=ir2* appears three times in our design (*Y1* is twice and *Y8* – one time).

We assume that each dotted arc has a weight equal to *0* and we do not write zero weights in our connection graph. Each source of the connection graph has a weight written on the left of this source. This weight is equal to the sum of weights of arcs outgoing from the source. We will use these weights later in the optimal encoding of the MUX inputs. In the Connection graph in Fig. 8 we use the abbreviation *mem0* for *m0[m0_adr], mem1* for *m1[m1_adr]* and *bor* for *bor[bor_adr].*

Sometimes, when a graphic representation of a connection graph is too complicated, we can present it as a list (Fig. 9). In this list, weights on the left are the weights of sources and weights on the right are the weights of arcs. Thus, the weight on the right which is equal to zero corresponds to the direct connection. Synthagate automatically constructs this file from file *Funcmi.mrk*.

```
weight : sources                  targets : weight
     0 : alu                         ralu : 0

     5 : bor[bor_adr]                  br : 3
                                      ir2 : 1
                                       pc : 1

     3 : br                       alu_in1 : 0
                             bor[bor_adr] : 1
                                 ialu_in2 : 0
                                      ir2 : 2

     0 : data_in                     inpr : 0

     4 : ext_adr                   m0_adr : 2
                                   m1_adr : 2

     0 : ext_out              m0[m0_adr] : 0
                              m1[m1_adr] : 0

     0 : ialu                       rialu : 0

     1 : inpr                bor[bor_adr] : 1

     5 : ir2                      alu_in2 : 0
                                       br : 1
```

```
                          ialu_in1 : 0
                            m1_adr : 3
                                pc : 1

2 : m0[m0_adr]              ext_in : 1
                               ir1 : 0
                               ir2 : 1

4 : m1[m1_adr]                  br : 2
                            ext_in : 1
                                pc : 1

2 : pc                      m0_adr : 2

1 : ralu              bor[bor_adr] : 1

1 : rialu                      ir2 : 1
```

Figure 9. Connection Graph as a list

3.1.4 List of parallel (concurrent) microoperations

The next important object that we use in design of data path is the *list of parallel (concurrent) microoperations* (Fig. 10 for the sixteen-bit transfers). In this list, we include microinstructions, containing two or more microoperations, marked by 16 in the third column of Fig. 7. I remind you that if several microoperations are in one microinstruction, they are implemented concurrently (at the same clock).

```
Y1     : y1    br:=m1[m1_adr]
         y2    m1_adr:=ir2

Y5     : y9    alu_in1:=br                d
         y10   alu_in2:=ir2               d
         y11   ralu:=alu                  d

Y8     : y2    m1_adr:=ir2
         y14   pc:=m1[m1_adr]

Y15    : y20   m1[m1_adr]:=ext_out        d
         y21   m1_adr:=ext_adr

Y16    : y21   m1_adr:=ext_adr
         y22   ext_in:=m1[m1_adr]

Y17    : y23   m0[m0_adr]:=ext_out        d
         y24   m0_adr:=ext_adr

Y18    : y24   m0_adr:=ext_adr
         y25   ext_in:=m0[m0_adr]

Y20    : y27   ialu_in1:=ir2              d
         y28   ialu_in2:=br               d
         y29   rialu:=ialu                d
```

```
Y22        : y31      ir2:=m0[m0_adr]
             y32      m0_adr:=pc

Y23        : y32      m0_adr:=pc
             y33      ir1:=m0[m0_adr]          d
```

Figure 10. Parallel microoperations before considering direct connections

Let us shortly discuss construction of this list from Fig. 7. We didn't insert microinstruction *Y2* in this list because it contains only one 16 bit microoperation. Microinstruction Y5 contains four microoperations, but only three of them are marked by 16 in the third column of Fig. 7:

```
y9      alu_in1:=br
y10     alu_in2:=ir2
y11     ralu:=alu
```

We can compress the list of parallel microoperations (Fig. 10), if we remove microoperations corresponding to direct connections in the connection graph (dotted arcs in Fig. 8), or, that is the same, microoperations with zero target weights in its representation as a list (right column in Fig. 9). We have nine such microoperations, they are marked by *d* (*direct*) in Fig. 10 in the right column. After such reduction, three microinstructions – *Y15*, *Y17* and *Y23* contain only one microoperation, so we can remove them as well (it is similar to example 4 in Fig. 2, return to this example). The final list of parallel microoperations is shown in Fig. 11.

```
Y1         : y1       br:=m1[m1_adr]
             y2       m1_adr:=ir2

Y8         : y2       m1_adr:=ir2
             y14      pc:=m1[m1_adr]
Y16        : y21      m1_adr:=ext_adr
             y22      ext_in:=m1[m1_adr]

Y18        : y24      m0_adr:=ext_adr
             y25      ext_in:=m0[m0_adr]

Y22        : y31      ir2:=m0[m0_adr]
             y32      m0_adr:=pc
```

Figure 11. Parallel microoperations after considering direct connections

3.1.5 Design of the graph of incompatibility

In this Section I would like to show that the use of the connection graph and the list of parallel microoperations are sufficient to design the Data Path. For that we will use Fig. 9 and Fig. 11.

If we use MUXes for indirect connections between Processor units, we can connect the output of only one MUX with the input of the target. So, if we have two targets *A* and *C*, one MUX is sufficient to transfer information to these targets if we do not have parallel transfers to *A* and *C* from the different sources.

Let us now suppose that we have two transfers *A* := *B* and *C* := *D* that must be implemented concurrently. Then we must use two MUXes, the output of one of them will be connected to the input of target *A* and source *B* should be among the inputs of this MUX. The output of the second MUX will be connected to the input of target *C* and source *D* should be among the inputs of this MUX.

After this, our next steps are almost evident. First, we find all targets with nonzero weights of arcs from the connection graph in Fig. 9. These weights are written in the last column of this figure. We go along this column from the top to the bottom and write targets without repetition. Here they are:

br, ir2, pc, bor, m0_adr, m1_adr, ext_in. (1)

Next, I construct the *graph of incompatibility* (Fig. 12):

- Each vertex of this graph is a target from (1).
- We connect vertices (targets) by edge (line) if these targets are together in the same microinstruction in the set of parallel microoperations. For example, we connect *br* and *m1_adr* by edge because *br* and *m1_adr* are the targets in microinstruction *Y1* in Fig. 11:

```
Y1  : y1       br:=m1[m1_adr]
      y2       m1_adr:=ir2
```

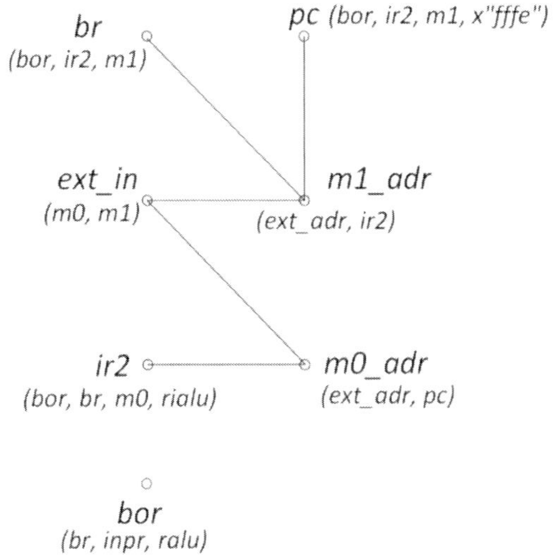

Figure 12. Graph of incompatibility

If two vertices (targets) are connected by edge in this graph we cannot pass information to these targets through the same MUX because these targets are written together in some set of concurrent microoperations with *different* sources. For example, target *m1_adr* cannot be acquired from the same MUX with *ext_in, br* and *pc,* since *m1_adr* is connected with these vertices by arcs. However, *m1_adr* can be acquired from the same MUX with *ir2, bor* and *m0_adr* – *m1_adr* is not connected with them in the graph of incompatibility.

3.1.6 Design of MUXes

To find the minimal number of MUXes in our design we must color this graph with a minimal number of colors in such a way that each two connected vertices are colored by different colors. The targets (vertices) colored by the same colors will be received from the same MUXes and the number of MUXes will be equal to the number of colors. And we will use *mux1, mux2, …* as colors for such a coloring.

The coloring process is presented in Table 1. It is reasonable to order vertices in such table according to their ranks – to the decreasing number of edges connected with each vertex (three such edges for m1*_adr*, two edges for *m0_adr* and *ext_in*, one edge for *br, pc* and *ir2* and zero edges for *bor)*. We place these vertices in the column *Forbidden vertices*.

Table 1. Coloring process for graph of incompatibility 16bit

Vertices	*Forbidden vertices*	*Colors*
m1_adr	*ext_in, br, pc*	*mux1*
m0_adr	*ext_in, ir2*	*mux1*
ext_in	*m1_adr, m0_adr*	*mux2*
br	*m1_adr*	*mux2*
pc	*m1_adr*	*mux2*
ir2	*m0_adr*	*mux2*
bor	-	*mux1*

We color the first vertex *m1_adr* with color *mux1.* Since the second vertex *m0_adr* is not connected to *m1_adr (m0_adr* has not *m1_adr* in the column *Forbidden vertices),* we color *m0_adr* with the same color *mux1.* We cannot color *ext_in, br, pc* and *ir2* with *mux1,* because these vertices are connected with vertex *m1_adr* or *m0_adr* colored with *mux1.* Continue until the end of the list with color *mux1* we use this color for *bor.*

In the next step, taking color *mux2* for *ext_in,* we go down the list and color *br, pc* and *ir2* with *mux2.* Now all vertices are colored. The total number of MUXes (colors) is equal to two.

Thus, we got the outputs of MUXes by coloring process. To get inputs to these MUXes we should refer to the connection graph in Fig. 9. Let us discuss MUX2 with outputs *br, ext_in, ir2* and *pc.* We go along the last but one column *targets* in this figure and search for target *br.* The first time *br* appears as a target with source *bor* with the target weight equal *3* (last column in Fig. 9).

So we include *bor* as an input with input weight equal to *3* (Fig. 13,a). Then we continue to descend and find *br* with source *ir2*, its target weight is equal to *1*. We put the second input to MUX2. Going down with target *br* we find input *m1* (weight = *2*).

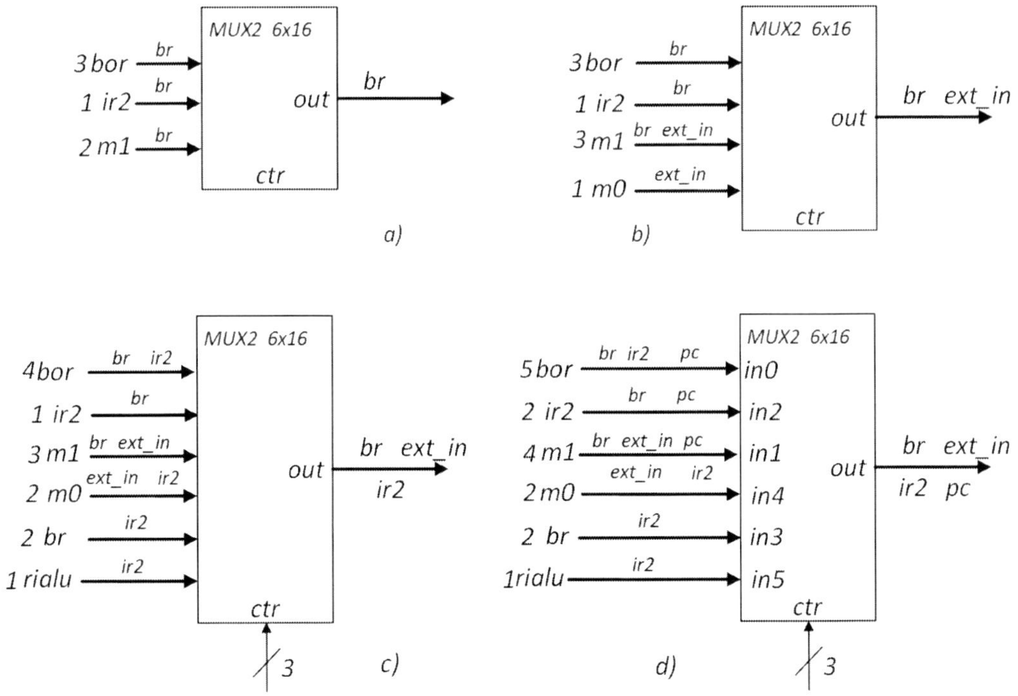

Figure 13. Inputs in *MUX2*

Recall that the weight of microoperation *br:=bor* is equal to the number of appearances of this microoperation in the combined functional ASM. This means that *bor* is used three times as the source for target *br*, or which is the same, *br* is three times the target for *bor*. Thus, when we talk about a pair (*source, target*), their weights are equal. On the other hand, the weight in the left column of Fig. 9 is the total weight of the source for all targets. For example, weight 5 on the left of *bor* is the sum of corresponding weights of source *bor* with all targets written on the right side. The zero weight there means that the direct connection is used for the corresponding transfer.

Now we should repeat the same for target *ext_in*. The first appearance of *ext_in* in column *targets* is with input *m0*, target weight *1*. Thus, we add m0 as an input with this weight (Fig. 13,b). The next appearance of *ext_in* in column *targets* is with input *m1*, target weight *1*.

Since we already have such input in MUX2, we add the new weight *1* to the old weight 2 (the weight of input *m1* becomes equal to *3*) and write *ext_in* over the arrow for *m1* near *br* to show that this source *m1* sends information to *br* and *ext_in* using MUX2 (Fig. 13,b). Coming down with target *ext_in*, we don't see more appearance of this target below m1. Continuing in the same way, we constructed Fig. 13,c and 13,d.

Fig. 14 presents the same procedure for MUX1. Both 16bit MUXes are in Fig. 15. Of course, Synthagate constructs MUXes automatically.

Note, that the same input can appear in the different MUXes if such input has several targets distributed between several MUXes. For example, *br* sends information to *bor* through MUX1, to *ir2* – through MUX2. Input *ir2* occurs in both MUXes as well. That allows to increase the speed of a digital systems. We will talk about input encoding later.

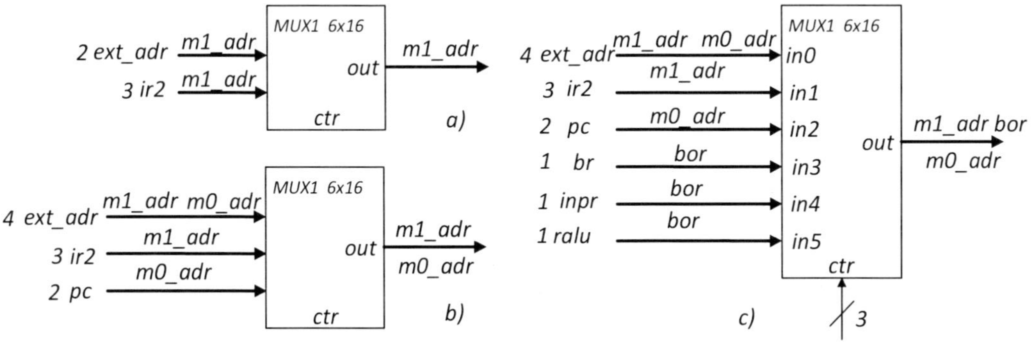

Figure 14. Inputs in *MUX1*

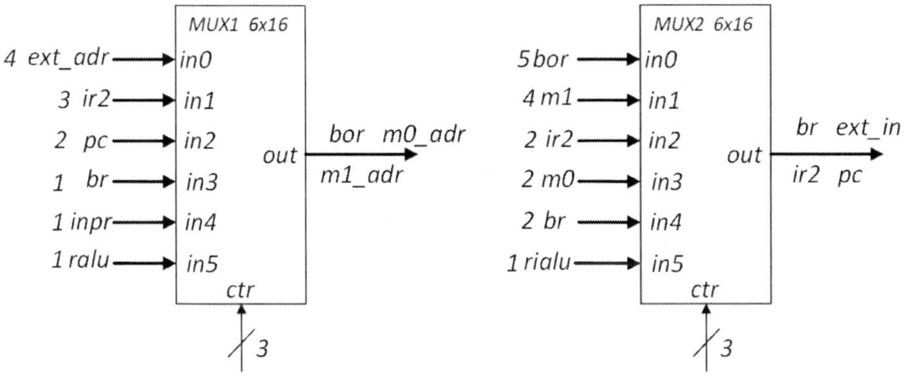

Figure 15. Muxes 16bit

The list of direct connections, constructed by using zero entries in the last column of Connection graph in Fig. 8, is shown in Fig. 16.

SOURCES	TARGETS
alu	ralu
br	alu_in1 ialu_in2

```
data_in                 inpr

ext_out                 m0[m0_adr]
                        m1[m1_adr]

        ialu                rialu

        ir2                 alu_in2
                            ialu_in1

        m0[m0_adr]          ir1
```

Figure 16. Direct connections

Synthagate constructs MUXes automatically in two forms – as a text file (Fig. 17) and a file in XML (to save place I gave only MUX1 in Fig. 18).

```
MUX1
   OUTPUT:
      bor[bor_adr]
      m0_adr
      m1_adr
    INPUT:
      ext_adr        4    000     in0    m0_adr
                                         m1_adr
      ir2            3    001     in1    m1_adr
      pc             2    010     in2    m0_adr
      br             1    100     in4    bor[bor_adr]
      inpr           1    011     in3    bor[bor_adr]
      ralu           1    101     in5    bor[bor_adr]
MUX2
   OUTPUT:
      br
      ext_in
      ir2
      pc
    INPUT:
      bor[bor_adr]   5    000     in0    br
                                         ir2
                                         pc
      m1[m1_adr]     4    001     in1    br
                                         ext_in
                                         pc
      ir2            2    010     in2    br
                                         pc
      m0[m0_adr]     2    100     in4    ext_in
                                         ir2
      br             2    011     in3    ir2
      rialu          1    101     in5    ir2
```

Figure 17. 16bit MUXes as a text file

```
<Mux name="MUX1" ctr_width="3">
      <Outputs>
        <Output name="bor[bor_adr]" />
        <Output name="m0_adr" />
        <Output name="m1_adr" />
      </Outputs>
      <Inputs>
        <Input name="ext_adr" weight="4" code="000" in="0">
          <Target name="m0_adr" />
          <Target name="m1_adr" />
        </Input>
        <Input name="ir2" weight="3" code="001" in="1">
          <Target name="m1_adr" />
        </Input>
        <Input name="pc" weight="2" code="010" in="2">
          <Target name="m0_adr" />
        </Input>
        <Input name="br" weight="1" code="100" in="4">
          <Target name="bor[bor_adr]" />
        </Input>
        <Input name="inpr" weight="1" code="011" in="3">
          <Target name="bor[bor_adr]" />
        </Input>
        <Input name="ralu" weight="1" code="101" in="5">
          <Target name="bor[bor_adr]" />
        </Input>
      </Inputs>
    </Mux>
```

Figure 18. MUX1 in XML

The same design for 4-bit transfers is trivial. Fig. 19 presents connection graph as a graph (a) and as a list (b).

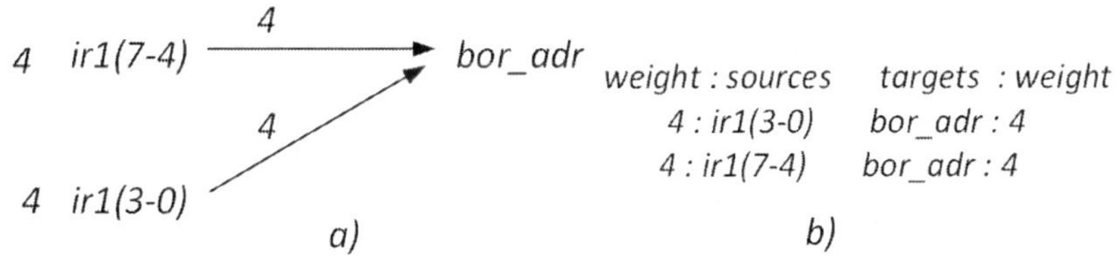

Figure 19. Connection graph for 4-bit transfers

The list of parallel microoperations for 4-bit transfer is empty. Graph incompatibility (Fig. 20) contains only one vertex.

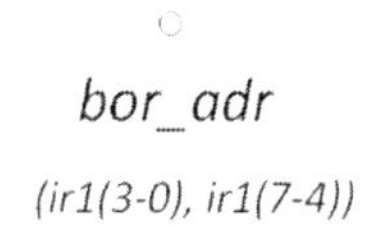

Figure 20. Graph incompatibility for 4bit transfers

Table 2 presents the coloring process for graph in Fig. 20.

Table 2. Coloring process for 4-bit transfers

Vertices	Forbidden vertices	Colors
bor_adr	-	mux1

One MUX for 4-bit transfers is on Fig. 21.

```
MUX0
    OUTPUT:
        bor_adr
     INPUT:
        ir1(3-0)                  4    0          in0     bor_adr
        ir1(7-4)                  4    1          in1     bor_adr
```

Figure 21. MUX for 4-bit transfers

We don't have MUX for 5-bit transfers and have only one direct connection:

SOURCES	TARGETS
ir1(15-11)	alu_ctr

3.1.7 Design of Data Path

After constructing MUXes and the list of direct connections, it is very simple to draw data path (Fig. 22). To do that, I drew the units of data path on the left side and the main MUXes on the right side of this figure. Each input of each MUX was connected to the output of the corresponding unit in accordance with the name of the MUX input. Each output of each MUX was connected to the inputs of the corresponding units in accordance with the targets written at the output of MUX. Direct connections are drawn by dotted lines in accordance with the list of direct connections in Fig. 17. I hope that you understood – designer should not draw pictures from this section. I gave them only for understanding of corresponding processes. Synthagate constructs all VHDL codes for RTL automatically.

VHDL code of *DP*, constructed by Synthagate is presented in Fig. 23.

Refer to Figure 22 (Chapter 3) in HLS-Figures-and-Tables.pdf

Figure 22. VHDL code of Data Path

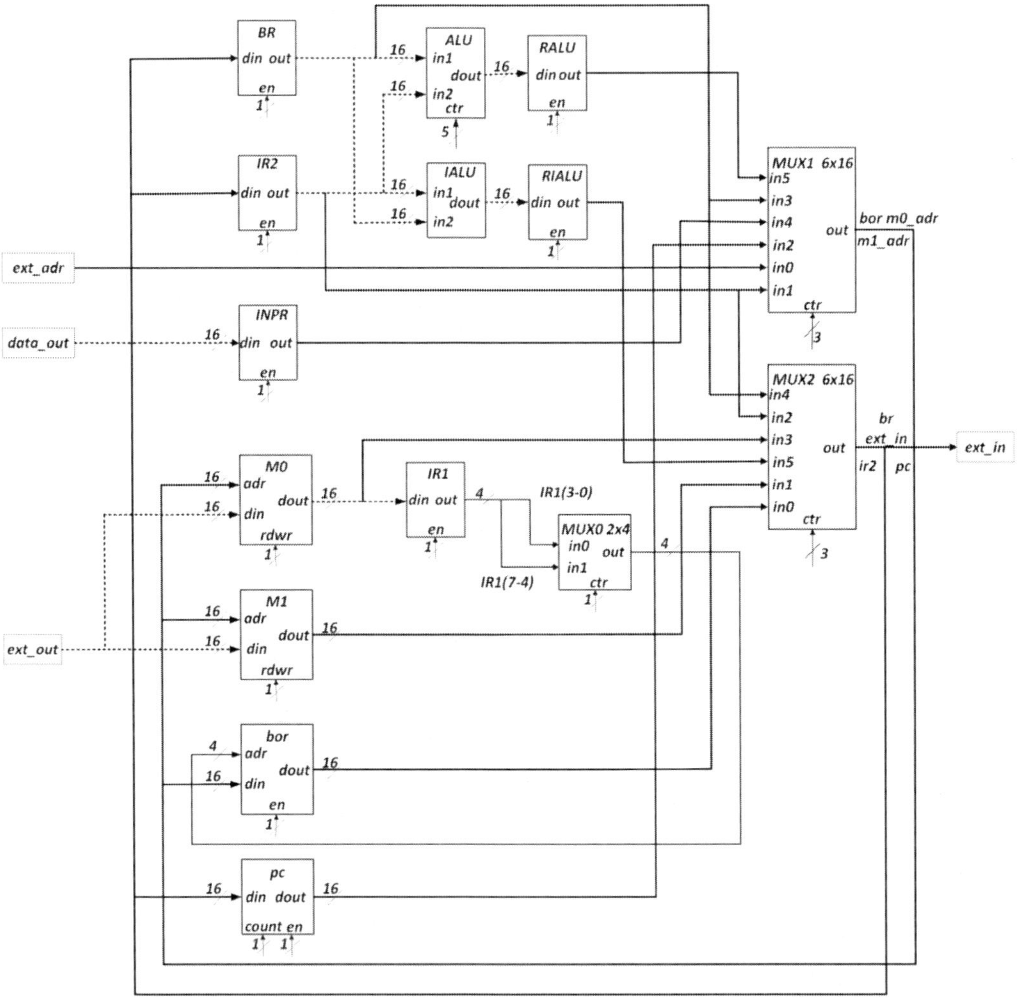

Figure 23. Data Path for ALBI

You will find all components of Data path for this and the following examples *here* (file *ALBI.zip* for ALBI).

To design VHDL code of Data path Synthagate automatically designs the External Specifications (file *ExtSpec.xml*):

```
<external_specifications xmlns="ExtSpec">
    <essential_files>
        <txt path="Funcmi_t.txt" />
        <tab path="Structm.tab" />
        <mrk path="Funcmi_t.mrk" />
        <spec path="Funcmi_t.spec" />
        <mux_files>
            <mux path="funcmi_t16b-mux.xml" bits="16" />
            <mux path="funcmi_t4b-mux.xml" bits="4" />
            <mux path="funcmi_t5b-mux.xml" bits="5" />
        </mux_files>
    </essential_files>
    <settings>
        <bit_range direction="Down" />
    </settings>
    <dp_to_out_and_out_to_dp>
        <signal name="clk" in_or_out="in" width="1" />
        <signal name="rst" in_or_out="in" width="1" />
        <signal name="ext_in" in_or_out="out" width="16" />
        <signal name="ext_adr" in_or_out="in" width="16" />
        <signal name="ext_out" in_or_out="in" width="16" />
        <signal name="data_in" in_or_out="in" width="16" />
    </dp_to_out_and_out_to_dp>
    <components>
        <external>
            <!-- Add external components (and their path)
                  that you would like to use in your design -->
            <component path="Components\alub.vhd"     global="">
                        <class      name="alu"  >
                              <signal     name="%name%_in1" />
                              <signal     name="%name%_in2" />
                              <signal     name="%name%_ctr" />
                              <signal     name="%name%"           />
                        </class>
                        <instances>
                              <instance   name="ALU"        />
                        </instances>
                  </component>

            <component  path="Components\ialub.vhd" global="">
                        <class      name="ialu" >
                              <signal     name="%name%_in1" />
                              <signal     name="%name%_in2" />
                              <signal     name="%name%"           />
                        </class>
                        <instances>
                              <instance   name="IALU"       />
                        </instances>
                  </component>
```

```
    </external>
<automatic>
    <generator type="register" global="clk, rst">
        <class>
            <signal name="%name%" />
            <signal name="%name%_en" />
            <signal name="%name%" />
        </class>
        <instances>
            <instance name="ir2" />
            <instance name="br" />
            <instance name="ir1" />
            <instance name="rialu" />
            <instance name="ralu" />
            <instance name="inpr" />
        </instances>
    </generator>
    <generator type="bor" global="clk, rst">
        <class>
            <signal name="%name%_adr" />
            <signal name="%name%[%name%_adr]" />
            <signal name="%name%_en" />
            <signal name="%name%[%name%_adr]" />
        </class>
        <instances>
            <instance name="bor" />
        </instances>
    </generator>
    <generator type="ram" global="clk">
        <class>
            <signal name="%name%_adr" />
            <signal name="%name%[%name%_adr]" />
            <signal name="%name%_rdwr" />
            <signal name="%name%[%name%_adr]" />
        </class>
        <instances>
            <instance name="m0" />
            <instance name="m1" />
        </instances>
    </generator>
    <generator type="counter_p" global="clk, rst">
        <class>
            <signal name="%name%_en" />
            <signal name="%name%_count" />
            <signal name="%name%" />
            <signal name="%name%" />
        </class>
        <instances>
            <instance name="pc" />
        </instances>
```

```
            </generator>
            <generator type="generic_comparator" global="clk, rst">
                <class>
                    <signal name="%name%_in1" />
                    <signal name="%name%_in2" />
                    <signal name="%name%_out" />
                </class>
                <instances>
                    <instance name="comp4_1" />
                </instances>
            </generator>
        </automatic>
    </components>
</external_specifications>
```

3.2 Control Unit Design

3.2.1. Transformation of functional ASM into structural ASM

At this stage Synthagate transfers functional operators from file *Funcmi.mrk* (Fig. 24, to simplify reading I repeat this file here) into structural operators in file *Funcmi.smo* (Fig.25). In file *Funcmi.smo*, each microoperation corresponds to signals of *DP*, constructed in the previous Section. We will postpone consideration of input encoding for MUXes and will use codes from Fig. 17 and Fig. 21.

```
Y1      y1      16      br:=m1[m1_adr]
        y2      16      m1_adr:=ir2

Y2      y3       4      bor_adr:=ir1(7-4)
        y4      16      br:=bor[bor_adr]

Y3      y5       4      bor_adr:=ir1(3-0)
        y6      16      ir2:=bor[bor_adr]
Y4      y7      16      bor[bor_adr]:=ralu
        y3       4      bor_adr:=ir1(7-4)

Y5      y8       5      alu_ctr:=ir1(15-11)
        y9      16      alu_in1:=br
        y10     16      alu_in2:=ir2
        y11     16      ralu:=alu

Y6      y12     16      ir2:=br

Y7      y13     16      pc:=ir2

Y8      y2      16      m1_adr:=ir2
        y14     16      pc:=m1[m1_adr]

Y9      y5       4      bor_adr:=ir1(3-0)
```

	y15	16	pc:=bor[bor_adr]
Y10	y16	16	inpr:=data_in
Y11	y17	16	bor[bor_adr]:=inpr
	y3	4	bor_adr:=ir1(7-4)
Y12	y18	16	bor[bor_adr]:=br
	y3	4	bor_adr:=ir1(7-4)
Y13	y5	4	bor_adr:=ir1(3-0)
	y4	16	br:=bor[bor_adr]
Y14	y19	16	br:=ir2
Y15	y20	16	m1[m1_adr]:=ext_out
	y21	16	m1_adr:=ext_adr
Y16	y22	16	ext_in:=m1[m1_adr]
	y21	16	m1_adr:=ext_adr
Y17	y23	16	m0[m0_adr]:=ext_out
	y24	16	m0_adr:=ext_adr
Y18	y25	16	ext_in:=m0[m0_adr]
	y24	16	m0_adr:=ext_adr
Y19	y26	16	ir2:=rialu
Y20	y27	16	ialu_in1:=ir2
	y28	16	ialu_in2:=br
	y29	16	rialu:=ialu
Y21	y30	0	pc:=pc+1
Y22	y31	16	ir2:=m0[m0_adr]
	y32	16	m0_adr:=pc
Y23	y33	16	ir1:=m0[m0_adr]
	y32	16	m0_adr:=pc

Figure 24. Functional process table *Funcmi.mrk*

Let we have a functional microoperation $A := B$. To implement this assignment, we must *read* information from B and *write* it to A. Now, once again, we will discuss reading and writing information at the functional level in our design.

Reading. We will consider three cases of information reading:

Read1. When source B is a combinational circuit or a register, we should not supply special signals to read information from such devices. This information is always at its output. Examples:

ralu:=alu; ir2:=br; m1_adr:=ir2.

Read2. Source *B* is *bor* (Block of Registers). To choose the register from *bor*, the Control unit should give address to *bor_adr* and send information from its output to the target. Examples:

bor_adr:=ir1(7-4); br:=bor[bor_adr].

Read3. Source *B* is a memory (*m0* or *m1*). As a memory is a source, ALBI should send an address to the address bus *m0_adr* or *m1_adr*. Then the corresponding word of the memory *m0[m0_adr]* or *m1[m1_adr]* will appear at the output of *m0* or *m1*. Examples:

m0_adr:=pc; ir2:=m0[m0_adr].

m1_adr:=ir2; pc:=m1[m1_adr].

Writing. We will consider three cases of writing as well:

Write1. Target *A* is a register. To write information from the source to the register we shouldn't supply any additional information. Examples:

inpr:=data_in; pc:=ir2.

Write2. Target *A* is *bor*. To write information to *bor* from some source we must provide an address to the address bus *bor_adr*. The information from the input of *bor* will be written into *bor* with a given address. Example:

bor_adr:=ir1(7-4); bor[bor_adr]:=ralu.

Write3. Target *A* is a memory. To write information to the memory from some source we must provide an address to the address bus *m0_adr* for *m0* or *m1_adr* for *m1*. The information from the input of the memory will be written into the memory word with a given address. *Examples:*

m0_adr:=ext_adr; m0[m0_adr]:=ext_out.

m1_adr:=ext_adr; m1[m1_adr]:=ext_out.

In such a manner, we present the transfer information at the high (the functional) level. Let us discuss several examples of transformation of functional microinstructions into structural ones. Really, it is very similar to the transformation in our first simple structure – see Fig. 1 and Fig. 2.

1. Operator *Y6* in Fig. 24 contains microoperation:

ir2:=br. Case ***Read1 – Write1***.

The content of register *br* should be written into *ir2*. At the first step we must find whether the connection between *br* and *ir2* is direct or indirect (via MUXes). For that we apply to 16-bit direct connections in Fig. 16. There is not direct connection between *br* and *ir2*. Then we must find 16-bit MUX (Fig. 17) with output *ir2* because *ir2* is a target in this microoperation. It is *MUX2*. To pass information from *br* to *ir2* through *MUX2* we must supply signal *ctr_mux2:=011* (Fig. 17), because input *br* of *MUX2* has code *011*. The signal *ir2_en:=1* will write information from the output of *MUX2* into *ir2*. Finally, we use the following microoperations at the structure level:

ctr_mux2:=011; ir2_en:=1 (see operator *Y6* in Fig. 25).

2. Operator *Y2* in Fig. 24 contains microoperations:

bor_adr:=ir1(7-4); br:=bor[bor_adr]. Case ***Read2 – Write1***.

To pass information from *ir1(7-4)* to *bor_adr* through *MUX0* we must give signal *ctr_mux0:=1* (Fig. 21), because input *ir1(7-4)* of *MUX0* has code *1*. To pass information from *bor* to *br* through *MUX2* we must supply signal *ctr_mux2:=000* (Fig. 17), because input *bor* of *MUX2* has code *000*. The signal *br_en:=1* will write information from the output of *MUX2* into *br*. Finally, we use the following microoperations at the structure level:

ctr_mux0:=1; ctr_mux2:=000; br_en:=1

(see operator *Y2* in Fig. 25).

```
Y1        m1_rdwr:=0
          ctr_mux2:=001
          br_en:=1
          ctr_mux1:=001

Y2        ctr_mux0:=1
          ctr_mux2:=000
          br_en:=1

Y3        ctr_mux0:=0
          ctr_mux2:=000
          ir2_en:=1

Y4        ctr_mux1:=101
          bor_en:=1
          ctr_mux0:=1

Y5        ralu_en:=1

Y6        ctr_mux2:=011
          ir2_en:=1

Y7        ctr_mux2:=010
          pc_en:=1

Y8        ctr_mux1:=001
```

	m1_rdwr:=0 ctr_mux2:=001 pc_en:=1
Y9	ctr_mux0:=0 ctr_mux2:=000 pc_en:=1
Y10	inpr_en:=1
Y11	ctr_mux1:=011 bor_en:=1 ctr_mux0:=1
Y12	ctr_mux1:=100 bor_en:=1 ctr_mux0:=1
Y13	ctr_mux0:=0 ctr_mux2:=000 br_en:=1
Y14	ctr_mux2:=010 br_en:=1
Y15	m1_rdwr:=1 ctr_mux1:=000
Y16	m1_rdwr:=0 ctr_mux2:=001 ctr_mux1:=000
Y17	m0_rdwr:=1 ctr_mux1:=000
Y18	m0_rdwr:=0 ctr_mux2:=100 ctr_mux1:=000
Y19	ctr_mux2:=101 ir2_en:=1
Y20	rialu_en:=1
Y21	pc_count:=1
Y22	m0_rdwr:=0 ctr_mux2:=100 ir2_en:=1 ctr_mux1:=010
Y23	m0_rdwr:=0 ir1_en:=1 ctr_mux1:=010

Figure 25. Structural process table *Funcmi.smo*

3. Operator *Y4* in Fig. 24 contains microoperations:

bor_adr:=ir1(7-4); bor[bor_adr]:=ralu. Case ***Read1 – Write2***.

As in point 2, to pass information from *ir1(7-4)* to *bor_adr* through *MUX0* we must give signal *ctr_mux0:=1* (Fig. 21), because input *ir1(7-4)* of *MUX0* has code *1*. To pass information from *ralu* to *bor* through *MUX1* we must supply signal *ctr_mux1:=101* (Fig. 17), because input *ralu* of *MUX1* has code *101*. The signal *bor_en:=1* will write information from the output of *MUX1* into *bor*. Finally, we use the following microoperations at the structure level:

ctr_mux0:=1; ctr_mux1:=101; bor_en:=1 (see operator *Y4* in Fig. 25).

4. Operator *Y15* in Fig. 24 contains microoperations:

m1_adr:=ext_adr; m1[m1_adr]:=ext_out. Case ***Read1 – Write3***.

To pass information from *ext_adr* to *m1_adr* through *MUX1* we must give signal *ctr_mux1:=000* (Fig. 17), because input *ext_adr* of *MUX1* has code *000*. Because *ext_out* is connected directly with *m1* (Fig. 16, Direct connections) no *MUX* is used to pass information from *ext_out* to *m1*. To write information into *m1* it is sufficient to supply signal *m1_rdwr:=1*. Finally, we use the following microoperations at the structure level:

m1_rdwr:=1; ctr_mux1:=000 (see operator *Y15* in Fig. 25).

5. Operator *Y22* in Fig. 24 contains microoperations:

m0_adr:=pc; ir2:=m0[m0_adr]. Case ***Read3 – Write1***.

To pass information from *pc* to *m0_adr* through *MUX1* we must give signal *ctr_mux1:=010* (Fig. 17), because input *pc* of *MUX1* has code *010*. Signal *m0_rdwr=0* defines reading from *m0*. To pass information from *m0* to *ir2* through *MUX2* we must supply signal *ctr_mux2:=100* (Fig. 17), because input *m0* of *MUX2* has code *100*. The signal *ir2_en:=1* will write information from the output of *MUX2* into *ir2*. Finally, we use the following microoperations at the structure level:

m0_rdwr:=0; ctr_mux1:=010; ctr_mux2:=100; ir2_en:=1

(see operator *Y22* in Fig. 25).

In this manner, Synthagate automatically constructs file *Funcmi.smo* in Fig. 25. Extension *smo* in this file means *structural microoperations*.

3.2.2 Reduction of the number of microoperations

Let's come back to FSM synthesis. On Fig. 26 and in Table 3, I repeat ASM *G1* marked for the Mealy FSM synthesis (Fig. 7 from Chapter 1) and the transition table of Mealy FSM *S1* (Table 2 from Chapter 1). I remind you that if some microinstruction, for example, *Y5* = *{y1, y3}* is written in the operator vertex, it means that *y1* = *y3* = *1* and other microoperations are equal to zero. Our understanding of output signals in FSM is just like this. If *y1* and *y3* are written in the column for output signals (see row 1, column 4 in Table 3), only these signals are equal to one at the transition from *a1* to *a2* with the input signal *x1*x2*x3*, but other output signals are equal to zero. Really, it is the same as when we constructed some of products from the truth table, we were interesting only in output signals equal to one.

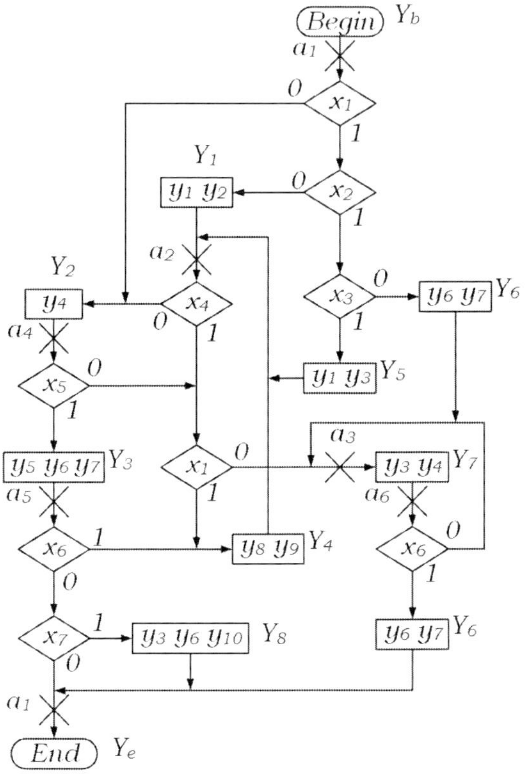

Figure 26. ASM *G1* marked for the Mealy FSM synthesis

In consideration of this, Synthagate constructs file *Structm.tab* (Fig. 27) from file *Funcmi.smo* (Fig.25) using only microoperations and component of microoperations equal to one. Look, for example, at microinstruction *Y3* at the functional level (*Funcmi.mrk* in Fig. 24):

bor_adr:=ir1(3-0); ir2:=bor[bor_adr].

Y3 in file *Structm.smo* in Fig. 25 contains three microoperations:

ctr_mux0:=0; ctr_mux2:=000; ir2_en:=1,

but *Y3* in file *Structm.tab* in Fig. 27 – only one:

ir2_en:=1.

As a result, Synthagate reduces the number of microoperations almost twice in file *Structm.tab* on Fig. 27.

Table 3. Direct transition table of Mealy FSM S_1

a_m	a_s	$X(a_m,a_s)$	$Y(a_m,a_s)$	H
a_1	a_2	$x_1x_2x_3$	y_1y_3	1
	a_3	x_1x_2~x_3	y_6y_7	2
	a_2	x_1~x_2	y_1y_2	3
	a_4	~x_1	y_4	4
a_2	a_2	x_4x_1	y_8y_9	5
	a_6	x_4~x_1	y_3y_4	6
	a_4	~x_4	y_4	7
a_3	a_6	1	y_3y_4	8
a_4	a_5	x_5	$y_5y_6y_7$	9
	a_2	~x_5x_1	y_8y_9	10
	a_6	~x_5~x_1	y_3y_4	11
a_5	a_2	x_6	y_8y_9	12
	a_1	~x_6x_7	$y_3y_6y_{10}$	13
	a_1	~x_6~x_7	-	14
a_6	a_1	x_6	y_6y_7	15
	a_6	~x_6	y_3y_4	16

```
Y1        y1        ctr_mux2[0] <= 1
          y2        br_en       <= 1
          y3        ctr_mux1[0] <= 1

Y2        y4        ctr_mux0    <= 1
          y2        br_en       <= 1

Y3        y5        ir2_en      <= 1

Y4        y6        ctr_mux1[2] <= 1
          y3        ctr_mux1[0] <= 1
          y7        bor_en      <= 1
          y4        ctr_mux0    <= 1

Y5        y8        ralu_en     <= 1
```

```
Y6      y9      ctr_mux2[1] <= 1
        y1      ctr_mux2[0] <= 1
        y5      ir2_en      <= 1

Y7      y9      ctr_mux2[1] <= 1
        y10     pc_en       <= 1

Y8      y3      ctr_mux1[0] <= 1
        y1      ctr_mux2[0] <= 1
        y10     pc_en       <= 1

Y9      y10     pc_en       <= 1

Y10     y11     inpr_en     <= 1

Y11     y12     ctr_mux1[1] <= 1
        y3      ctr_mux1[0] <= 1
        y7      bor_en      <= 1
        y4      ctr_mux0    <= 1

Y12     y6      ctr_mux1[2] <= 1
        y7      bor_en      <= 1
        y4      ctr_mux0    <= 1

Y13     y2      br_en       <= 1
Y14     y9      ctr_mux2[1] <= 1
        y2      br_en       <= 1

Y15     y13     m1_rdwr     <= 1

Y16     y1      ctr_mux2[0] <= 1

Y17     y14     m0_rdwr     <= 1

Y18     y15     ctr_mux2[2] <= 1

Y19     y15     ctr_mux2[2] <= 1
        y1      ctr_mux2[0] <= 1
        y5      ir2_en      <= 1

Y20     y16     rialu_en    <= 1

Y21     y17     pc_count    <= 1

Y22     y15     ctr_mux2[2] <= 1
        y5      ir2_en      <= 1
        y12     ctr_mux1[1] <= 1

Y23     y18     ir1_en      <= 1
        y12     ctr_mux1[1] <= 1
```

Figure 27. File *Structm.tab*

3.2.3 Design of Control Unit

Exactly as at the functional level (High level), to construct Control unit at the structural level (RTL), Synthagate needs two files *Structm.gsa* and *Structm.txt*.

0	Begin	1	0
1	x5	2	1
2	x4	3	4
3	x9	5	6
4	Y23	7	0
5	x8	8	9
6	x8	10	11
7	Y21	12	0
8	Y15	13	0
9	Y17	13	0
10	Y16	13	0
11	Y18	13	0
12	x6	14	15
13	End	0	0
14	x7	16	17
15	x2	18	19
16	Y10	20	0
17	x2	18	21
18	Y22	22	0
19	x7	23	24
20	Y11	13	0
21	Y9	13	0
22	Y21	25	0
23	Y13	26	0
24	Y3	27	0
25	x3	28	29
26	x1	30	31
27	x1	32	33
28	x6	34	35
29	x1	36	37
30	Y6	38	0
31	Y12	13	0
32	Y1	39	0
33	Y2	40	0
34	Y7	13	0
35	x7	41	33
36	Y1	42	0
37	x10	43	44
38	x7	32	33
39	x7	31	30
40	Y5	45	0
41	Y14	31	0
42	Y6	37	0
43	x6	46	32
44	Y13	47	0
45	Y4	13	0
46	Y8	13	0
47	Y20	48	0
48	Y19	43	0

Figure 28. Structural ASM Structm.gsa

ASM in file *Structm.gsa* (Fig. 28) is equal to the functional ASM *Funcmi.gsa* (Fig. 27 in Chapter 2).

Synthagate only renumbered vertices in these ASMs but these ASMs are really equivalent. File *Structm.txt* (Fig. 28) was constructed by Synthagate using file *Structm.tab* in Fig. 27. Finite State Machine *Structm.t1* is in Fig. 30. It is equal to FSM Funcmi.t1 on Fig. 3-30. The Control unit for ALBI is presented on Fig. 31.

```
Micro Instructions:
Y1 = y1 y2 y3
Y2 = y2 y4
Y3 = y5
Y4 = y3 y4 y6 y7
Y5 = y8
Y6 = y1 y5 y9
Y7 = y9 y10
```

```
Y8 = y1 y3 y10
Y9 = y10
Y10 = y11
Y11 = y3 y4 y7 y12
Y12 = y4 y6 y7
Y13 = y2
Y14 = y2 y9
Y15 = y13
Y16 = y1
Y17 = y14
Y18 = y15
Y19 = y1 y5 y15
Y20 = y16
Y21 = y17
Y22 = y5 y12 y15
Y23 = y12 y18
```

```
Micro Operations:              Logical Conditions:
y1  : ctr_mux2_0:=1            File   Draw
y2  : br_en:=1                 x1  : ir1_9
y3  : ctr_mux1_0:=1            x2  : ir1_10
y4  : ctr_mux0:=1              x3  : ir1_8
y5  : ir2_en:=1                x4  : dma
y6  : ctr_mux1_2:=1            x5  : s
y7  : bor_en:=1                x6  : bit0
y8  : ralu_en:=1               x7  : bit1
y9  : ctr_mux2_1:=1            x8  : m
y10  : pc_en:=1                x9  : ext_rdwr
y11  : inpr_en:=1              x10 : comp4_1_dout
y12  : ctr_mux1_1:=1
y13  : m1_rdwr:=1
y14  : m0_rdwr:=1
y15  : ctr_mux2_2:=1
y16  : rialu_en:=1
y17  : pc_count:=1
y18  : ir1_en:=1
```

Figure 29. Structural ASM *Structm.txt*

a1	a1	x5*x4*x9*x8	y13	1
a1	a1	x5*x4*x9*~x8	y14	2
a1	a1	x5*x4*~x9*x8	y1	3
a1	a1	x5*x4*~x9*~x8	y15	4
a1	a2	x5*~x4	y12y18	5
a1	a1	~x5	--	6
a2	a3	1	y17	7
a3	a4	x6*x7	y11	8
a3	a5	x6*~x7*x2	y5y12y15	9
a3	a1	x6*~x7*~x2	y10	10

a3	a5	~x6*x2	y5y12y15	11
a3	a7	~x6*~x2*x7	y2	12
a3	a8	~x6*~x2*~x7	y5	13
a4	a1	1	y3y4y7y12	14
a5	a6	1	y17	15
a6	a1	x3*x6	y9y10	16
a6	a14	x3*~x6*x7	y2y9	17
a6	a11	x3*~x6*~x7	y2y4	18
a6	a12	~x3*x1	y1y2y3	19
a6	a1	~x3*~x1*x10*x6	y1y3y10	20
a6	a10	~x3*~x1*x10*~x6	y1y2y3	21
a6	a16	~x3*~x1*~x10	y2	22
a7	a9	x1	y1y5y9	23
a7	a1	~x1	y4y6y7	24
a8	a10	x1	y1y2y3	25
a8	a11	~x1	y2y4	26
a9	a10	x7	y1y2y3	27
a9	a11	~x7	y2y4	28
a10	a1	x7	y4y6y7	29
a10	a9	~x7	y1y5y9	30
a11	a13	1	y8	31
a12	a15	1	y1y5y9	32
a13	a1	1	y3y4y6y7	33
a14	a1	1	y4y6y7	34
a15	a1	x10*x6	y1y3y10	35
a15	a10	x10*~x6	y1y2y3	36
a15	a16	~x10	y2	37
a16	a17	1	y16	38
a17	a18	1	y1y5y15	39
a18	a1	x6	y1y3y10	40
a18	a10	~x6	y1y2y3	41

Figure 30. FSM *Structm.t1* for Control unit

Refer to Figure 31 (Chapter 3) in HLS-Figures-and-Tables.pdf

Figure 31. Control Unit for *ALBI in VHDL*

3.2.4 Encoding of inputs of MUXes

My goal in this section is to minimize the number of outputs $y_1, \ldots, y_N$ in FSM table or, which is the same, in the Control unit. To explain this, we appeal to the rows with microinstructions *Y2* and *Y9* in file *Funcmi.mrk* in Fig. 24. We used code *000* for input *bor[bor_adr]* in *MUX2* and therefore the components of vector *ctr_mux2* didn't appear in file *Structm.tab* in Fig. 27 when we turned from the file *Structm.smo* to the minimized structural microinstructions in *Structm.tab*. If, for example, we used code *111* for the same input *bor[bor_adr]* of *MUX2*, we would get *ctr_mux2:=111* instead of *ctr_mux2 := 000* in *Structm.smo* (see Fig. 25). This leads to appearance of three additional microoperations in *Structm.tab* (*ctr_mux2[0] := 1, ctr_mux2[1] := 1, ctr_mux2[2] := 1)*. It entails three additional outputs in the transition table of the finite state machine.

```
MUX2
   OUTPUT:
      br
      ext_in
      ir2
      pc
    INPUT:
      bor[bor_adr]          5    000       in0    br
                                                  ir2
                                                  pc
      m1[m1_adr]            4    001       in1    br
                                                  ext_in
                                                  pc
      ir2                   2    010       in2    br
                                                  pc
      m0[m0_adr]            2    100       in4    ext_in
                                                  ir2
      br                    2    011       in3    ir2
      rialu                 1    101       in5    ir2
```

Figure 32. *MUX2* as a list

The algorithm for the input encoding is absolutely the same as in the state assignment of FSM, presented in my book "*Finite State Machines and Algorithmic State Machines*". Let's return to *MUX2* in Fig. 32. First, we used the zero code for input *bor[bor_adr]* because it used maximum times (5 in column 2) as the input of this mux. Then we used codes with one "1" for inputs *m1[m1_adr], ir2* and *m0[m0_adr]* with the following maximum appearances in *MUX2* etc. In the same manner we encoded *MUX0* and *MUX1* – see Fig. 17 and Fig.21.

3.3 Top Design

Thus, we constructed Data path and Control unit. Our next step is to combine two components – Control unit and Data path in one final block. The top level of *ALBI* as a composition of Control unit and Data path is presented in Fig. 33.

VHDL code of the top level constructed by Synthagate is in Fig. 34. Top level contains two components – *Structm* for Control unit and *dp* for Data path.

Refer to Figure 33 (Chapter 3) in HLS-Figures-and-Tables.pdf

Figure 33. Top level of *ALBI* in VHDL

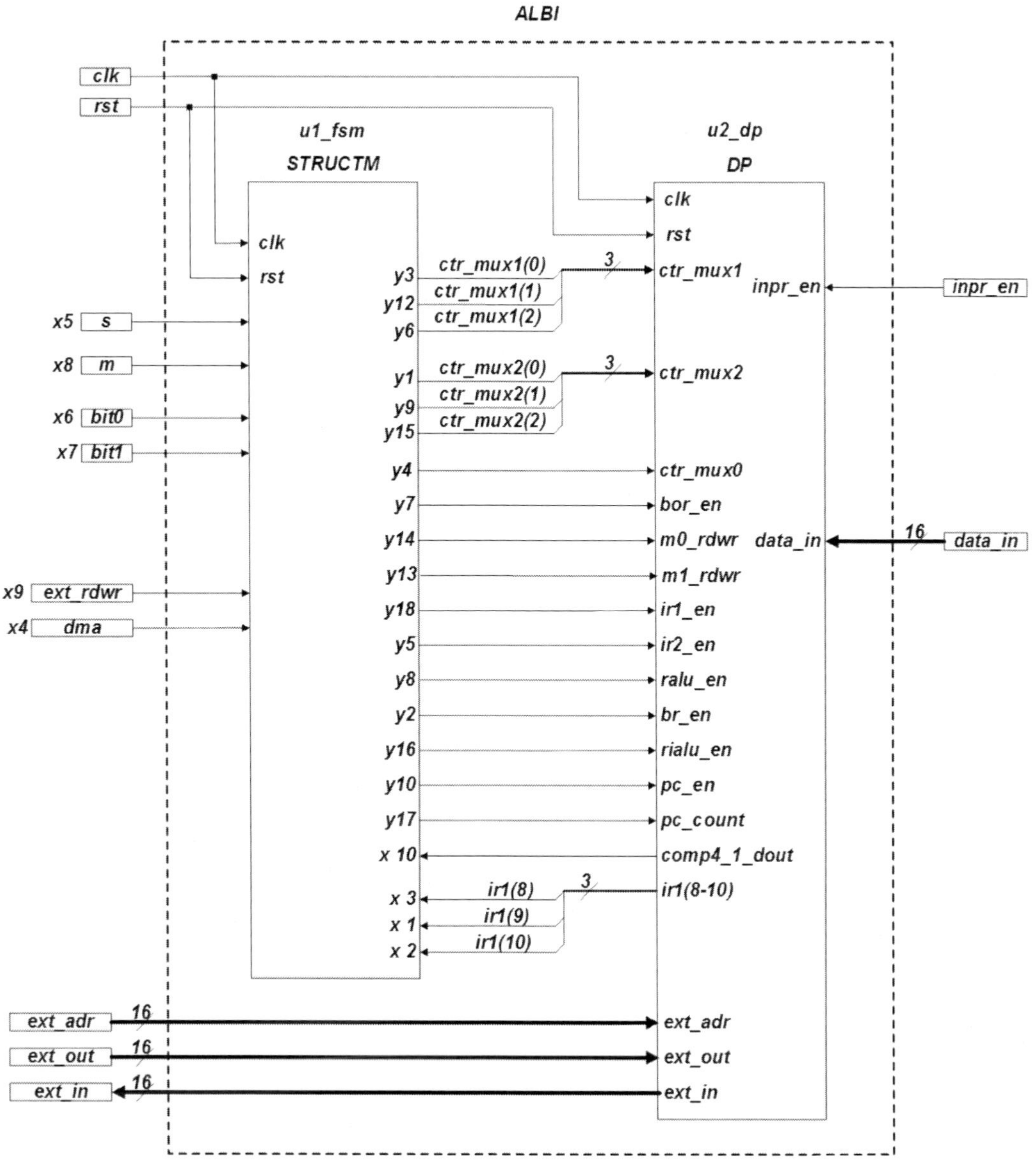

Figure 34. Top level of *ALBI*

4 CASE STUDY. EXAMPLES FROM THE BOOK OF ENOCH HWANG

In his interesting book "Digital Logic and Microprocessor Design with VHDL" Prof. Enoch Hwang gave examples of dedicated microprocessors. I strongly advise beginning hardware designers to read this book. Prof. Enoch Hwang defines such microprocessors as application specific integrated circuits (ASICs), are dedicated to performing only one task. In this Chapter I will show designs of the same microprocessors using design methodology presented in the previous chapters. And, of course, I will use my tool Synthagate to realize these designs automatically in several seconds. Moreover, after that I will construct a processor which can perform all functions of the previous four dedicated microprocessors. In all examples from this section you will see that for such design it is enough to present the behavior of the design system at the High Level with Algorithmic State Machines.

All designs presented in this and the following chapters you will find at www.synthezza.com/examples-of-hls-and-rtl-design. Moreover, I gave there the same designs where I begin from ASMs presented in System C and VHDL. Synthagate transforms these ASMs in the same internal forms as after beginning from GUI in ASM Creator. The readers of this book can download these examples and play with them. As well, they can download *ASM Creator* at www.synthezza.com/asm-creator-short-manual.

4.1 Sum of Inputs

In this design, a user enters 8-bit numbers until the number x"00" appears at the input. The sum of the entered numbers will be on the output of the system. The ASM *Sum* for this behavior is on Fig. 1.

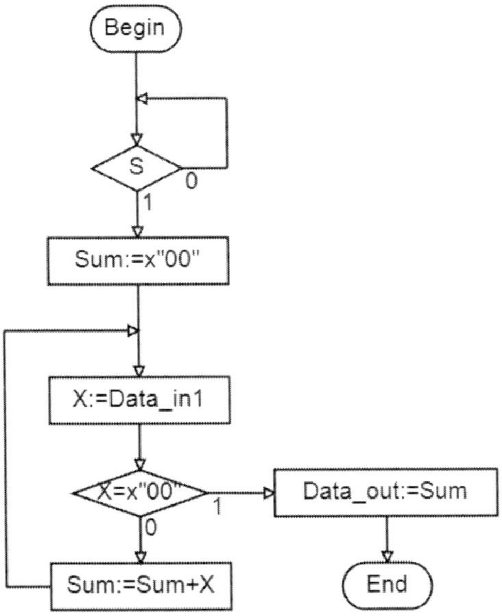

Figure 1. ASM for Sum of inputs

This ASM is very simple – its file *sum.txt* is presented on Fig. 2. ASM *Sum* contains only four operators (*Y1* – *Y4*), four microoperations (*y1* – *y4*) and two logical conditions (*x1, x2*).

```
Micro Instructions:
Y1 = y1
Y2 = y2
Y3 = y3
Y4 = y4

Micro Operations:
y1   :   Sum:=x"00"
y2   :   Data_out:=Sum
y3   :   Sum:=Sum+X
y4   :   X:=Data_in1

Logical Conditions:
File    Draw
x1   : X=x"00"
x2   : S
```

Figure 2. Txt file for ASM Sum

A marked ASM Sum is presented in Fig. 3. In this ASM I replaced microoperations and logical conditions of ASM in Fig. 1 by *y1, ..., y4* and *x1, x2* from Fig. 2. If you forgot, how to design FSM from ASM, return to Section 1.2 from the first Chapter. The Functional FSM *Funcmi.t1* with only three states is shown in Table 1.

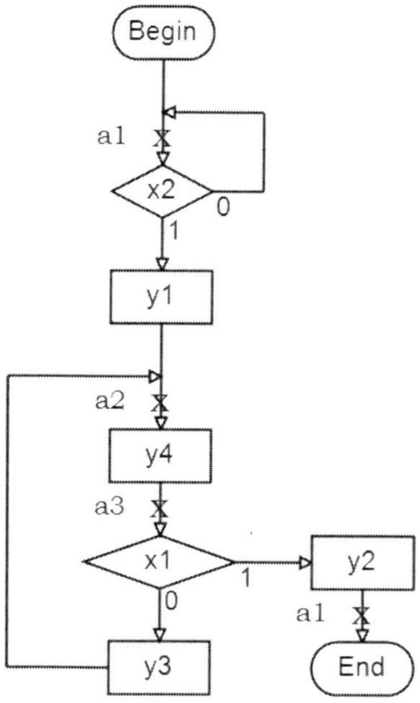

Figure 3. ASM marked for Mealy FSM

Table 1. Transition table of the functional FSM for Sum

a1	a2	x2	y1	1
a1	a1	~x2	--	2
a2	a3	1	y4	3
a3	a1	x1	y2	4
a3	a2	~x1	y3	5

Automatically constructed functional specifications is presented in file *Sum.spec* (Fig. 4). It contains only 14 rows.

```
<functional_specifications>
    <declarations>
        <port name="data_in1" width="8" direction="in" />
        <port name="data_out" width="8" direction="out" />
        <port name="s" width="1" direction="in" />
        <signal name="sum" width="8" />
        <signal name="x" width="8" />
    </declarations>
    <required_libraries>
        <vhdl>
            <library name="my_package" />
        </vhdl>
    </required_libraries>
</functional_specifications>
```

Figure 4. Functional specifications

Functional design at the High level (file *Fincmi.vhd* constructed by Synthagate) is presented on Fig. 5. It is a small design – file contains only 71 lines.

```
library ieee;
use ieee.std_logic_1164.all;
use ieee.numeric_std.all;
use work.my_package.all;

entity Funcmi is
      port (
            clk          : in std_logic;
            data_in1     : in std_logic_vector(7 downto 0);
            data_out     : out std_logic_vector(7 downto 0);
            idle         : out std_logic;
            rst          : in std_logic;
            s            : in std_logic
      );
end Funcmi;
```

```
architecture ARC_Funcmi of Funcmi is

	type FSMStates is (
		a1, a2, a3
	);

	signal currentState : FSMStates;
	signal sum : std_logic_vector(7 downto 0);
	signal x : std_logic_vector(7 downto 0);
begin
	process (clk , rst)

	procedure proc_Funcmi is
	begin

	case currentState is
	when a1 =>
		if (s) = '1' then
			sum <= x"00";
			currentState <= a2;
		else
			currentState <= a1;
			idle <= '1';
		end if;
	when a2 =>
			x <= data_in1;
			currentState <= a3;
	when a3 =>
		if (x = x"00") then
			data_out <= sum;
			currentState <= a1;
			idle <= '1';
		else
			sum<=std_logic_vector(unsigned(sum)+ unsigned(x));
			currentState <= a2;
		end if;
	end case;
	end proc_Funcmi;

	begin
		if (rst = '1') then
			data_out <= (others => '0');
			idle <= '0';
			sum <= (others => '0');
			x <= (others => '0');

			currentState <= a1;
			idle <= '1';

		elsif (clk'event and clk = '1') then
```

```
                idle <= '0';
                proc_Funcmi;
            end if;
        end process;
end ARC_Funcmi;
```

Figure 5. High Level Synthesis for Sum

This design is so simple that I wouldn't like to give here the connection graphs and graphs of incompatibility. You can easily construct them from Functional ASM table in Fig. 6. The list of parallel microoperations is empty. The only 8-bit MUX is shown in Fig. 7. External specifications (61 lines) are in Fig. 8. Data path for this design (Fig. 9) contains 4 components, the total number of instantiated components is equal to 6. VHDL code for the Control unit is in Fig. 10. The top design, combining Control unit and Data path is shown in Fig. 11.

```
Y1    y1    8    sum:=x"00"
Y2    y2    8    data_out:=sum
Y3    y3    8    sum:=tempReg8_1
Y4    y4    8    x:=data_in1

Y5    y5    4    alu8_1_ctr:="0001"
      y6    8    alu8_1_in1:=sum
      y7    8    alu8_1_in2:=x
      y8    8    tempReg8_1:=alu8_1_out
```

Figure 6. Functional ASM Table Funcmi.mrk

```
INDIRECT CONNECTIONS:

MUX0
   OUTPUT:
      sum
    INPUT:
      tempReg8_1              1    0        in0    sum
      x"00"                   1    1        in1    sum


DIRECT CONNECTIONS:

        SOURCES                        TARGETS

     alu8_1_out                     tempReg8_1

       data_in1                              x

            sum                     alu8_1_in1
                                      data_out

              x                     alu8_1_in2
```

Figure 7. 8-bit MUX and direct connections for Sum

```
<external_specifications xmlns="ExtSpec">
    <essential_files>
        <txt path="Funcmi_t.txt" />
        <tab path="Structm.tab" />
        <mrk path="Funcmi_t.mrk" />
        <spec path="Funcmi_t.spec" />
        <mux_files>
            <mux path="funcmi_t4b-mux.xml" bits="4" />
            <mux path="funcmi_t8b-mux.xml" bits="8" />
        </mux_files>
    </essential_files>
    <settings>
        <bit_range direction="Down" />
    </settings>
    <dp_to_out_and_out_to_dp>
        <signal name="clk" in_or_out="in" width="1" />
        <signal name="rst" in_or_out="in" width="1" />
        <signal name="data_in1" in_or_out="in" width="8" />
        <signal name="data_out" in_or_out="out" width="8" />
    </dp_to_out_and_out_to_dp>
    <components>
        <external>
            <!-- Add external components (and their path) that you would like to use in your design -->
        </external>
        <automatic>
            <generator type="register" global="clk, rst">
                <class>
                    <signal name="%name%" />
                    <signal name="%name%_en" />
                    <signal name="%name%" />
                </class>
                <instances>
                    <instance name="sum" />
                    <instance name="x" />
                    <instance name="tempreg8_1" />
                </instances>
            </generator>
            <generator type="generic_comparator" global="clk, rst">
                <class>
                    <signal name="%name%_in1" />
                    <signal name="%name%_in2" />
                    <signal name="%name%_out" />
                </class>
                <instances>
                    <instance name="comp8_1" />
                </instances>
            </generator>
            <generator type="alu" global="clk, rst">
                <class>
```

```
                    <signal name="%name%_in1" />
                    <signal name="%name%_in2" />
                    <signal name="%name%_ctr" />
                    <signal name="%name%_out" />
                </class>
                <instances>
                    <instance name="alu8_1" />
                </instances>
            </generator>
        </automatic>
    </components>
</external_specifications>
```

Figure 8. External specifications for Sum

```
-----------------------------
library IEEE;
use IEEE.std_logic_1164.all;
use IEEE.numeric_std.all;
use work.components.all;
-----------------------------
entity dp is
      port
            (

            -- Inputs from control unit
            ctr_mux0                  :      in    std_logic;  --(y1)
            sum_en                    :      in    std_logic;  --(y2)
            x_en                      :      in    std_logic;  --(y3)
            tempreg8_1_en             :      in    std_logic;  --(y4)

            -- Inputs from outside
            clk                       :      in    std_logic;
            rst                       :      in    std_logic;
            data_in1                  :      in      std_logic_vector(7
downto 0);

            -- Outputs to control unit
            comp8_1_dout              :      out   std_logic;  --(x1)

            -- Outputs to outside
            data_out                  :      out     std_logic_vector(7
downto 0)
            );

end dp;
----------------------------------------------
architecture arc_dp of dp is
      signal mux0_dout          :  std_logic_vector (7 downto 0);
      signal alu8_1_dout        :  std_logic_vector (7 downto 0);
      signal sum_dout           :  std_logic_vector (7 downto 0);
      signal tempreg8_1_dout    :  std_logic_vector (7 downto 0);
```

```
        signal x_dout                  :  std_logic_vector (7 downto 0);
begin

        ---------
        -- Mux 0
        ---------
        u1_mux0  : mux_2x8 port map (tempreg8_1_dout, x"00", ctr_mux0,
mux0_dout);

        ---------
        -- sum
        ---------
        u2_sum    :  reg_8bit  port  map  (clk,  rst,  mux0_dout,  sum_en,
sum_dout);

        ---------
        -- x
        ---------
        u3_x     : reg_8bit port map (clk, rst, data_in1, x_en, x_dout);

        ---------
        -- tempreg8_1
        ---------
        u4_tempreg8_1: reg_8bit port map (clk, rst, alu8_1_dout,
                                  tempreg8_1_en, tempreg8_1_dout);

        ---------
        -- comp8_1
        ---------
        u5_comp8_1 : g_comp generic map (comp_kind => "eq", size => 8)
                         port map (x_dout, x"00", comp8_1_dout);

        ---------
        -- alu8_1
        ---------
        u6_alu8_1  :  alu_8bit  port  map  (sum_dout,  x_dout,  "0001",
alu8_1_dout);

        -----------------------
        -- Additional Signals
        -----------------------

        data_out          <=    sum_dout;
end  arc_dp;
----------------------------------------------
configuration cfg_dp of dp is
        for arc_dp
        end for;
end cfg_dp;
------------------------------
```

Figure 9. Data Path for Sum

Of course, Synthagate automatically constructed VHDL codes of components instantiated in Data Path – register (*reg_8bit*), comparator (*g_comp*), ALU (*alu_8bit*) and MUX with two inputs (*mux_2x8*).

```
library ieee;
use ieee.std_logic_1164.all;
use ieee.numeric_std.all;
use work.components.all;
entity Structm is
      port (
            clk             : in std_logic;
            comp8_1_dout    : in std_logic;
            ctr_mux0        : out std_logic;
            idle            : out std_logic;
            rst             : in std_logic;
            s               : in std_logic;
            sum_en          : out std_logic;
            tempreg8_1_en   : out std_logic;
            x_en            : out std_logic
      );
end Structm;
architecture ARC_Structm of Structm is
      type FSMStates is (
            a1, a2, a3, a4
      );
      signal currentState : FSMStates;
begin
      process (clk , rst)
      procedure proc_Structm is
      begin
      ctr_mux0 <= '0';
      idle <= '0';
      sum_en <= '0';
      tempreg8_1_en <= '0';
      x_en <= '0';
      case currentState is
      when a1 =>
            if (s) = '1' then
                  ctr_mux0 <= '1';
                  sum_en <= '1';
                  currentState <= a2;
            else
                  currentState <= a1;
                  idle <= '1';
            end if;
      when a2 =>
                  x_en <= '1';
                  currentState <= a3;
      when a3 =>
            if (comp8_1_dout) = '1' then
                  currentState <= a1;
                  idle <= '1';
            else
```

```
                    tempreg8_1_en <= '1';
                    currentState <= a4;
              end if;
        when a4 =>

                    sum_en <= '1';
                    currentState <= a2;
        end case;
        end proc_Structm;
        begin
              if (rst = '1') then
                    ctr_mux0 <= '0';
                    idle <= '0';
                    sum_en <= '0';
                    tempreg8_1_en <= '0';
                    x_en <= '0';
                    currentState <= a1;
                    idle <= '1';
              elsif (clk'event and clk = '0') then
                    idle <= '0';
                    proc_Structm;
              end if;
        end process;
end ARC_Structm;
```

Figure 10. Control Unit

```
library IEEE;
use IEEE.std_logic_1164.all;
----------------------------------------------
entity top is
    port
      (
        clk        : in  std_logic;
        data_in1   : in  std_logic_vector(7 downto 0);
        data_out   : out std_logic_vector(7 downto 0);
        idle       : out std_logic;
        rst        : in  std_logic;
        s          : in  std_logic
      );
end top;
----------------------------------------------
architecture arc_top of top is
component Structm is
      port (
            clk             : in std_logic;
            comp8_1_dout    : in std_logic;
            ctr_mux0        : out std_logic;
            idle            : out std_logic;
            rst             : in std_logic;
            s               : in std_logic;
            sum_en          : out std_logic;
```

```
            tempreg8_1_en : out std_logic;
            x_en          : out std_logic
      );
end component;

component dp is
      port
            (

            -- Inputs from control unit
            ctr_mux0      :    in    std_logic;  --(y1)
            sum_en        :    in    std_logic;  --(y2)
            x_en          :    in    std_logic;  --(y3)
            tempreg8_1_en:     in    std_logic;  --(y4)

            -- Inputs from outside
            clk           :    in    std_logic;
            rst           :    in    std_logic;
            data_in1      :    in    std_logic_vector(7 downto 0);

            -- Outputs to control unit
            comp8_1_dout :     out  std_logic;   --(x1)

            -- Outputs to outside
            data_out      :    out std_logic_vector(7 downto 0)
            );

end component;

    -- output of  control unit
    signal ctr_mux0         : std_logic;
    signal sum_en           : std_logic;
    signal x_en             : std_logic;
    signal tempreg8_1_en    : std_logic;

    -- output of operational unit
    signal comp8_1_dout     : std_logic;

begin
    u1_fsm : structm port map
      (
            clk            => clk           ,
            comp8_1_dout   => comp8_1_dout  ,
            ctr_mux0       => ctr_mux0      ,
            idle           => idle          ,
            rst            => rst           ,
            s              => s             ,
            sum_en         => sum_en        ,
            tempreg8_1_en  => tempreg8_1_en ,
            x_en           => x_en
```

```
      );

    u2_dp : dp port map
      (
            clk            => clk            ,
            rst            => rst            ,
            data_in1       => data_in1       ,
            ctr_mux0       => ctr_mux0       ,
            sum_en         => sum_en         ,
            x_en           => x_en           ,
            tempreg8_1_en  => tempreg8_1_en  ,
            data_out       => data_out       ,
            comp8_1_dout   => comp8_1_dout
      );
end arc_top;
-----------------------------------
configuration cfg_top of top is
      for arc_top
      end for;
end cfg_top;
-----------------------------------
```

Figure 11. Top as a composition of Control Unit and Data Path

The whole design from ASM to RTL took less than four seconds. Here the time report from Synthagate is: `HLS Total Time: 00:00:03.8414845.`

4.2 Greatest Common Divisor

I will design here a system in which a user enters two 8-bit unsigned numbers *X* and *Y*. The greatest common divisor (GCD) of these numbers should be on the output of the system. The ASM *Divider* for this behavior is on Fig. 12.

That ASM is very simple too – its file *divider.txt* is presented on Fig. 13. ASM *Divider* contains only four operators (*Y1* – *Y4*), five microoperations (*y1* – *y5*) and three logical conditions (*x1, x2, x3*).

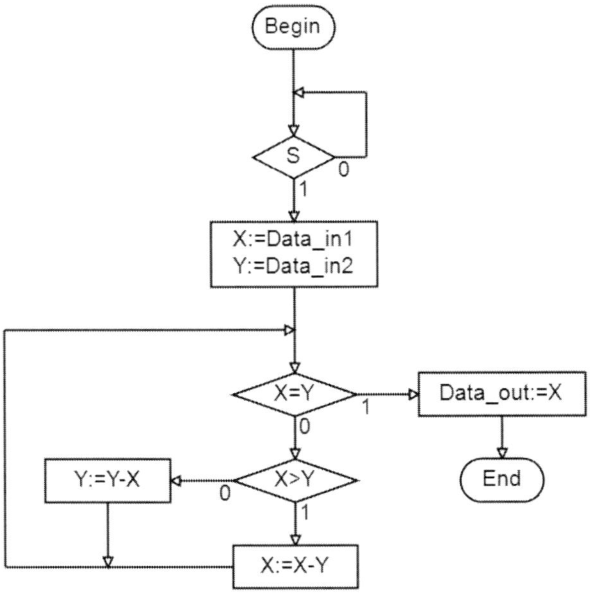

Figure 12. ASM for Divider

Micro Instructions:	Micro Operations:	Logical Conditions:
Y1 = y1	y1 : Data_out:=X	File Draw
Y2 = y2	y2 : X:=X-Y	x1 : X>Y
Y3 = y3	y3 : Y:=Y-X	x2 : X=Y
Y4 = y4 y5	y4 : X:=Data_in1	x3 : S
	y5 : Y:=Data_in2	

Figure 13. Txt file for ASM Divider

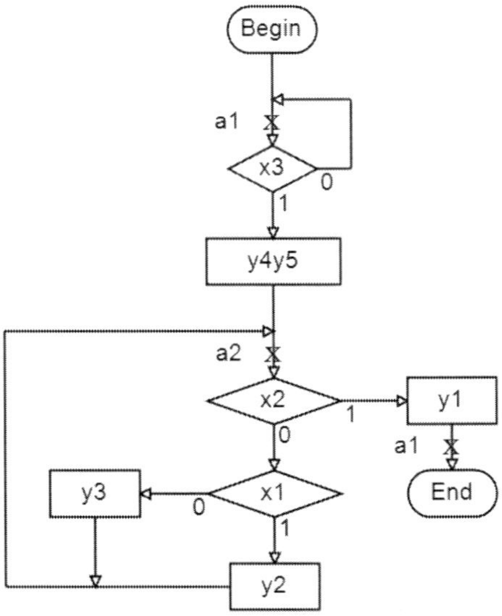

Figure 14. ASM marked for Mealy FSM

A marked ASM Divider is presented in Fig. 14. In this ASM I replaced microoperations and logical conditions of ASM in Fig. 12 by *y1, ..., y5* and *x1, x2* and *x3* from Fig.13. If you forgot, how to design FSM from ASM, return to Section 1.2 from the first Chapter. The Functional FSM *Funcmi.t1* with only two states is shown in Table 2.

Table 2. Transition table of Functional FSM for Divider

a1	a2	x3	y4y5	1
a1	a1	~x3	--	2
a2	a1	x2	y1	3
a2	a2	~x2*x1	y2	4
a2	a2	~x2*~x1	y3	5

Automatically constructed functional specifications is presented in file *Divider.spec* (Fig. 15). It contains only 15 rows.

```
<functional_specifications>
    <declarations>
        <port name="data_in1" width="8" direction="in" />
        <port name="data_in2" width="8" direction="in" />
        <port name="data_out" width="8" direction="out" />
        <port name="s" width="1" direction="in" />
        <signal name="x" width="8" />
        <signal name="y" width="8" />
    </declarations>
    <required_libraries>
        <vhdl>
            <library name="my_package" />
        </vhdl>
    </required_libraries>
</functional_specifications>
```

Figure 15. Functional specifications

Functional design at High level (file *Fincmi.vhd* constructed by Synthagate) is presented on Fig. 16. It is a small design – file contains only 70 lines.

```
library ieee;
use ieee.std_logic_1164.all;
use ieee.numeric_std.all;
use work.my_package.all;

entity Funcmi is
      port (
            clk         : in std_logic;
            data_in1    : in std_logic_vector(7 downto 0);
            data_in2    : in std_logic_vector(7 downto 0);
            data_out    : out std_logic_vector(7 downto 0);
```

```
        idle            : out std_logic;
        rst             : in std_logic;
        s               : in std_logic
    );
end Funcmi;

architecture ARC_Funcmi of Funcmi is

    type FSMStates is (
        a1, a2
    );
    signal currentState : FSMStates;
    signal x : std_logic_vector(7 downto 0);
    signal y : std_logic_vector(7 downto 0);
begin
    process (clk , rst)

    procedure proc_Funcmi is
    begin
    case currentState is
    when a1 =>
        if (s) = '1' then
            x <= data_in1;
            y <= data_in2;
            currentState <= a2;
        else
            currentState <= a1;
            idle <= '1';
        end if;
    when a2 =>
        if (x = y) then
            data_out <= x;
            currentState <= a1;
            idle <= '1';

        elsif (not (x = y) and x > y) then
            x <= std_logic_vector(unsigned(x) - unsigned(y));
            currentState <= a2;

        else
            y <= std_logic_vector(unsigned(y) - unsigned(x));
            currentState <= a2;
        end if;
    end case;
    end proc_Funcmi;
    begin
        if (rst = '1') then
```

```
                data_out <= (others => '0');
                idle <= '0';
                x <= (others => '0');
                y <= (others => '0');
                currentState <= a1;
                idle <= '1';
          elsif (clk'event and clk = '1') then
                idle <= '0';
                proc_Funcmi;
          end if;
    end process;
end ARC_Funcmi;
```

Figure 16. High Level Synthesis for Divider

Functional ASM table is shown in Fig. 17, Connection graph – in Fig.18, the list of parallel microoperations before and after considering direct connections – in Fig. 19.

```
Y1     y1       8      data_out:=x

Y2     y2       8      x:=tempReg8_1

Y3     y3       8      y:=tempReg8_1

Y4     y4       8      x:=data_in1
       y5       8      y:=data_in2

Y5     y6       4      alu8_1_ctr:="0010"
       y7       8      alu8_1_in1:=y
       y8       8      alu8_1_in2:=x
       y9       8      tempReg8_1:=alu8_1_out

Y6     y6       4      alu8_1_ctr:="0010"
       y10      8      alu8_1_in1:=x
       y11      8      alu8_1_in2:=y
       y9       8      tempReg8_1:=alu8_1_out
```

Figure 17. Functional ASM Table Funcmi.mrk

```
weight : sources         targets : weight
     0 : alu8_1_out   tempReg8_1 : 0

     1 : data_in1              x : 1

     1 : data_in2              y : 1

     2 : tempReg8_1            x : 1
                               y : 1

     2 : x            alu8_1_in1 : 1
```

```
                     alu8_1_in2 : 1
                       data_out : 0

2 : y                alu8_1_in1 : 1
                     alu8_1_in2 : 1
```

Figure 18. Connection graph for 8-bit connections

Parallel Microoperations before considering direct connections:

```
Y4      : y4     x:=data_in1
          y5     y:=data_in2

Y5      : y7     alu8_1_in1:=y
          y8     alu8_1_in2:=x
          y9     tempReg8_1:=alu8_1_out

Y6      : y9     tempReg8_1:=alu8_1_out
          y10    alu8_1_in1:=x
          y11    alu8_1_in2:=y
```

Parallel Microoperations after considering direct connections:

```
Y4      : y4     x:=data_in1
          y5     y:=data_in2

Y5      : y7     alu8_1_in1:=y
          y8     alu8_1_in2:=x

Y6      : y10    alu8_1_in1:=x
          y11    alu8_1_in2:=y
```

Figure 19. 8-bit parallel microoperations for Divider

The graph of incompatibility, constructed from the connection graph (Fig. 18) and the list of parallel microoperations (Fig.19), is presented in Fig. 20. 8-bit MUXes and direct connections are shown in Fig. 21.

```
alu8_1_in1 -> alu8_1_in2
( x, y )

alu8_1_in2 -> alu8_1_in1
( x, y )

x -> y
( data_in1, tempReg8_1 )

y -> x
( data_in2, tempReg8_1 )
```

Figure 20. Graph of Incompatibility for 8-bit connections

```
MUX0
   OUTPUT:
      alu8_1_in1
      x
    INPUT:
      data_in1                      1    00        in0    x
      tempReg8_1                    1    01        in1    x
      x                             1    10        in2    alu8_1_in1
      y                             1    11        in3    alu8_1_in1

MUX1
   OUTPUT:
      alu8_1_in2
      y
    INPUT:
      data_in2                      1    00        in0    y
      tempReg8_1                    1    01        in1    y
      x                             1    10        in2    alu8_1_in2
      y                             1    11        in3    alu8_1_in2


DIRECT CONNECTIONS:

        SOURCES                            TARGETS

     alu8_1_out                         tempReg8_1

             x                            data_out
```

Figure 21. 8-bit MUXes and direct connections

External specifications (64 lines) are in Fig. 22. Data path for this design (Fig. 23) contains 4 components, the total number of instantiated components is equal to 8. VHDL code for the Control unit is in Fig. 24. The top design, combining Control unit and Data path is shown in Fig. 25.

```
<external_specifications xmlns="ExtSpec">
    <essential_files>
        <txt path="Funcmi_t.txt" />
        <tab path="Structm.tab" />
        <mrk path="Funcmi_t.mrk" />
        <spec path="Funcmi_t.spec" />
        <mux_files>
            <mux path="funcmi_t4b-mux.xml" bits="4" />
            <mux path="funcmi_t8b-mux.xml" bits="8" />
        </mux_files>
    </essential_files>
    <settings>
        <bit_range direction="Down" />
    </settings>
```

```
    <dp_to_out_and_out_to_dp>
        <signal name="clk" in_or_out="in" width="1" />
        <signal name="rst" in_or_out="in" width="1" />
        <signal name="data_in1" in_or_out="in" width="8" />
        <signal name="data_in2" in_or_out="in" width="8" />
        <signal name="data_out" in_or_out="out" width="8" />
    </dp_to_out_and_out_to_dp>
    <components>
        <external>
        <!-- Add external components (and their path) that you would
like to use in your design -->
        </external>
        <automatic>
            <generator type="register" global="clk, rst">
                <class>
                    <signal name="%name%" />
                    <signal name="%name%_en" />
                    <signal name="%name%" />
                </class>
                <instances>
                    <instance name="x" />
                    <instance name="y" />
                    <instance name="tempreg8_1" />
                </instances>
            </generator>
            <generator type="generic_comparator" global="clk, rst">
                <class>
                    <signal name="%name%_in1" />
                    <signal name="%name%_in2" />
                    <signal name="%name%_out" />
                </class>
                <instances>
                    <instance name="comp8_1" />
                    <instance name="comp8_2" />
                </instances>
            </generator>
            <generator type="alu" global="clk, rst">
                <class>
                    <signal name="%name%_in1" />
                    <signal name="%name%_in2" />
                    <signal name="%name%_ctr" />
                    <signal name="%name%_out" />
                </class>
                <instances>
                    <instance name="alu8_1" />
                </instances>
            </generator>
```

```
        </automatic>
    </components>
</external_specifications>
```

Figure 22. External specifications for Divider

Of course, Synthagate automatically constructed VHDL codes of components instantiated in Data Path – register (*reg_8bit*), comparator (*g_comp*), ALU (*alu_8bit*) and MUX with four inputs (*mux_4x8*).

```
-----------------------------
library IEEE;
use IEEE.std_logic_1164.all;
use IEEE.numeric_std.all;
use work.components.all;
-----------------------------
entity dp is
      port
            (

            -- Inputs from control unit
            ctr_mux0_0      :  in    std_logic;  --(y1)
            x_en            :  in    std_logic;  --(y2)
            ctr_mux1_0      :  in    std_logic;  --(y3)
            y_en            :  in    std_logic;  --(y4)
            ctr_mux0_1      :  in    std_logic;  --(y5)
            ctr_mux1_1      :  in    std_logic;  --(y6)
            tempreg8_1_en   :  in    std_logic;  --(y7)

            -- Inputs from outside
            clk             :  in    std_logic;
            rst             :  in    std_logic;
            data_in1        :  in    std_logic_vector(7 downto 0);
            data_in2        :  in    std_logic_vector(7 downto 0);

            -- Outputs to control unit
            comp8_1_dout    :  out   std_logic;  --(x1)
            comp8_2_dout    :  out   std_logic;  --(x2)

            -- Outputs to outside
            data_out        :  out   std_logic_vector(7 downto 0)
            );

end dp;
-----------------------------------------------
architecture arc_dp of dp is
      signal mux0_dout           :    std_logic_vector (7 downto 0);
      signal mux1_dout           :    std_logic_vector (7 downto 0);
      signal alu8_1_dout         :    std_logic_vector (7 downto 0);
      signal tempreg8_1_dout     :    std_logic_vector (7 downto 0);
      signal x_dout              :    std_logic_vector (7 downto 0);
      signal y_dout              :    std_logic_vector (7 downto 0);
      signal ctr_mux0            :    std_logic_vector (1 downto 0);
```

```
	signal ctr_mux1		:  std_logic_vector (1 downto 0);
begin

	---------
	-- Mux 0
	---------
	u1_mux0 : mux_4x8 port map (data_in1, tempreg8_1_dout, x_dout,
			y_dout, ctr_mux0, mux0_dout);

	---------
	-- Mux 1
	---------
	u2_mux1 : mux_4x8  port map (data_in2, tempreg8_1_dout,
			x_dout, y_dout, ctr_mux1, mux1_dout);

	---------
	-- x
	---------
	u3_x : reg_8bit port map (clk, rst, mux0_dout, x_en, x_dout);

	---------
	-- y
	---------
	u4_y : reg_8bit  port map (clk, rst, mux1_dout, y_en, y_dout);

	---------
	-- tempreg8_1
	---------
	u5_tempreg8_1 : reg_8bit port map (clk, rst, alu8_1_dout,
			tempreg8_1_en, tempreg8_1_dout);

	---------
	-- comp8_1
	---------
	u6_comp8_1	: g_comp generic map (comp_kind => "gr", size =>
			8) port map (x_dout, y_dout, comp8_1_dout);

	---------
	-- comp8_2
	---------
	u7_comp8_2	: g_comp generic map (comp_kind => "eq", size =>
			8) port map (x_dout, y_dout, comp8_2_dout);

	---------
	-- alu8_1
	---------
	u8_alu8_1	: alu_8bit port map (mux0_dout, mux1_dout, "0010",
			alu8_1_dout);

	-----------------------
	-- Additional Signals
	-----------------------

	ctr_mux0	<= ctr_mux0_1 & ctr_mux0_0;
```

```
      ctr_mux1  <= ctr_mux1_1 & ctr_mux1_0;
      data_out  <= x_dout;

end  arc_dp;
-------------------
configuration cfg_dp of dp is
      for arc_dp
      end for;
end cfg_dp;

-----------------------------
```

Figure 23. Data Path

```
library ieee;
use ieee.std_logic_1164.all;
use ieee.numeric_std.all;
use work.components.all;

entity Structm is
      port (
            clk            : in std_logic;
            comp8_1_dout   : in std_logic;
            comp8_2_dout   : in std_logic;
            ctr_mux0_0     : out std_logic;
            ctr_mux0_1     : out std_logic;
            ctr_mux1_0     : out std_logic;
            ctr_mux1_1     : out std_logic;
            idle           : out std_logic;
            rst            : in std_logic;
            s              : in std_logic;
            tempreg8_1_en  : out std_logic;
            x_en           : out std_logic;
            y_en           : out std_logic
      );
end Structm;

architecture ARC_Structm of Structm is

      type FSMStates is (
            a1, a2, a3, a4
      );

      signal currentState : FSMStates;

begin

      process (clk , rst)

      procedure proc_Structm is
      begin

      ctr_mux0_0 <= '0';
```

```
ctr_mux0_1 <= '0';
ctr_mux1_0 <= '0';
ctr_mux1_1 <= '0';
idle <= '0';
tempreg8_1_en <= '0';
x_en <= '0';
y_en <= '0';

case currentState is
when a1 =>
      if (s) = '1' then
            x_en <= '1';
            y_en <= '1';
            currentState <= a2;

      else
            currentState <= a1;
            idle <= '1';

      end if;

when a2 =>
      if (comp8_2_dout) = '1' then
            currentState <= a1;
            idle <= '1';

      elsif (not comp8_2_dout and comp8_1_dout) = '1' then
            ctr_mux1_0 <= '1';
            ctr_mux0_1 <= '1';
            ctr_mux1_1 <= '1';
            tempreg8_1_en <= '1';
            currentState <= a3;

      else
            ctr_mux0_0 <= '1';
            ctr_mux0_1 <= '1';
            ctr_mux1_1 <= '1';
            tempreg8_1_en <= '1';
            currentState <= a4;

      end if;

when a3 =>

            ctr_mux0_0 <= '1';
            x_en <= '1';
            currentState <= a2;

when a4 =>

            ctr_mux1_0 <= '1';
            y_en <= '1';
            currentState <= a2;
```

```
       end case;
       end proc_Structm;

       begin
            if (rst = '1') then
                 ctr_mux0_0 <= '0';
                 ctr_mux0_1 <= '0';
                 ctr_mux1_0 <= '0';
                 ctr_mux1_1 <= '0';
                 idle <= '0';
                 tempreg8_1_en <= '0';
                 x_en <= '0';
                 y_en <= '0';

                 currentState <= a1;
                 idle <= '1';

            elsif (clk'event and clk = '0') then
                 idle <= '0';
                 proc_Structm;
            end if;
       end process;

end ARC_Structm;
```

Figure 24. Control Unit

```
library IEEE;
use IEEE.std_logic_1164.all;
----------------------------------------------
entity top is
    port
      (
        clk         : in  std_logic;
        data_in1    : in  std_logic_vector(7 downto 0);
        data_in2    : in  std_logic_vector(7 downto 0);
        data_out    : out std_logic_vector(7 downto 0);
        idle        : out std_logic;
        rst         : in  std_logic;
        s           : in  std_logic
      );
end top;
----------------------------------------------
architecture arc_top of top is
component Structm is
      port (
            clk            : in std_logic;
            comp8_1_dout   : in std_logic;
            comp8_2_dout   : in std_logic;
            ctr_mux0_0     : out std_logic;
            ctr_mux0_1     : out std_logic;
            ctr_mux1_0     : out std_logic;
```

```
            ctr_mux1_1    : out std_logic;
            idle          : out std_logic;
            rst           : in std_logic;
            s             : in std_logic;
            tempreg8_1_en : out std_logic;
            x_en          : out std_logic;
            y_en          : out std_logic
      );
end component;

component dp is
      port
            (

            -- Inputs from control unit
            ctr_mux0_0     :  in    std_logic;  --(y1)
            x_en           :  in    std_logic;  --(y2)
            ctr_mux1_0     :  in    std_logic;  --(y3)
            y_en           :  in    std_logic;  --(y4)
            ctr_mux0_1     :  in    std_logic;  --(y5)
            ctr_mux1_1     :  in    std_logic;  --(y6)
            tempreg8_1_en  :  in    std_logic;  --(y7)

            -- Inputs from outside
            clk            :  in    std_logic;
            rst            :  in    std_logic;
            data_in1       :  in    std_logic_vector(7 downto 0);
            data_in2       :  in    std_logic_vector(7 downto 0);

            -- Outputs to control unit
            comp8_1_dout   :  out   std_logic;  --(x1)
            comp8_2_dout   :  out   std_logic;  --(x2)

            -- Outputs to outside
            data_out          : out   std_logic_vector(7 downto 0)
            );

end component;

     -- output of  control unit
     signal ctr_mux0_0     : std_logic;
     signal x_en           : std_logic;
     signal ctr_mux1_0     : std_logic;
     signal y_en           : std_logic;
     signal ctr_mux0_1     : std_logic;
     signal ctr_mux1_1     : std_logic;
     signal tempreg8_1_en  : std_logic;

     -- output of operational unit
     signal comp8_1_dout   : std_logic;
```

```
    signal comp8_2_dout   : std_logic;

begin

    u1_fsm : structm port map
      (
            clk              => clk            ,
            comp8_1_dout     => comp8_1_dout   ,
            comp8_2_dout     => comp8_2_dout   ,
            ctr_mux0_0       => ctr_mux0_0     ,
            ctr_mux0_1       => ctr_mux0_1     ,
            ctr_mux1_0       => ctr_mux1_0     ,
            ctr_mux1_1       => ctr_mux1_1     ,
            idle             => idle           ,
            rst              => rst            ,
            s                => s              ,
            tempreg8_1_en    => tempreg8_1_en  ,
            x_en             => x_en           ,
            y_en             => y_en
      );

    u2_dp : dp port map
      (
            clk              => clk            ,
            rst              => rst            ,
            data_in1         => data_in1       ,
            data_in2         => data_in2       ,
            ctr_mux0_0       => ctr_mux0_0     ,
            x_en             => x_en           ,
            ctr_mux1_0       => ctr_mux1_0     ,
            y_en             => y_en           ,
            ctr_mux0_1       => ctr_mux0_1     ,
            ctr_mux1_1       => ctr_mux1_1     ,
            tempreg8_1_en    => tempreg8_1_en  ,
            data_out         => data_out       ,
            comp8_1_dout     => comp8_1_dout   ,
            comp8_2_dout     => comp8_2_dout
      );
end arc_top;
-----------------------------------
configuration cfg_top of top is
      for arc_top
      end for;
end cfg_top;
------------------------------------
```

Figure 25. Top as a composition of Control Unit and Data Path

4.3 High-Low Guessing Game

I will design here a system for playing the high-low guessing game. The user picks a number between 0 and 99, and our processor *Game* will use the binary search algorithm to guess the number. After each guess, the user tells the processor whether the guess is high or low compared to the picked number.

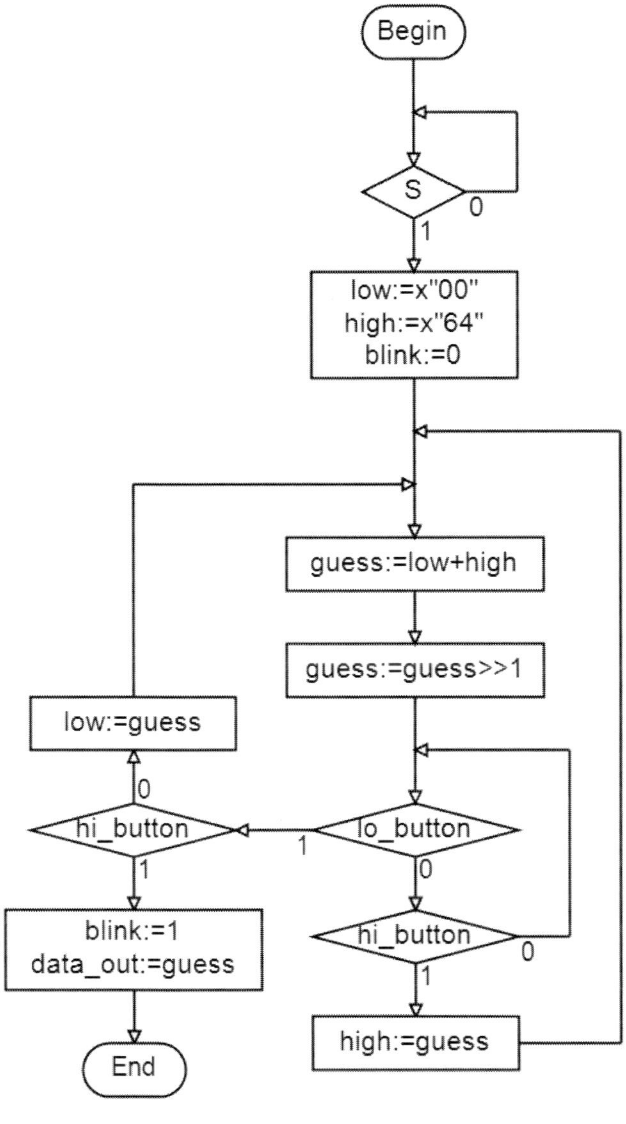

Figure 26. ASM for Game

Two push buttons, *hi_button* and *lo_button*, are used for the user to tell the processor whether the guess is too high, too low, or correct. The *hi_button* is pressed if the guess is too high, and the *lo_button* is pressed if the guess is too low. When both buttons are pressed, the *guess* is correct and it arrives at the output. At the same time the signal *blink* will be equal to one. The ASM *Game* for this behavior is on Fig. 26.

```
Micro                 Micro Operations:               Logical Conditions:
Instructions:         y1  :  blink:=1                 File   Draw
Y1 = y1 y2            y2  :  data_out:=guess          x1  : s
Y2 = y3               y3  :  guess:=guess>>1          x2  : hi_button
Y3 = y4 y5 y6         y4  :  low:=x"00"               x3  : lo_button
Y4 = y7               y5  :  high:=x"64"
Y5 = y8               y6  :  blink:=0
Y6 = y9               y7  :  guess:=low+high
                      y8  :  high:=guess
                      y9  :  low:=guess
```

Figure 27. Txt file for ASM Game

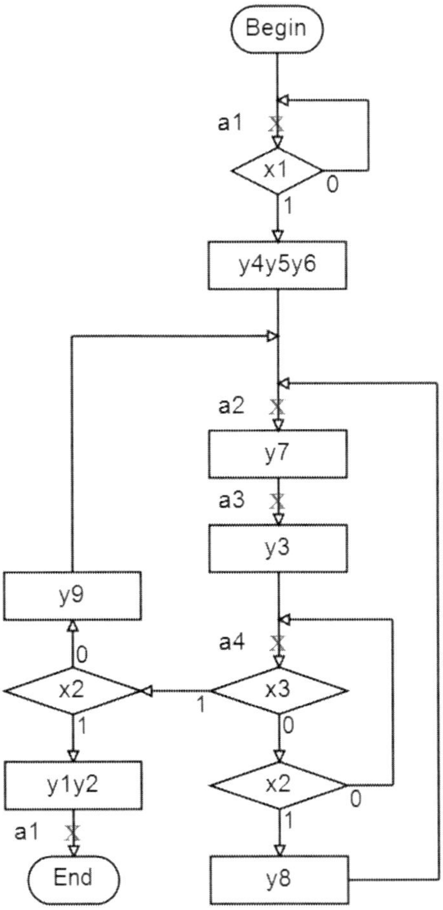

Figure 28. ASM marked for Mealy FSM

That ASM is a little bit more than the previous ones – its file *game.txt* is presented on Fig. 27. ASM *Game* contains six operators (*Y1 – Y6*), nine microoperations (*y1 – y9*) and three logical conditions (*x1, x2, x3*).

A marked ASM Game is presented in Fig. 28. In this ASM I replaced microoperations and logical conditions of ASM in Fig. 26 by *y1, ..., y9* and *x1, x2* and *x3* from Fig.27. If you forgot, how to design FSM from ASM, return to Section 1.2 from the first Chapter. The Functional FSM Funcmi.t1 with four states is shown in Table 3.

Table 3. Transition table of Functional FSM for Game

a1	a2	x1	y4y5y6	1
a1	a1	~x1	--	2
a2	a3	1	y7	3
a3	a4	1	y3	4
a4	a1	x2*x3	y1y2	5
a4	a2	x2*~x3	y8	6
a4	a2	~x2*x3	y9	7
a4	a4	~x2*~x3	--	8

Automatically constructed functional specifications is presented in file *Game.spec* (Fig. 29). It contains only 17 rows.

```
<functional_specifications>
        <declarations>
            <port name="blink" width="1" direction="out" />
            <port name="data_out" width="8" direction="out" />
            <port name="hi_button" width="1" direction="in" />
            <port name="lo_button" width="1" direction="in" />
            <port name="s" width="1" direction="in" />
            <signal name="guess" width="8" />
            <signal name="high" width="8" />
            <signal name="low" width="8" />
        </declarations>
        <required_libraries>
            <vhdl>
                <library name="my_package" />
            </vhdl>
        </required_libraries>
    </functional_specifications>
```

Figure 29. Functional specifications

Functional design at High level (file *Fincmi.vhd* constructed by Synthagate) is presented on Fig. 30. It is a small design too – file contains only 82 lines.

```
library ieee;
use ieee.std_logic_1164.all;
use ieee.numeric_std.all;
use work.my_package.all;

entity Funcmi is
      port (
            blink         : out std_logic;
            clk           : in std_logic;
            data_out      : out std_logic_vector(7 downto 0);
            hi_button     : in std_logic;
            idle          : out std_logic;
            lo_button     : in std_logic;
            rst           : in std_logic;
            s             : in std_logic
      );
end Funcmi;

architecture ARC_Funcmi of Funcmi is
      type FSMStates is (
            a1, a2, a3, a4
      );
      signal currentState : FSMStates;
      signal guess : std_logic_vector(7 downto 0);
      signal high : std_logic_vector(7 downto 0);
      signal low : std_logic_vector(7 downto 0);

begin
      process (clk , rst)

      procedure proc_Funcmi is
      begin

      case currentState is
      when a1 =>
            if (s) = '1' then
                  low <= x"00";
                  high <= x"64";
                  blink <= '0';
                  currentState <= a2;
            else
                  currentState <= a1;
                  idle <= '1';
            end if;
      when a2 =>
            guess<=std_logic_vector(unsigned(low) + unsigned(high));
                  currentState <= a3;
      when a3 =>
            guess <= std_logic_vector(unsigned(guess) srl 1);
                  currentState <= a4;
```

```
        when a4 =>
              if (hi_button and lo_button) = '1' then
                    blink <= '1';
                    data_out <= guess;
                    currentState <= a1;
                    idle <= '1';
              elsif (hi_button and not lo_button) = '1' then
                    high <= guess;
                    currentState <= a2;
              elsif (not hi_button and lo_button) = '1' then
                    low <= guess;
                    currentState <= a2;
              else
                    currentState <= a4;
              end if;
        end case;
        end proc_Funcmi;

        begin
              if (rst = '1') then
                    blink <= '0';
                    data_out <= (others => '0');
                    guess <= (others => '0');
                    high <= (others => '0');
                    idle <= '0';
                    low <= (others => '0');
                    currentState <= a1;
                    idle <= '1';
              elsif (clk'event and clk = '1') then
                    idle <= '0';
                    proc_Funcmi;
              end if;

        end process;
end ARC_Funcmi;
```

Figure 30. High Level Synthesis for Game

Here I strongly advise you to come back to Sections 3.1.3 – 3.1.6 to remember how to construct the connection graph, the list of parallel microoperations, the graph of incompatibility and multiplexers. Four bits connection graph is very simple here – its design you can use as an exercise.

8-bit Functional ASM table is shown in Fig. 31, The 8-bit connection graph is on Fig. 32, the list of parallel microoperations for 8-bit connections before and after considering direct connections – on Fig. 33.

```
Y1    y1     0    blink:=1
      y2     8    data_out:=guess

Y2    y3     8    guess:=tempReg8_1

Y3    y4     0    blink:=0
      y5     8    high:=x"64"
      y6     8    low:=x"00"

Y4    y7     4    alu8_1_ctr:="0001"
      y8     8    alu8_1_in1:=low
      y9     8    alu8_1_in2:=high
      y10    8    guess:=alu8_1_out

Y5    y11    8    high:=guess

Y6    y12    8    low:=guess

Y7    y13    4    alu8_1_ctr:="1100"
      y14    8    alu8_1_in1:=guess
      y15    8    alu8_1_in2:=x"01"
      y16    8    tempReg8_1:=alu8_1_out
```

Figure 31. Functional ASM Table Funcmi.mrk

```
weight : sources          targets : weight
     1 : alu8_1_out         guess : 1
                       tempReg8_1 : 0
     3 : guess         alu8_1_in1 : 1
                         data_out : 0
                             high : 1
                              low : 1
     1 : high          alu8_1_in2 : 1
     1 : low           alu8_1_in1 : 1
     1 : tempReg8_1         guess : 1
     1 : x"00"                low : 1
     1 : x"01"         alu8_1_in2 : 1
     1 : x"64"               high : 1
```

Figure 32. Connection graph for 8-bit connections

```
Parallel Microoperations before considering direct connections:

        Y3      : y5     high:=x"64"
                  y6     low:=x"00"

        Y4      : y8     alu8_1_in1:=low
                  y9     alu8_1_in2:=high
                  y10    guess:=alu8_1_out

        Y7      : y14    alu8_1_in1:=guess
                  y15    alu8_1_in2:=x"01"
                  y16    tempReg8_1:=alu8_1_out


Parallel Microoperations after considering direct connections:
        Y3      : y5     high:=x"64"
                  y6     low:=x"00"

        Y4      : y8     alu8_1_in1:=low
                  y9     alu8_1_in2:=high
                  y10    guess:=alu8_1_out

        Y7      : y14    alu8_1_in1:=guess
                  y15    alu8_1_in2:=x"01"
```

Figure 33. 8-bit parallel microoperations for *Game*

The graph of incompatibility, constructed from the connection graph (Fig. 32) and the list of parallel microoperations (Fig.33), is presented in Fig. 34. 8-bit MUXes and direct connections are shown in Fig. 35.

```
alu8_1_in1 -> alu8_1_in2, guess
( guess, low )

alu8_1_in2 -> alu8_1_in1, guess
( high, x"01" )

guess -> alu8_1_in1, alu8_1_in2
( alu8_1_out, tempReg8_1 )

high -> low
( guess, x"64" )

low -> high
( guess, x"00" )
```

Figure 34. Graph of Incompatibility for 8-bit connections

```
MUX1
   OUTPUT:
      alu8_1_in1
      high
    INPUT:
      guess            2    00        in0    alu8_1_in1
                                             high
      low              1    01        in1    alu8_1_in1
      x"64"            1    10        in2    high

MUX2
   OUTPUT:
      alu8_1_in2
      low
    INPUT:
      guess           1    00        in0    low
      high            1    01        in1    alu8_1_in2
      x"00"           1    10        in2    low
      x"01"           1    11        in3    alu8_1_in2

MUX3
   OUTPUT:
      guess
    INPUT:
      alu8_1_out      1    0         in0    guess
      tempReg8_1      1    1         in1    guess

DIRECT CONNECTIONS:

        SOURCES                        TARGETS

     alu8_1_out                     tempReg8_1
          guess                       data_out
```

Figure 35. 8-bit MUXes and direct connections

External specifications (62 lines) are in Fig. 36. Data path for this design (Fig. 37) contains 7 components, the total number of instantiated components is equal to 10. VHDL code for the Control unit is in Fig. 38. The top design, combining Control unit and Data path is shown in Fig. 39.

```
<external_specifications xmlns="ExtSpec">
    <essential_files>
        <txt path="Funcmi_t.txt" />
        <tab path="Structm.tab" />
        <mrk path="Funcmi_t.mrk" />
        <spec path="Funcmi_t.spec" />
        <mux_files>
            <mux path="funcmi_t4b-mux.xml" bits="4" />
            <mux path="funcmi_t8b-mux.xml" bits="8" />
        </mux_files>
    </essential_files>
```

```
    <settings>
        <bit_range direction="Down" />
    </settings>
    <dp_to_out_and_out_to_dp>
        <signal name="clk" in_or_out="in" width="1" />
        <signal name="rst" in_or_out="in" width="1" />
        <signal name="blink" in_or_out="out" width="1" />
        <signal name="data_out" in_or_out="out" width="8" />
    </dp_to_out_and_out_to_dp>
    <components>
        <external>
            <!-- Add external components (and their path) that you
            would like to use in your design -->
        </external>
        <automatic>
            <generator type="rsff" global="clk, rst">
                <class>
                    <signal name="%name%_reset" />
                    <signal name="%name%_set" />
                    <signal name="%name%" />
                </class>
                <instances>
                    <instance name="blink" />
                </instances>
            </generator>
            <generator type="register" global="clk, rst">
                <class>
                    <signal name="%name%" />
                    <signal name="%name%_en" />
                    <signal name="%name%" />
                </class>
                <instances>
                    <instance name="guess" />
                    <instance name="low" />
                    <instance name="high" />
                    <instance name="tempreg8_1" />
                </instances>
            </generator>
            <generator type="alu" global="clk, rst">
                <class>
                    <signal name="%name%_in1" />
                    <signal name="%name%_in2" />
                    <signal name="%name%_ctr" />
                    <signal name="%name%_out" />
                </class>
                <instances>
                    <instance name="alu8_1" />
                </instances>
            </generator>
        </automatic>
    </components>
</external_specifications>
```

Figure 36. External specifications for Game

```
-----------------------------
library IEEE;
use IEEE.std_logic_1164.all;
use IEEE.numeric_std.all;
use work.components.all;
-----------------------------
entity dp is
      port
            (
            -- Inputs from control unit
            blink_set          :     in    std_logic;  --(y1)
            ctr_mux3           :     in    std_logic;  --(y2)
            guess_en           :     in    std_logic;  --(y3)
            blink_reset        :     in    std_logic;  --(y4)
            ctr_mux1_1         :     in    std_logic;  --(y5)
            high_en            :     in    std_logic;  --(y6)
            ctr_mux2_1         :     in    std_logic;  --(y7)
            low_en             :     in    std_logic;  --(y8)
            ctr_mux1_0         :     in    std_logic;  --(y9)
            ctr_mux2_0         :     in    std_logic;  --(y10)
            ctr_mux0           :     in    std_logic;  --(y11)
            tempreg8_1_en      :     in    std_logic;  --(y12)

            -- Inputs from outside
            clk                :     in    std_logic;
            rst                :     in    std_logic;

            -- Outputs to control unit

            -- Outputs to outside
            blink      :   out   std_logic;
            data_out   :   out   std_logic_vector(7 downto 0)
            );
end dp;
-----------------------------------------------
architecture arc_dp of dp is
      signal mux0_dout         :    std_logic_vector (3 downto 0);
      signal mux1_dout         :    std_logic_vector (7 downto 0);
      signal mux2_dout         :    std_logic_vector (7 downto 0);
      signal mux3_dout         :    std_logic_vector (7 downto 0);
      signal alu8_1_dout       :    std_logic_vector (7 downto 0);
      signal guess_dout        :    std_logic_vector (7 downto 0);
      signal high_dout         :    std_logic_vector (7 downto 0);
      signal low_dout          :    std_logic_vector (7 downto 0);
      signal tempreg8_1_dout   :    std_logic_vector (7 downto 0);
      signal ctr_mux1          :    std_logic_vector (1 downto 0);
      signal ctr_mux2          :    std_logic_vector (1 downto 0);
```

```
begin
      ---------
      -- Mux 0
      ---------
      u1_mux0 :mux_2x4 port map ("0001", "1100",ctr_mux0, mux0_dout);

      ---------
      -- Mux 1
      ---------
      u2_mux1 : mux_3x8 port map (guess_dout, low_dout, x"64",
                ctr_mux1, mux1_dout);

      ---------
      -- Mux 2
      ---------
      u3_mux2 : mux_4x8 port map (guess_dout, high_dout, x"00", x"01",
                ctr_mux2, mux2_dout);
      ---------
      -- Mux 3
      ---------
      u4_mux3 : mux_2x8 port map (alu8_1_dout, tempreg8_1_dout,
                ctr_mux3, mux3_dout);

      ---------
      -- blink
      ---------
      u5_blink : rsff port map (clk, blink_reset, blink_set, rst,
                blink);

      ---------
      -- guess
      ---------
      u6_guess : reg_8bit port map (clk, rst, mux3_dout, guess_en,
                guess_dout);

      ---------
      -- low
      ---------
      u7_low : reg_8bit port map (clk, rst, mux2_dout, low_en,
                low_dout);

      ---------
      -- high
      ---------
      u8_high : reg_8bit port map (clk, rst, mux1_dout, high_en,
                high_dout);

      ---------
      -- tempreg8_1
      ---------
```

```
      u9_tempreg8_1 : reg_8bit port map (clk, rst, alu8_1_dout,
                  tempreg8_1_en, tempreg8_1_dout);

      ---------
      -- alu8_1
      ---------
      u10_alu8_1 : alu_8bit port map (mux1_dout, mux2_dout,
                  mux0_dout, alu8_1_dout);

      -----------------------
      -- Additional Signals
      -----------------------
      ctr_mux1          <=    ctr_mux1_1 & ctr_mux1_0;
      ctr_mux2          <=    ctr_mux2_1 & ctr_mux2_0;
      data_out          <=    guess_dout;

end  arc_dp;
-----------------------------------------------
configuration cfg_dp of dp is
      for arc_dp
      end for;
end cfg_dp;
-----------------------------
```

Figure 37. Data Path

Of course, Synthagate automatically constructed VHDL codes of components instantiated in Data Path – register (*reg_8bit*), ALU (*alu_8bit*), 4 MUXes and *rs* flip-flop.

```
library ieee;
use ieee.std_logic_1164.all;
use ieee.numeric_std.all;
use work.my_package.all;

entity Structm is
      port (
            blink_reset    : out std_logic;
            blink_set      : out std_logic;
            clk            : in std_logic;
            ctr_mux0       : out std_logic;
            ctr_mux1_0     : out std_logic;
            ctr_mux1_1     : out std_logic;
            ctr_mux2_0     : out std_logic;
            ctr_mux2_1     : out std_logic;
            ctr_mux3       : out std_logic;
            guess_en       : out std_logic;
            hi_button      : in std_logic;
            high_en        : out std_logic;
            idle           : out std_logic;
            lo_button      : in std_logic;
            low_en         : out std_logic;
            rst            : in std_logic;
```

```
            s              : in std_logic;
            tempreg8_1_en : out std_logic
      );
end Structm;

architecture ARC_Structm of Structm is

      type FSMStates is (
            a1, a2, a3, a4, a5
      );

      signal currentState : FSMStates;
begin
      process (clk , rst)

      procedure proc_Structm is
      begin

      blink_reset <= '0';
      blink_set <= '0';
      ctr_mux0 <= '0';
      ctr_mux1_0 <= '0';
      ctr_mux1_1 <= '0';
      ctr_mux2_0 <= '0';
      ctr_mux2_1 <= '0';
      ctr_mux3 <= '0';
      guess_en <= '0';
      high_en <= '0';
      idle <= '0';
      low_en <= '0';
      tempreg8_1_en <= '0';

      case currentState is
      when a1 =>
            if (s) = '1' then
                  blink_reset <= '1';
                  ctr_mux1_1 <= '1';
                  high_en <= '1';
                  ctr_mux2_1 <= '1';
                  low_en <= '1';
                  currentState <= a2;
            else
                  currentState <= a1;
                  idle <= '1';
            end if;
      when a2 =>
                  guess_en <= '1';
                  ctr_mux1_0 <= '1';
                  ctr_mux2_0 <= '1';
                  currentState <= a3;
```

```
when a3 =>
                  ctr_mux2_1 <= '1';
                  ctr_mux2_0 <= '1';
                  ctr_mux0 <= '1';
                  tempreg8_1_en <= '1';
                  currentState <= a4;
      when a4 =>
                  ctr_mux3 <= '1';
                  guess_en <= '1';
                  currentState <= a5;
      when a5 =>
            if (hi_button and lo_button) = '1' then
                  blink_set <= '1';
                  currentState <= a1;
                  idle <= '1';
            elsif (hi_button and not lo_button) = '1' then
                  high_en <= '1';
                  currentState <= a2;
            elsif (not hi_button and lo_button) = '1' then
                  low_en <= '1';
                  currentState <= a2;
            else
                  currentState <= a5;

            end if;
      end case;
      end proc_Structm;

      begin
            if (rst = '1') then
                  blink_reset <= '0';
                  blink_set <= '0';
                  ctr_mux0 <= '0';
                  ctr_mux1_0 <= '0';
                  ctr_mux1_1 <= '0';
                  ctr_mux2_0 <= '0';
                  ctr_mux2_1 <= '0';
                  ctr_mux3 <= '0';
                  guess_en <= '0';
                  high_en <= '0';
                  idle <= '0';
                  low_en <= '0';
                  tempreg8_1_en <= '0';
                  currentState <= a1;
                  idle <= '1';
            elsif (clk'event and clk = '0') then
                  idle <= '0';
                  proc_Structm;
            end if;
      end process;

end ARC_Structm;
```

Figure 38. Control Unit

```
library IEEE;
use IEEE.std_logic_1164.all;
----------------------------------------------
entity top is
    port
      (
        blink      : out std_logic;
        clk        : in  std_logic;
        data_out   : out std_logic_vector(7 downto 0);
        hi_button  : in  std_logic;
        idle       : out std_logic;
        lo_button  : in  std_logic;
        rst        : in  std_logic;
        s          : in  std_logic
      );
end top;
----------------------------------------------
architecture arc_top of top is

component Structm is
      port (
            blink_reset   : out std_logic;
            blink_set     : out std_logic;
            clk           : in std_logic;
            ctr_mux0      : out std_logic;
            ctr_mux1_0    : out std_logic;
            ctr_mux1_1    : out std_logic;
            ctr_mux2_0    : out std_logic;
            ctr_mux2_1    : out std_logic;
            ctr_mux3      : out std_logic;
            guess_en      : out std_logic;
            hi_button     : in std_logic;
            high_en       : out std_logic;
            idle          : out std_logic;
            lo_button     : in std_logic;
            low_en        : out std_logic;
            rst           : in std_logic;
            s             : in std_logic;
            tempreg8_1_en : out std_logic
      );
end component;

component dp is
      port
            (
            -- Inputs from control unit
            blink_set        :      in    std_logic;  --(y1)
            ctr_mux3         :      in    std_logic;  --(y2)
            guess_en         :      in    std_logic;  --(y3)
            blink_reset      :      in    std_logic;  --(y4)
            ctr_mux1_1       :      in    std_logic;  --(y5)
            high_en          :      in    std_logic;  --(y6)
            ctr_mux2_1       :      in    std_logic;  --(y7)
            low_en           :      in    std_logic;  --(y8)
```

```
            ctr_mux1_0        :      in    std_logic;   --(y9)
            ctr_mux2_0        :      in    std_logic;   --(y10)
            ctr_mux0          :      in    std_logic;   --(y11)
            tempreg8_1_en     :      in    std_logic;   --(y12)

            -- Inputs from outside
            clk               :      in    std_logic;
            rst               :      in    std_logic;

            -- Outputs to control unit

            -- Outputs to outside
            blink           :  out   std_logic;
            data_out        :  out   std_logic_vector(7 downto 0)
            );
end component;
    -- output of  control unit
    signal blink_set      : std_logic;
    signal ctr_mux3       : std_logic;
    signal guess_en       : std_logic;
    signal blink_reset    : std_logic;
    signal ctr_mux1_1     : std_logic;
    signal high_en        : std_logic;
    signal ctr_mux2_1     : std_logic;
    signal low_en         : std_logic;
    signal ctr_mux1_0     : std_logic;
    signal ctr_mux2_0     : std_logic;
    signal ctr_mux0       : std_logic;
    signal tempreg8_1_en  : std_logic;

    -- output of operational unit
begin
    u1_fsm : structm port map
      (
            blink_reset    => blink_reset   ,
            blink_set      => blink_set     ,
            clk            => clk           ,
            ctr_mux0       => ctr_mux0      ,
            ctr_mux1_0     => ctr_mux1_0    ,
            ctr_mux1_1     => ctr_mux1_1    ,
            ctr_mux2_0     => ctr_mux2_0    ,
            ctr_mux2_1     => ctr_mux2_1    ,
            ctr_mux3       => ctr_mux3      ,
            guess_en       => guess_en      ,
            hi_button      => hi_button     ,
            high_en        => high_en       ,
            idle           => idle          ,
            lo_button      => lo_button     ,
            low_en         => low_en        ,
            rst            => rst           ,
            s              => s             ,
            tempreg8_1_en  => tempreg8_1_en
      );
```

```
    u2_dp : dp port map
      (
            clk             => clk          ,
            rst             => rst          ,
            blink_set       => blink_set    ,
            ctr_mux3        => ctr_mux3     ,
            guess_en        => guess_en     ,
            blink_reset     => blink_reset  ,
            ctr_mux1_1      => ctr_mux1_1   ,
            high_en         => high_en      ,
            ctr_mux2_1      => ctr_mux2_1   ,
            low_en          => low_en       ,
            ctr_mux1_0      => ctr_mux1_0   ,
            ctr_mux2_0      => ctr_mux2_0   ,
            ctr_mux0        => ctr_mux0     ,
            tempreg8_1_en   => tempreg8_1_en ,
            blink           => blink        ,
            data_out        => data_out
      );
end arc_top;
-----------------------------------
configuration cfg_top of top is
      for arc_top
      end for;
end cfg_top;
------------------------------------
```

Figure 39. Top as a composition of Control Unit and Data Path

The whole design from ASM to RTL took only 3.5 seconds. Here the time report from Synthagate is: `HLS Total Time: 00:00:03.5425893`

4.4 Finding Largest Number

I will design here a system in which a user enters 8-bit numbers until the number x"00" appears at the input. The largest of the entered numbers should be on the output of the system. The ASM *Largnumb* for this behavior is on Fig. 40.

That ASM is very simple – its file Largnumb.*txt* is presented on Fig. 41. ASM *Largnumb* contains only four operators (*Y1* – *Y4*), five microoperations (*y1* – *y5*) and three logical conditions (*x1, x2, x3*).

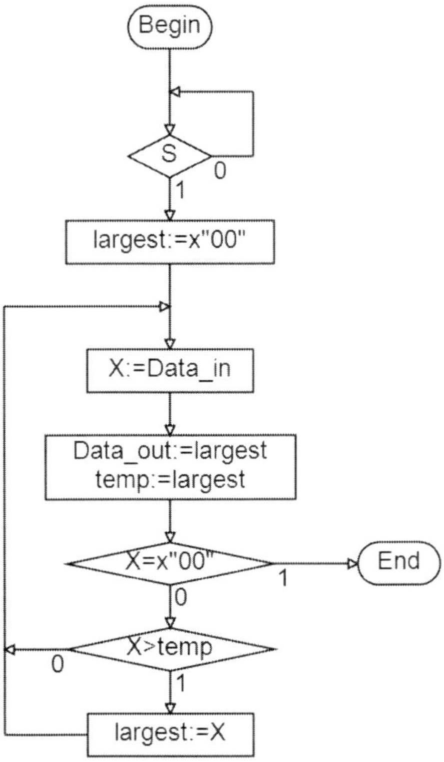

Figure 40. ASM for *Largnumb*

A marked ASM *LargNumb* is presented in Fig. 42. In this ASM I replaced microoperations and logical conditions of ASM in Fig. 40 by *y1, ..., y5* and *x1, x2* and *x3* from Fig. 41. If you forgot, how to design FSM from ASM, return to Section 1.2 from the first Chapter. The Functional FSM Funcmi.t1 with only three states is shown in Table 4.

```
Micro Instructions: Micro Operations:             Logical
Y1 = y1 y2          y1  :  Data_out:=largest      Conditions:
Y2 = y3             y2  :   temp:=largest         File    Draw
Y3 = y4             y3  :   largest:=X            x1   : X=x"00"
Y4 = y5             y4  :   X:=Data_in            x2   : X>temp
                    y5  :   largest:=x"00"        x3   : S
```

Figure 41. Txt file for ASM *Largnumb*

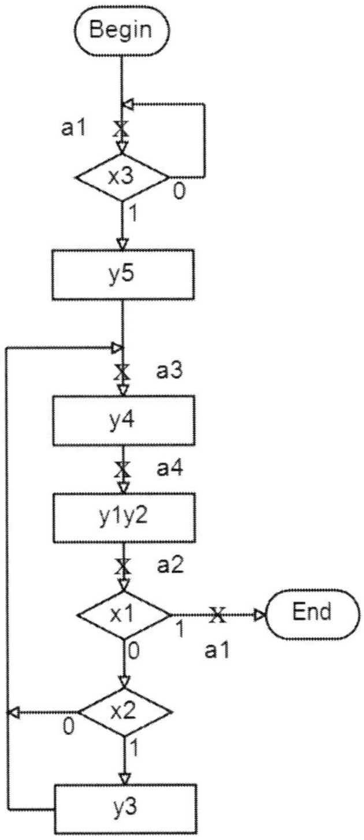

Figure 42. ASM marked for Mealy FSM

Table 4. Transition table of Functional FSM for Largnumb

a1	a3	x3	y5	1
a1	a1	~x3	--	2
a2	a1	x1	--	3
a2	a3	~x1*x2	y3	4
a2	a4	~x1*~x2	y4	5
a3	a4	1	y4	6
a4	a2	1	y1y2	7

Automatically constructed functional specifications is presented in file *Largnumb.spec* (Fig. 43). It contains only 15 rows.

```
<functional_specifications>
        <declarations>
          <port name="data_in" width="8" direction="in" />
          <port name="data_out" width="8" direction="out" />
          <port name="s" width="1" direction="in" />
          <signal name="largest" width="8" />
          <signal name="temp" width="8" />
          <signal name="x" width="8" />
        </declarations>
        <required_libraries>
            <vhdl>
```

```
            <library name="my_package" />
        </vhdl>
    </required_libraries>
</functional_specifications>
```

Figure 43. Functional specifications

Functional design at High level (file *Fincmi.vhd* constructed by Synthagate) is presented on Fig. 44. It is a small design – file contains only 76 lines.

```
library ieee;
use ieee.std_logic_1164.all;
use ieee.numeric_std.all;
use work.my_package.all;

entity Funcmi is
      port (
            clk             : in std_logic;
            data_in         : in std_logic_vector(7 downto 0);
            data_out        : out std_logic_vector(7 downto 0);
            idle            : out std_logic;
            rst             : in std_logic;
            s               : in std_logic
      );
end Funcmi;

architecture ARC_Funcmi of Funcmi is

      type FSMStates is (
            a1, a2, a3, a4
      );

      signal currentState  : FSMStates;
      signal largest       : std_logic_vector(7 downto 0);
      signal temp            : std_logic_vector(7 downto 0);
      signal x             : std_logic_vector(7 downto 0);
begin
      process (clk , rst)
      procedure proc_Funcmi is
      begin
      case currentState is
      when a1 =>
            if (s) = '1' then
                  largest <= x"00";
                  currentState <= a3;
            else
                  currentState <= a1;
                  idle <= '1';
            end if;
      when a2 =>
```

```
            if (x = x"00") then
                    currentState <= a1;
                    idle <= '1';
            elsif (not (x = x"00") and x > temp) then
                    largest <= x;
                    currentState <= a3;
            else
                    x <= data_in;
                    currentState <= a4;
            end if;
        when a3 =>
                    x <= data_in;
                    currentState <= a4;
        when a4 =>
                    data_out <= largest;
                    temp <= largest;
                    currentState <= a2;
        end case;
        end proc_Funcmi;
           begin
            if (rst = '1') then
                    data_out <= (others => '0');
                    idle <= '0';
                    largest <= (others => '0');
                    temp <= (others => '0');
                    x <= (others => '0');

                    currentState <= a1;
                    idle <= '1';

            elsif (clk'event and clk = '1') then
                    idle <= '0';
                    proc_Funcmi;
            end if;
        end process;
end ARC_Funcmi;
```

Figure 44. High Level Synthesis for LargNumb

Functional ASM table is shown in Fig. 45, Connection graph – in Fig.46, The list of parallel microoperations after considering direct connections is empty. One MUX and three direct connections are in Fig. 47.

```
Y1    y1    8    data_out:=largest
      y2    8    temp:=largest

Y2    y3    8    largest:=x

Y3    y4    8    x:=data_in
```

```
Y4    y5    8    largest:=x"00"
```

Figure 45. Functional ASM Table Funcmi.mrk

```
weight : sources     targets : weight
     0 : data_in           x : 0

     0 : largest    data_out : 0
                        temp : 0

     1 : x           largest : 1

     1 : x"00"       largest : 1
```

Figure 46. Connection graph for 8-bit connections

```
INDIRECT CONNECTIONS:

MUX0
   OUTPUT:
      largest
    INPUT:
      x                     1    0        in0    largest
      x"00"                 1    1        in1    largest

DIRECT CONNECTIONS:

        SOURCES                             TARGETS

        data_in                                   x
        largest                            data_out
                                               temp
```

Figure 47. One MUX and direct connections

External specifications (50 lines) are in Fig. 48. Data path for this design (Fig. 49) contains 3 components, the total number of instantiated components is equal to 6. VHDL code for the Control unit is in Fig. 50. The top design, combining Control unit and Data path is shown in Fig. 51.

```
<external_specifications xmlns="ExtSpec">
    <essential_files>
        <txt path="Funcmi_t.txt" />
        <tab path="Structm.tab" />
        <mrk path="Funcmi_t.mrk" />
        <spec path="Funcmi_t.spec" />
        <mux_files>
            <mux path="funcmi_t8b-mux.xml" bits="8" />
        </mux_files>
    </essential_files>
    <settings>
        <bit_range direction="Down" />
```

```
    </settings>
    <dp_to_out_and_out_to_dp>
        <signal name="clk" in_or_out="in" width="1" />
        <signal name="rst" in_or_out="in" width="1" />
        <signal name="data_out" in_or_out="out" width="8" />
        <signal name="data_in" in_or_out="in" width="8" />
    </dp_to_out_and_out_to_dp>
    <components>
        <external>
            <!-- Add external components (and their path)
            that you would like to use in your design -->
        </external>
        <automatic>
            <generator type="register" global="clk, rst">
                <class>
                    <signal name="%name%" />
                    <signal name="%name%_en" />
                    <signal name="%name%" />
                </class>
                <instances>
                    <instance name="x" />
                    <instance name="largest" />
                    <instance name="temp" />
                </instances>
         </generator>
         <generator type="generic_comparator" global="clk,
                rst">
                <class>
                    <signal name="%name%_in1" />
                    <signal name="%name%_in2" />
                    <signal name="%name%_out" />
                </class>
                <instances>
                    <instance name="comp8_1" />
                    <instance name="comp8_2" />
                </instances>
            </generator>
        </automatic>
    </components>
</external_specifications>
```

Figure 48. External specifications for *Largnumb*

Of course, Synthagate automatically constructed VHDL codes of components instantiated in Data Path – register (*reg_8bit*) and comparator (*g_comp)*.

```
-----------------------------
library IEEE;
use IEEE.std_logic_1164.all;
use IEEE.numeric_std.all;
use work.components.all;
-----------------------------
entity dp is
```

```
        port
              (
              -- Inputs from control unit
              temp_en           :  in    std_logic;   --(y1)
              largest_en        :  in    std_logic;   --(y2)
              x_en              :  in    std_logic;   --(y3)
              ctr_mux0          :  in    std_logic;   --(y4)

              -- Inputs from outside
              clk            :  in    std_logic;
              rst            :  in    std_logic;
              data_in        :  in    std_logic_vector(7 downto 0);

              -- Outputs to control unit
              comp8_2_dout:  out   std_logic;  --(x1)
              comp8_1_dout:  out   std_logic;  --(x2)

              -- Outputs to outside
              data_out    :  out   std_logic_vector(7 downto 0)
              );

end dp;
----------------------------------------------
architecture arc_dp of dp is
      signal mux0_dout        :  std_logic_vector (7 downto 0);
      signal largest_dout     :  std_logic_vector (7 downto 0);
      signal temp_dout        :  std_logic_vector (7 downto 0);
      signal x_dout           :  std_logic_vector (7 downto 0);
begin
      ---------
      -- Mux 0
      ---------
      u1_mux0   :   mux_2x8    port map (x_dout, x"00", ctr_mux0,
                    mux0_dout);

      ---------
      -- x
      ---------
      u2_x     :  reg_8bit   port map (clk, rst, data_in, x_en,
                   x_dout);

      ---------
      -- largest
      ---------
      u3_largest  :  reg_8bit   port map (clk, rst, mux0_dout,
                         largest_en, largest_dout);

      ---------
      -- temp
      ---------
      u4_temp    :  reg_8bit   port map (clk, rst, largest_dout,
                         temp_en, temp_dout);

      ---------
```

```
      -- comp8_1
      ---------
      u5_comp8_1 :g_comp  generic map (comp_kind => "gr", size
            => 8) port map (x_dout, temp_dout, comp8_1_dout);

      ---------
      -- comp8_2
      ---------
      u6_comp8_2 :g_comp     generic map (comp_kind => "eq",
            size => 8) port map (x_dout, x"00", comp8_2_dout);

      -----------------------
      -- Additional Signals
      -----------------------
      data_out          <=    largest_dout;
end  arc_dp;
------------------------------
configuration cfg_dp of dp is
      for arc_dp
      end for;
end cfg_dp;
-----------------------------
```

Figure 49. Data Path

```
library ieee;
use ieee.std_logic_1164.all;
use ieee.numeric_std.all;
use work.components.all;
entity Structm is
      port (
            clk          : in std_logic;
            comp8_1_dout : in std_logic;
            comp8_2_dout : in std_logic;
            ctr_mux0     : out std_logic;
            idle         : out std_logic;
            largest_en   : out std_logic;
            s            : in std_logic;
            rst          : in std_logic;
            temp_en      : out std_logic;
            x_en         : out std_logic
      );
end Structm;
architecture ARC_Structm of Structm is
      type FSMStates is (
            a1, a2, a3, a4
      );
      signal currentState : FSMStates;
begin
      process (clk , rst)
      procedure proc_Structm is
      begin
      ctr_mux0 <= '0';
      idle <= '0';
```

```
      largest_en <= '0';
      temp_en <= '0';
      x_en <= '0';
      case currentState is
      when a1 =>
            if (s) = '1' then
                  largest_en <= '1';
                  ctr_mux0 <= '1';
                  currentState <= a2;
            else
                  currentState <= a1;
                  idle <= '1';
            end if;
      when a2 =>
                  x_en <= '1';
                  currentState <= a3;
      when a3 =>
                  temp_en <= '1';
                  currentState <= a4;
      when a4 =>
            if (comp8_2_dout) = '1' then
                  currentState <= a1;
                  idle <= '1';
            elsif (not comp8_2_dout and comp8_1_dout) = '1' then
                  largest_en <= '1';
                  currentState <= a2;
            else
                  x_en <= '1';
                  currentState <= a3;
            end if;
      end case;
      end proc_Structm;
      begin
            if (rst = '1') then
                  ctr_mux0 <= '0';
                  idle <= '0';
                  largest_en <= '0';
                  temp_en <= '0';
                  x_en <= '0';
                  currentState <= a1;
                  idle <= '1';
            elsif (clk'event and clk = '0') then
                  idle <= '0';
                  proc_Structm;
            end if;
end process;
end ARC_Structm;
```

Figure 50. Control Unit

```
library IEEE;
use IEEE.std_logic_1164.all;
----------------------
entity top is
```

```
    port
      (
        clk       : in  std_logic;
        data_in   : in  std_logic_vector(7 downto 0);
        data_out  : out std_logic_vector(7 downto 0);
        idle      : out std_logic;
        rst       : in  std_logic;
        s         : in  std_logic
      );
end top;
-----------------------
architecture arc_top of top is
component Structm is
      port (
            clk            : in std_logic;
            comp8_1_dout : in std_logic;
            comp8_2_dout : in std_logic;
            ctr_mux0      : out std_logic;
            idle           : out std_logic;
            largest_en    : out std_logic;
            rst            : in std_logic;
            s              : in std_logic;
            temp_en        : out std_logic;
            x_en           : out std_logic
      );
end component;
component dp is
      port
            (
            -- Inputs from control unit
            temp_en       :  in  std_logic;        --(y1)
            largest_en    :  in  std_logic;        --(y2)
            x_en          :  in  std_logic;        --(y3)
            ctr_mux0      :  in  std_logic;        --(y4)

            -- Inputs froooutside
            clk           :  in  std_logic;
            rst           :  in  std_logic;
            data_in       :  in  std_logic_vector(7 downto 0);

            -- Outputs to control unit
            comp8_2_dout :  out   std_logic;  --(x1)
            comp8_1_dout :  out   std_logic;  --(x2)
            -- Outputs to outside
            data_out     :  out   std_logic_vector(7 downto 0)
            );
end component;
    -- output of  control unit
    signal temp_en     : std_logic;
    signal largest_en  : std_logic;
```

```
    signal x_en        : std_logic;
    signal ctr_mux0    : std_logic;
    -- output of operational unit
    signal comp8_2_dout : std_logic;
    signal comp8_1_dout : std_logic;
begin
    u1_fsm : structm port map
      (
            clk            => clk          ,
            comp8_1_dout   => comp8_1_dout ,
            comp8_2_dout   => comp8_2_dout ,
            ctr_mux0       => ctr_mux0     ,
            idle           => idle         ,
            largest_en     => largest_en   ,
            rst            => rst          ,
            s              => s            ,
            temp_en        => temp_en      ,
            x_en           => x_en
      );
    u2_dp : dp port map
      (
            clk            => clk          ,
            rst            => rst          ,
            data_in        => data_in      ,
            temp_en        => temp_en      ,
            largest_en     => largest_en   ,
            x_en           => x_en         ,
            ctr_mux0       => ctr_mux0     ,
            data_out       => data_out     ,
            comp8_2_dout   => comp8_2_dout ,
            comp8_1_dout   => comp8_1_dout
      );
end arc_top;
----------------------------
configuration cfg_top of top is
      for arc_top
      end for;
end cfg_top;
----------------------------
```

Figure 51. Top as a composition of Control Unit and Data Path

The whole design from ASM to RTL took only a little bit more than two seconds. Here the time report from Synthagate is: `HLS Total Time: 00:00:02.3016812.`

4.5 Four together

I wanted to play a little bit more with these four examples from the book of Hwang and constructed one design implementing all these examples as its instructions.

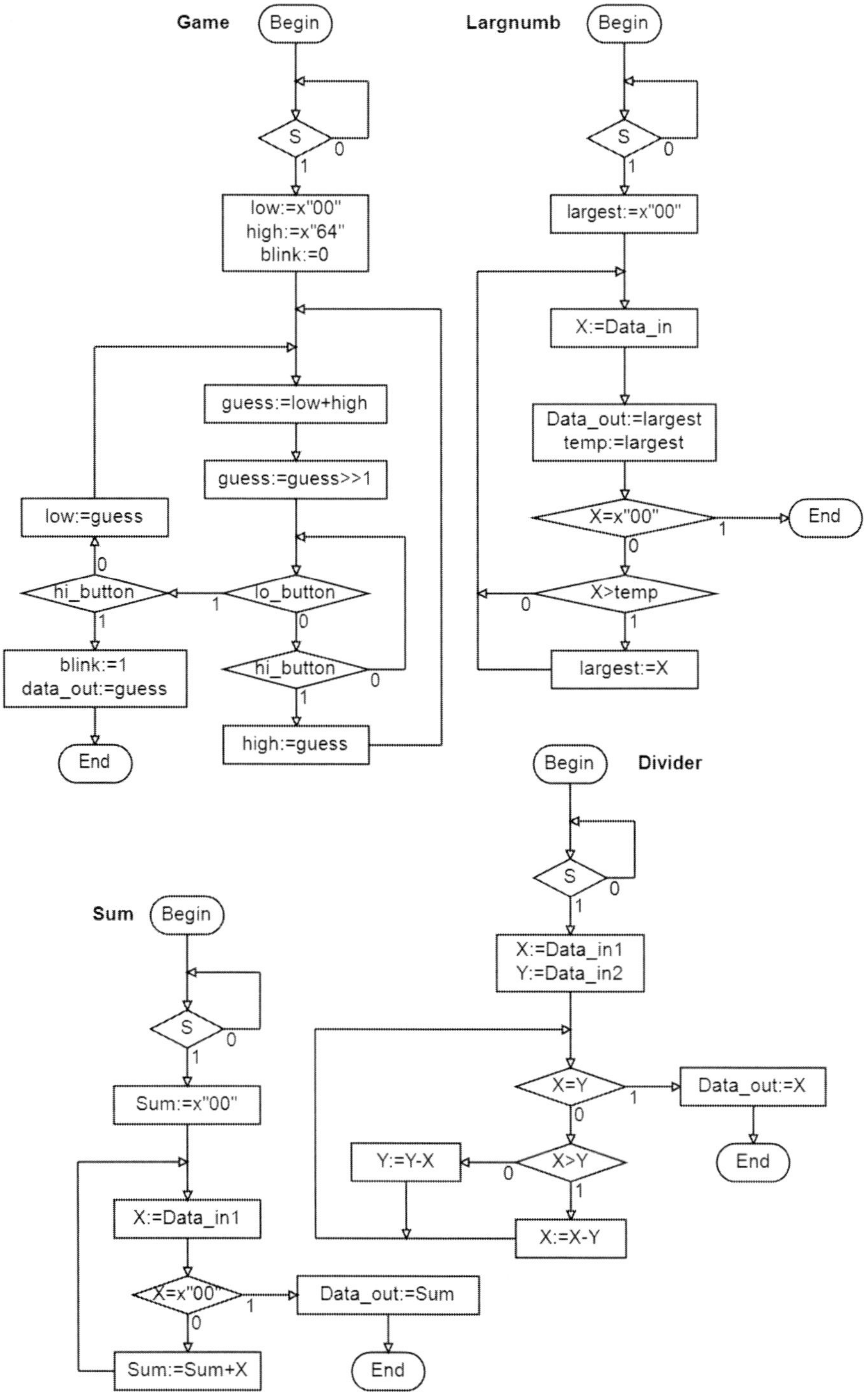

Figure 52. Four ASMs on one figure

I repeat four ASMs on Fig. 52 and I called this design *Fourtogether*. Synthagate used two variables *Bit0* and *Bit1* to encode four ASMs in the process of their combining:

divider – 00, game – 01, largnumb – 10 and sum – 11.

ASM *Fourtogether* as two-connected list is on Fig. 53, its file *Fourtogether.txt* is presented on Fig. 54. ASM *Fourtogether* contains nineteen operators (*Y1 – Y18*), twenty two microoperations (*y1 – y22*) and nine logical conditions (*x1 – x9*).

0	begin	23	0	16	Y16	19	0
1	Y1	19	0	17	Y17	18	0
2	Y2	27	0	18	Y18	31	0
3	Y3	27	0	19	end	0	0
4	Y4	27	0	20	x9	15	14
5	Y5	19	0	21	x9	7	4
6	Y6	30	0	22	x8	20	21
7	Y7	8	0	23	x3	22	23
8	Y8	6	0	24	x7	12	13
9	Y9	8	0	25	x6	19	24
10	Y10	8	0	26	x1	2	3
11	Y11	25	0	27	x2	1	26
12	Y12	13	0	28	x5	5	9
13	Y13	11	0	29	x5	10	29
14	Y14	13	0	30	x4	28	29
15	Y15	18	0	31	x6	16	17

Figure 53. GSA file for ASM *Fourtogether*

```
Micro
Instructions:
Y1 = y1
Y2 = y2
Y3 = y3
Y4 = y4 y5
Y5 = y6 y7
Y6 = y8
Y7 = y9 y10 y11
Y8 = y12
Y9 = y13
Y10 = y14
Y11 = y15 y16
Y12 = y17
Y13 = y18
Y14 = y19
Y15 = y20
Y16 = y21
Y17 = y22
Y18 = y4
```

```
Micro Operations:
y1  : Data_out:=X
y2  : X:=X-Y
y3  : Y:=Y-X
y4  : X:=Data_in1
y5  : Y:=Data_in2
y6  : blink:=1
y7  : data_out:=guess
y8  : guess:=guess>>1
y9  : low:=x"00"
y10  : high:=x"64"
y11  : blink:=0
y12  : guess:=low+high
y13  : high:=guess
y14  : low:=guess
y15  : Data_out:=largest
y16  : temp:=largest
y17  : largest:=X
y18  : X:=Data_in
y19  : largest:=x"00"
y20  : Sum:=x"00"
y21  : Data_out:=Sum
y22  : Sum:=Sum+X
```

```
Logical
Conditions:
File   Draw
x1  : X>Y
x2  : X=Y
x3  : S
x4  : hi_button
x5  : lo_button
x6  : X=x"00"
x7  : X>temp
x8  : Bit0
x9  : Bit1
```

Figure 54. TXT file for ASM Fourtogether

The Functional FSM Funcmi.t1 with ten states is shown in Table 5.

Table 5. Transition table of Functional FSM for Fourtogether

a1	a2	x3*x8*x9	y20	1
a1	a3	x3*x8*~x9	y19	2
a1	a4	x3*~x8*x9	y9y10y11	3
a1	a5	x3*~x8*~x9	y4y5	4
a1	a1	~x3	--	5
a2	a6	1	y4	6
a3	a7	1	y18	7
a4	a8	1	y12	8
a5	a1	x2	y1	9
a5	a5	~x2*x1	y2	10
a5	a5	~x2*~x1	y3	11
a6	a1	x6	y21	12
a6	a2	~x6	y22	13
a7	a9	1	y15y16	14
a8	a10	1	y8	15
a9	a1	x6	--	16
a9	a3	~x6*x7	y17	17
a9	a7	~x6*~x7	y18	18
a10	a1	x4*x5	y6y7	19
a10	a4	x4*~x5	y13	20
a10	a4	~x4*x5	y14	21
a10	a10	~x4*~x5	--	22

Functional specifications constructed automatically by Synthagate are presented in file *Fourtogether.spec* (Fig. 55). It contains 27 rows.

```
<functional_specifications>
        <declarations>
            <port name="bit0" width="1" direction="in" />
            <port name="bit1" width="1" direction="in" />
            <port name="blink" width="1" direction="out" />
            <port name="data_in" width="8" direction="in" />
            <port name="data_in1" width="8" direction="in" />
            <port name="data_in2" width="8" direction="in" />
            <port name="data_out" width="8" direction="out" />
            <port name="hi_button" width="1" direction="in" />
            <port name="lo_button" width="1" direction="in" />
            <port name="s" width="1" direction="in" />
            <signal name="guess" width="8" />
            <signal name="high" width="8" />
            <signal name="largest" width="8" />
            <signal name="low" width="8" />
            <signal name="sum" width="8" />
            <signal name="temp" width="8" />
            <signal name="x" width="8" />
            <signal name="y" width="8" />
        </declarations>
```

```
        <required_libraries>
           <vhdl>
               <library name="my_package" />
           </vhdl>
        </required_libraries>
    </functional_specifications>
```

Figure 55. Functional Specifications for *Fourtogether*

Functional design at High level (file *Fincmi.vhd* constructed by Synthagate) is presented on Fig. 56. It is a rather small design – file contains only 187 lines.

Refer to Figure 56 (Chapter 4) in HLS-Figures-and-Tables.pdf

Figure 56. High Level Synthesis for *Fourtogether*

Here I strongly advise you to come back to Sections 3.1.3 – 3.1.6 to remember how to construct the connection graph, the list of parallel microoperations, the graph of incompatibility and multiplexers. 4-bit connection graph is very simple here – its design you can use as an exercise.

8-bit Functional ASM table is shown in Fig. 57, The 8-bit connection graph is on Fig. 58, the list of parallel microoperations for 8-bit connections before and after considering direct connections – on Fig. 59. Only one microoperation

tempReg8_1:=alu8_1_out

was removed from this list.

```
Y1     y1     8     data_out:=x

Y2     y2     8     x:=tempReg8_1

Y3     y3     8     y:=tempReg8_1

Y4     y4     8     x:=data_in1
       y5     8     y:=data_in2

Y5     y6     0     blink:=1
       y7     8     data_out:=guess

Y6     y8     8     guess:=tempReg8_1

Y7     y9     0     blink:=0
       y10    8     high:=x"64"
       y11    8     low:=x"00"

Y8     y12    4     alu8_1_ctr:="0001"
       y13    8     alu8_1_in1:=low
       y14    8     alu8_1_in2:=high
```

```
      y15    8     guess:=alu8_1_out

Y9    y16    8     high:=guess

Y10   y17    8     low:=guess

Y11   y18    8     data_out:=largest
      y19    8     temp:=largest

Y12   y20    8     largest:=x

Y13   y21    8     x:=data_in

Y14   y22    8     largest:=x"00"

Y15   y23    8     sum:=x"00"

Y16   y24    8     data_out:=sum

Y17   y25    8     sum:=tempReg8_1

Y18   y4     8     x:=data_in1

Y19   y26    4     alu8_1_ctr:="0010"
      y27    8     alu8_1_in1:=x
      y28    8     alu8_1_in2:=y
      y29    8     tempReg8_1:=alu8_1_out

Y20   y26    4     alu8_1_ctr:="0010"
      y30    8     alu8_1_in1:=y
      y31    8     alu8_1_in2:=x
      y29    8     tempReg8_1:=alu8_1_out

Y21   y12    4     alu8_1_ctr:="0001"
      y32    8     alu8_1_in1:=sum
      y31    8     alu8_1_in2:=x
      y29    8     tempReg8_1:=alu8_1_out

Y22   y33    4     alu8_1_ctr:="1100"
      y34    8     alu8_1_in1:=guess
      y35    8     alu8_1_in2:=x"01"
      y29    8     tempReg8_1:=alu8_1_out
```

Figure 57. Functional ASM Table Funcmi.mrk

```
weight : sources          targets : weight
     1 : alu8_1_out         guess : 1
                      tempReg8_1 : 0

     1 : data_in                x : 1

     2 : data_in1               x : 2
```

```
1 : data_in2                  y : 1

4 : guess           alu8_1_in1 : 1
                      data_out : 1
                          high : 1
                           low : 1

1 : high            alu8_1_in2 : 1

1 : largest           data_out : 1
                          temp : 0

1 : low             alu8_1_in1 : 1

2 : sum             alu8_1_in1 : 1
                      data_out : 1

4 : tempReg8_1           guess : 1
                           sum : 1
                             x : 1
                             y : 1

5 : x               alu8_1_in1 : 1
                    alu8_1_in2 : 2
                      data_out : 1
                       largest : 1

3 : x"00"              largest : 1
                           low : 1
                           sum : 1

1 : x"01"           alu8_1_in2 : 1

1 : x"64"                 high : 1

2 : y               alu8_1_in1 : 1
                    alu8_1_in2 : 1
```

Figure 58. Connection graph for 8-bit connections

```
Parallel Microoperations before considering direct connections:

          Y4       : y4      x:=data_in1
                     y5      y:=data_in2

          Y7       : y10     high:=x"64"
                     y11     low:=x"00"

          Y8       : y13     alu8_1_in1:=low
                     y14     alu8_1_in2:=high
                     y15     guess:=alu8_1_out
```

```
Y11       : y18     data_out:=largest
            y19     temp:=largest

Y19       : y27     alu8_1_in1:=x
            y28     alu8_1_in2:=y
            y29     tempReg8_1:=alu8_1_out

Y20       : y29     tempReg8_1:=alu8_1_out
            y30     alu8_1_in1:=y
            y31     alu8_1_in2:=x

Y21       : y29     tempReg8_1:=alu8_1_out
            y31     alu8_1_in2:=x
            y32     alu8_1_in1:=sum

Y22       : y29     tempReg8_1:=alu8_1_out
            y34     alu8_1_in1:=guess
            y35     alu8_1_in2:=x"01"

Parallel Microoperations after considering direct connections:

Y4        : y4      x:=data_in1
            y5      y:=data_in2

Y7        : y10     high:=x"64"
            y11     low:=x"00"

Y8        : y13     alu8_1_in1:=low
            y14     alu8_1_in2:=high
            y15     guess:=alu8_1_out

Y19       : y27     alu8_1_in1:=x
            y28     alu8_1_in2:=y

Y20       : y30     alu8_1_in1:=y
            y31     alu8_1_in2:=x

Y21       : y31     alu8_1_in2:=x
            y32     alu8_1_in1:=sum

Y22       : y34     alu8_1_in1:=guess
            y35     alu8_1_in2:=x"01"
```

Figure 59. 8-bit parallel microoperations for *Fourtogether*

The graph of incompatibility, constructed from the connection graph (Fig. 58) and the list of parallel microoperations (Fig.59), is presented in Fig. 60. 8-bit MUXes and direct connections are shown in Fig. 61.

```
alu8_1_in1 -> alu8_1_in2, guess
( guess, low, sum, x, y )

alu8_1_in2 -> alu8_1_in1, guess
( high, x, x"01", y )

guess -> alu8_1_in1, alu8_1_in2
( alu8_1_out, tempReg8_1 )

high -> low
( guess, x"64" )

low -> high
( guess, x"00" )

x -> y
( data_in, data_in1, tempReg8_1 )

y -> x
( data_in2, tempReg8_1 )

sum ->
( tempReg8_1, x"00" )

largest ->
( x, x"00" )

data_out ->
( guess, largest, sum, x )
```

Figure 60. Graph of Incompatibility for 8-bit connections

```
INDIRECT CONNECTIONS:

MUX1
   OUTPUT:
      alu8_1_in1
      data_out
      high
      largest
      sum
      x
    INPUT:
      guess                     3    0000      in0    alu8_1_in1
                                                      data_out
                                                      high
      x                         3    0001      in1    alu8_1_in1
                                                      data_out
                                                      largest
```

```
      sum                          2    0010      in2     alu8_1_in1
                                                          data_out
      tempReg8_1                   2    0100      in4     sum
                                                          x
      data_in1                     2    1000      in8     x
      x"00"                        2    0011      in3     largest
                                                          sum
      largest                      1    0101      in5     data_out
      low                          1    0110      in6     alu8_1_in1
      data_in                      1    1001      in9     x
      x"64"                        1    1010      in10    high
      y                            1    0111      in7     alu8_1_in1

MUX2
   OUTPUT:
      alu8_1_in2
      low
      y
    INPUT:
      x                            2    000       in0     alu8_1_in2
      guess                        1    001       in1     low
      high                         1    010       in2     alu8_1_in2
      tempReg8_1                   1    100       in4     y
      data_in2                     1    011       in3     y
      x"00"                        1    101       in5     low
      x"01"                        1    110       in6     alu8_1_in2
      y                            1    111       in7     alu8_1_in2

MUX3
   OUTPUT:
      guess
    INPUT:
      alu8_1_out                   1    0         in0     guess
      tempReg8_1                   1    1         in1     guess

DIRECT CONNECTIONS:

        SOURCES                       TARGETS

      alu8_1_out                   tempReg8_1

        largest                          temp
```

Figure 61. 8-bit MUXes and direct connections

External specifications (83 lines) are in Fig. 62. Data path for this design (Fig. 63) contains 9 components, the total number of instantiated components is equal to 19. VHDL code for the Control unit is in Fig. 64. The top design, combining Control unit and Data path is shown in Fig. 65.

```
<external_specifications xmlns="ExtSpec">
    <essential_files>
        <txt path="Funcmi_t.txt" />
```

```
        <tab path="Structm.tab" />
        <mrk path="Funcmi_t.mrk" />
        <spec path="Funcmi_t.spec" />
        <mux_files>
            <mux path="funcmi_t4b-mux.xml" bits="4" />
            <mux path="funcmi_t8b-mux.xml" bits="8" />
        </mux_files>
    </essential_files>
    <settings>
        <bit_range direction="Down" />
    </settings>
    <dp_to_out_and_out_to_dp>
        <signal name="clk" in_or_out="in" width="1" />
        <signal name="rst" in_or_out="in" width="1" />
        <signal name="blink" in_or_out="out" width="1" />
        <signal name="data_in" in_or_out="in" width="8" />
        <signal name="data_in1" in_or_out="in" width="8" />
        <signal name="data_in2" in_or_out="in" width="8" />
        <signal name="data_out" in_or_out="out" width="8" />
    </dp_to_out_and_out_to_dp>
    <components>
        <external>
            <!-- Add external components (and their path) that you
would like to use in your design -->
        </external>
        <automatic>
            <generator type="rsff" global="clk, rst">
                <class>
                    <signal name="%name%_reset" />
                    <signal name="%name%_set" />
                    <signal name="%name%" />
                </class>
                <instances>
                    <instance name="blink" />
                </instances>
            </generator>
            <generator type="register" global="clk, rst">
                <class>
                    <signal name="%name%" />
                    <signal name="%name%_en" />
                    <signal name="%name%" />
                </class>
                <instances>
                    <instance name="guess" />
                    <instance name="high" />
                    <instance name="largest" />
                    <instance name="low" />
                    <instance name="sum" />
                    <instance name="temp" />
                    <instance name="tempreg8_1" />
                    <instance name="x" />
                    <instance name="y" />
                </instances>
            </generator>
```

```
            <generator type="generic_comparator" global="clk, rst">
                <class>
                    <signal name="%name%_in1" />
                    <signal name="%name%_in2" />
                    <signal name="%name%_out" />
                </class>
                <instances>
                    <instance name="comp8_1" />
                    <instance name="comp8_2" />
                    <instance name="comp8_3" />
                    <instance name="comp8_4" />
                </instances>
            </generator>
            <generator type="alu" global="clk, rst">
                <class>
                    <signal name="%name%_in1" />
                    <signal name="%name%_in2" />
                    <signal name="%name%_ctr" />
                    <signal name="%name%_out" />
                </class>
                <instances>
                    <instance name="alu8_1" />
                </instances>
            </generator>
        </automatic>
    </components>
</external_specifications>
```

Figure 62. External specifications for Fourtogether

Refer to Figure 63 (Chapter 4) in HLS-Figures-and-Tables.pdf

Figure 63. Data Path

Refer to Figure 64 (Chapter 4) in HLS-Figures-and-Tables.pdf

Figure 64. Control Unit

Refer to Figure 65 (Chapter 4) in HLS-Figures-and-Tables.pdf

Figure 65. Top as a composition of Control Unit and Data Path

The whole design from ASM to RTL took 5.8 seconds. Here the time report from Synthagate is: **HLS Total Time: 00:00:05.7812127**

5 CASE STUDY. DESIGN OF CODEC

This Chapter was written with Dr. Vadim Tkhor. As an example, we provide the design process for a lossless codec, which simply requires only generic knowledge of the algorithm. This codec implements a lossless compression based on the fact, that the locally dynamic range of data is lower than the maximum dynamic range for a whole data. The encoder splits a set of data samples on segments, measures the segment's dynamic range (dynamic_range = (maximum – minimum)), subtracts minimum values from each sample of data, assigns the corresponding code of words to samples and sends them to the channel together with values of the minimum and the number of bits to represent dynamic range. The decoder receives values of the minimum and the number of bits to represent the dynamic range of a segment, decodes a set of data samples of the segment and restores their original values by adding the minimum value to each sample of the data.

Design starts with sequence of steps describing the algorithm of the codec.

Coder algorithm:

1. Write 4 bytes (*x"FF"*) as a start code into memory *m2*.
2. Read predefined amount of bytes *S[i] (i=1,..., Nelem)* from an external file to the memory *m1*.
3. Read *NElem S[i] (i=1,..., Nelem)* bytes from *m1*.
4. Find minimal *rmin* and maximal *rmax* values of bytes in the segment.
5. Calculate dynamic range *D = rmax - rmin* of the segment.
6. Determine of how many bits is enough to represent a dynamic range value (*rLengthD*).
7. Write bytes representing *rmin* and *rLengthD* into memory *m2*.
8. Subtract *rmin* value from each sample *S[i]* of a segment *Dif[i] = S[i] – rmin (i=1,..., Nelem)*.
9. Pack *Dif[i] (i=1,..., Nelem)* bytes using *rLengthD* bits into memory *m2*.
10. Once NElem bytes are packed Go to 2.

Decoder algorithm:

1. Read bytes from *m2* until a start code (four *x"FF"* bytes) is reached.
2. Read bytes representing *rmin* and *rLengthD* values from *m2*.
3. Unpack *Dif[i] (i=1,..., Nelem)* data bytes by extracting *rLengthD* words from incoming bytes.
4. Add *rmin* value to unpacked byte to restore its original value, *S[i] = Dif[i] + rmin, (i=1,..., Nelem)*.
5. Write *NElem* restored bytes *S [i]* into *m3*.
6. Once *NElem* bytes are decoded, Goto 2.

Don't worry if you didn't understand what is written above, because you never designed codecs. Only follow the design process below beginning from ASMs in Figures 1-7.

5.1 Algorithmic State Machines for Codec

Thus, here we use Codec with two modes – *Coder* (Fig. 1a) and *Decoder* (Fig. 1b). In this Codec, uncompressed data is written into memory *M1*. Encoder reads this data from *M1*, compresses it and writes this compressed data into memory *M2*. Then decoder reads data from memory *M2*, decompresses it and writes decoded data into memory *M3*. Generalized operators (subASMs) are presented in Fig. 2-7.

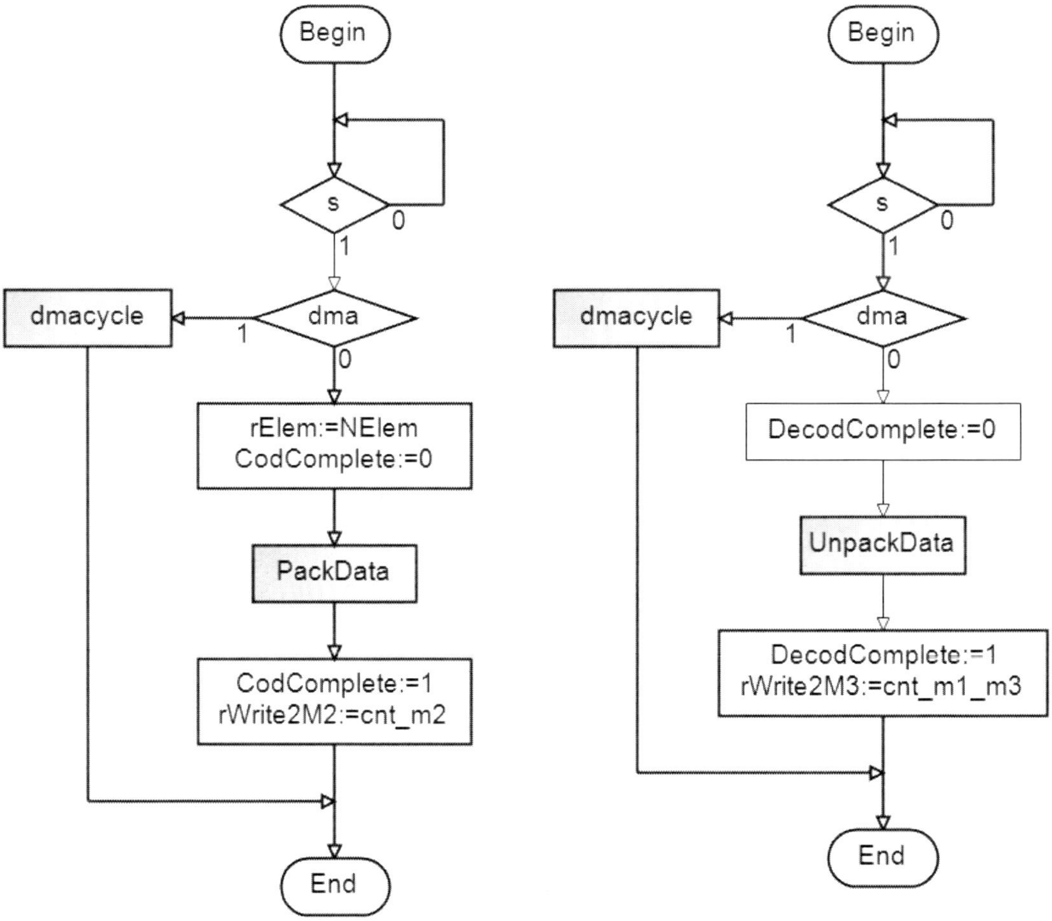

Figure 1. ASMs *maincoder* (a) and *maindecoder* (b)

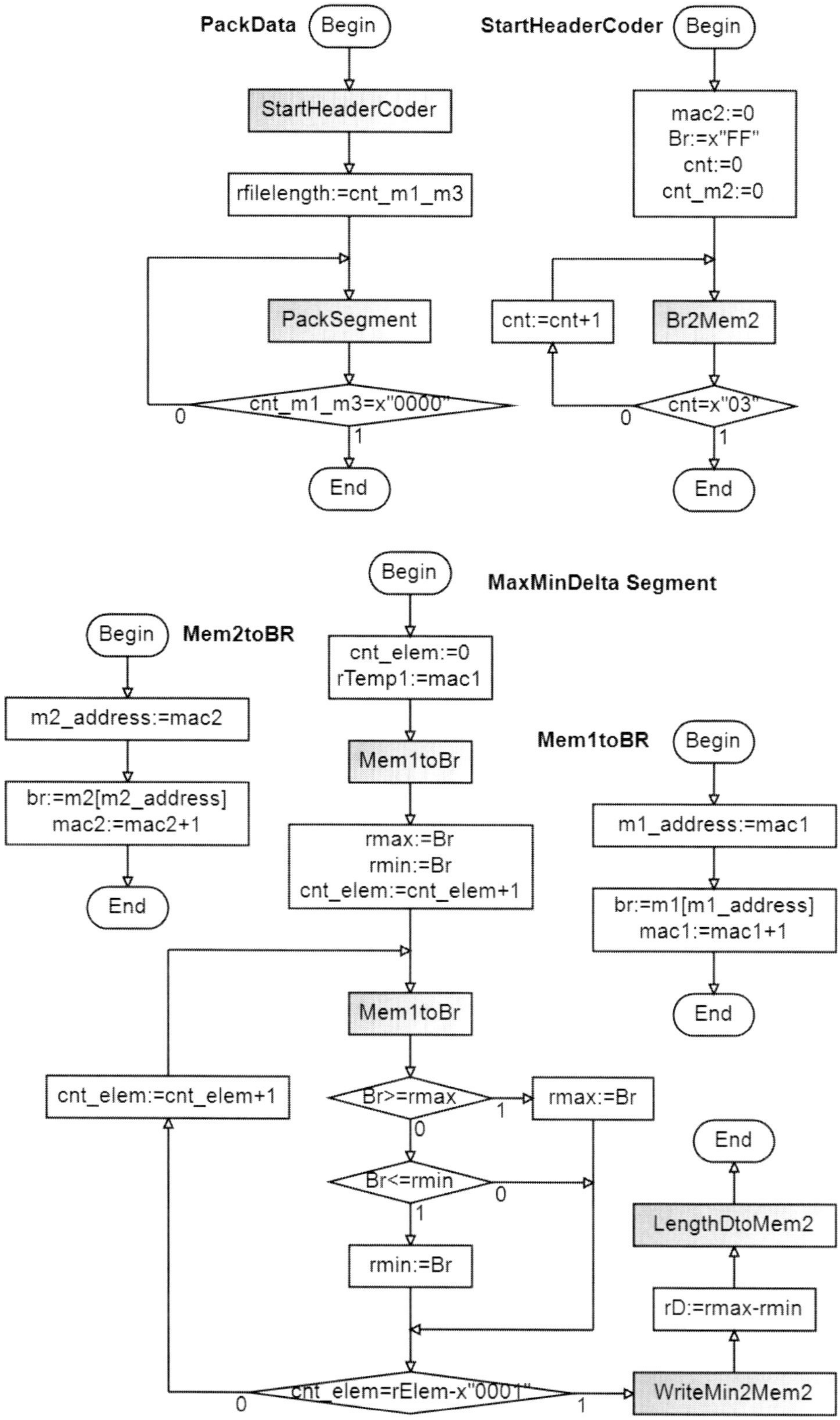

Figure 2. SubASMs ***PackData, StartHeaderCoder, Mem1toBr*** and ***Mem2toBr***

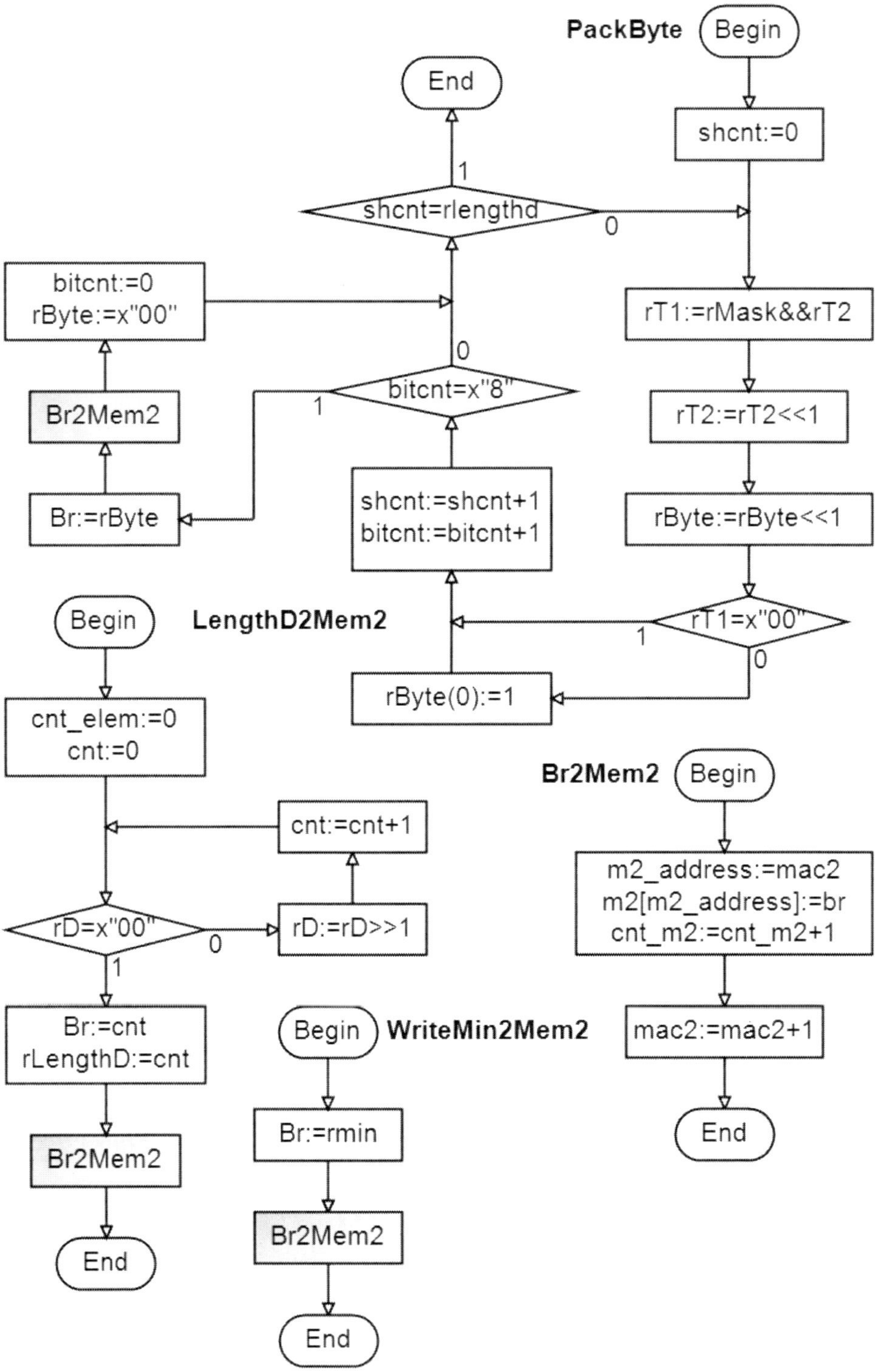

Figure 3. SubASMs *LengthD2Mem2, Br2Mem2, WriteMin2Mem2* and *PackByte*

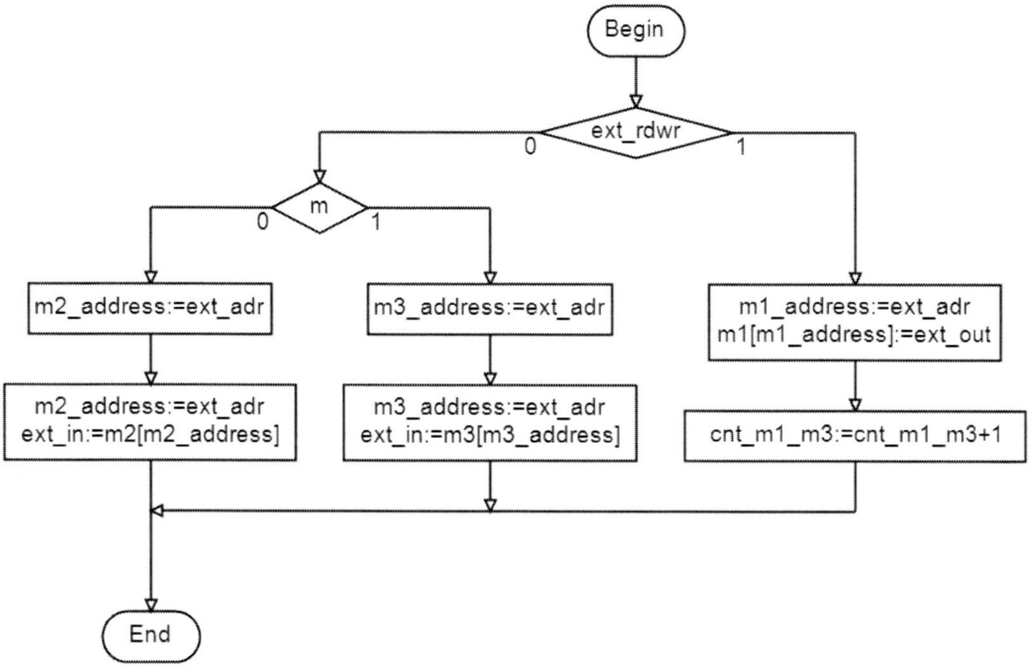

Figure 4. SubASM *DmaCycle*

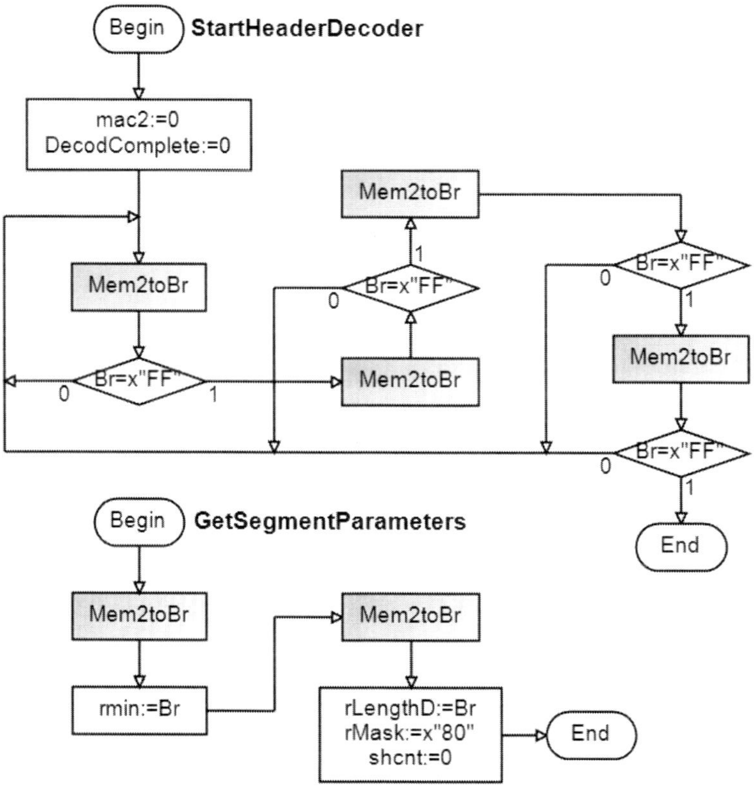

Figure 5. SubASMs *StartHeaderDecoder* and *GetSegmentParameters*

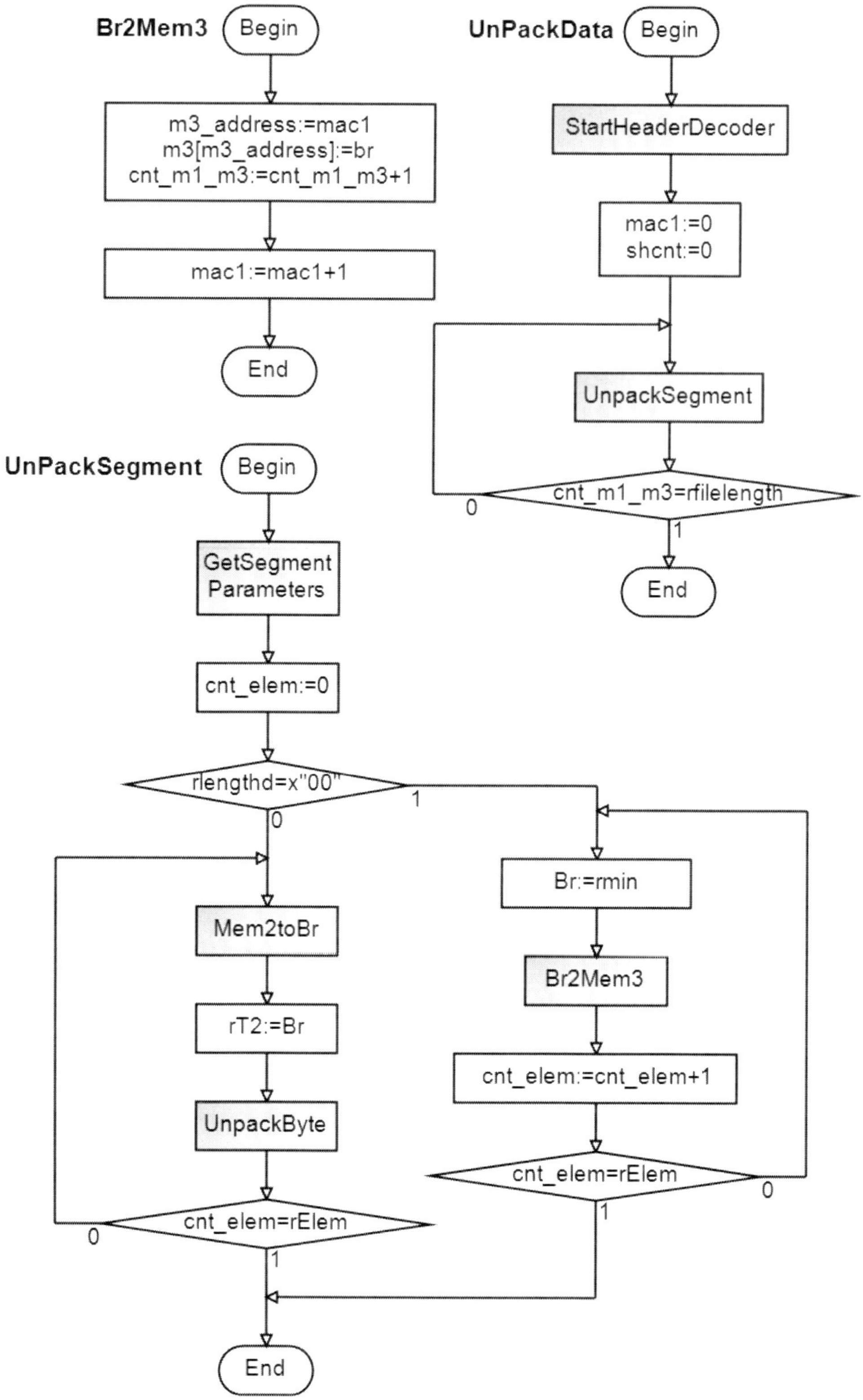

Figure 6. SubASMs *UnPackData, UnPackSegment* and *Br2Mem3*

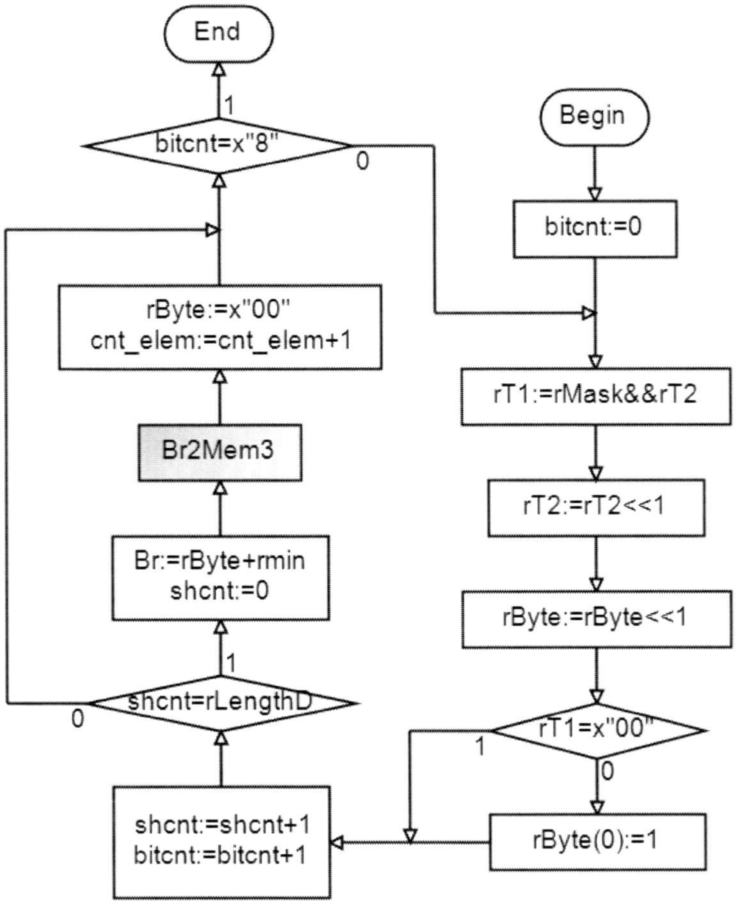

Figure 7. SubASM *UnpackByte*

ASM *Codec* as two-connected list is on Fig. 8. It was constructed after combining ASMs *Coder* and *Decoder* (Fig. 1), minimization of combined ASM and insertion of generalized operators from Fig. 2-7. Its file *Codec.txt* is presented on Fig. 9. ASM *Codec* contains fifty two operators (*Y1* – *Y52*), sixty two microoperations (*y1* – *y62*) and nineteen logical conditions (*x1*, ..., *x19*).

Refer to Figure 8 (Chapter 5) in HLS-Figures-and-Tables.pdf

Figure 8. Functional ASM as two-connected list

Refer to Figure 9 (Chapter 5) in HLS-Figures-and-Tables.pdf

Figure 9. List of Microinstructions, Microoperations and Logical conditions for *Codec*

5.2 High Level Synthesis

The Functional FSM *Funcmi.t1* with 77 states is shown in Table 1.

Table 1. Transition table of Functional FSM for Codec

a1	a7	x2*x1*x5	y11y12	1
a1	a6	x2*x1*~x5*x4	y9	2
a1	a8	x2*x1*~x5*~x4	y13	3
a1	a4	x2*~x1*x3	y7	4
a1	a3	x2*~x1*~x3	y3y4	5
a1	a1	~x2	--	6
a2	a13	1	y31y32y33	7
a3	a2	1	y19y20y21y22	8
a4	a5	1	y19y7	9
a5	a24	1	y31	10
a6	a1	1	y9y10	11
a7	a1	1	y8	12
a8	a1	1	y13y14	13
a9	a10	1	y29y50	14
a10	a48	1	y49	15
a11	a69	1	y54y34	16
a12	a11	1	y31	17
a13	a32	1	y34	18
a14	a1	x6	y1y2	19
a14	a10	~x6	y29y50	20
a15	a40	1	y43	21
a16	a15	1	y17	22
a17	a19	x16	y49	23
a17	a17	~x16	y44y39	24
a18	a19	1	y49	25
a19	a41	1	y47y48	26
a20	a16	1	y24y25	27
a21	a49	1	y54y34	28
a22	a50	1	y54y34	29
a23	a51	1	y54y34	30
a24	a52	1	y54y34	31
a25	a28	1	y36	32
a26	a29	x9	y30	33
a26	a31	~x9	y31	34
a27	a1	x12*x7	y5y6	35
a27	a11	x12*~x7	y31	36
a27	a29	~x12	y30	37
a28	a60	1	y43	38
a29	a30	1	y58y59y8	39
a30	a65	1	y48	40
a31	a53	1	y54y34	41
a32	a9	x8	y15	42
a32	a2	~x8	y18	43
a33	a37	x15	y39y40	44
a33	a39	~x15	y42	45
a34	a1	x14*x10*x6	y1y2	46
a34	a10	x14*x10*~x6	y29y50	47

a34	a18	x14*~x10	y26	48
a34	a40	~x14	y43	49
a35	a66	1	y34	50
a36	a35	1	y31y32y33	51
a37	a36	x13	y38	52
a37	a1	~x13*x14*x10*x6	y1y2	53
a37	a10	~x13*x14*x10*~x6	y29y50	54
a37	a18	~x13*x14*~x10	y26	55
a37	a40	~x13*~x14	y43	56
a38	a33	1	y35	57
a39	a37	1	y39y40	58
a40	a38	1	y41	59
a41	a20	1	y27	60
a42	a72	1	y31y32y33	61
a43	a75	x19	y61y62	62
a43	a73	~x19	y60	63
a44	a43	1	y29y21	64
a45	a47	1	y49	65
a46	a42	x10	y30	66
a46	a45	~x10	y26	67
a47	a67	1	y47y48	68
a48	a68	1	y47y48	69
a49	a22	x11	y31	70
a49	a24	~x11	y31	71
a50	a23	x11	y31	72
a50	a24	~x11	y31	73
a51	a12	x11	y16y17	74
a51	a24	~x11	y31	75
a52	a21	x11	y31	76
a52	a24	~x11	y31	77
a53	a25	1	y28	78
a54	a55	1	y58y59y8	79
a55	a71	1	y48	80
a56	a57	x15	y39y40	81
a56	a59	~x15	y42	82
a57	a54	x14	y55y17	83
a57	a1	~x14*x13*x12*x7	y5y6	84
a57	a11	~x14*x13*x12*~x7	y31	85
a57	a31	~x14*x13*~x12	y31	86
a57	a60	~x14*~x13	y43	87
a58	a56	1	y35	88
a59	a57	1	y39y40	89
a60	a58	1	y41	90
a61	a1	x13*x12*x7	y5y6	91
a61	a11	x13*x12*~x7	y31	92
a61	a31	x13*~x12	y31	93
a61	a60	~x13	y43	94
a62	a63	1	y31	95
a63	a70	1	y54y34	96
a64	a26	1	y29	97
a65	a27	1	y26	98
a66	a34	1	y36y37	99
a67	a46	x18	y53	100
a67	a46	~x18*x17	y52	101

a67	a42	~x18*~x17*x10	y30	102
a67	a45	~x18*~x17*~x10	y26	103
a68	a45	1	y53y52y26	104
a69	a62	1	y52	105
a70	a64	1	y56y57y17	106
a71	a61	1	y37y26	107
a72	a76	1	y34	108
a73	a43	1	y18	109
a74	a77	1	y34	110
a75	a74	1	y31y32y33	111
a76	a44	1	y51	112
a77	a14	x9	y23	113
a77	a17	~x9	y17y45y46	114

Functional specifications constructed automatically by Synthagate are presented in file *Codec.spec* (Fig. 10). It contains 48 rows.

```
<functional_specifications>
    <declarations>
        <port name="bit0" width="1" direction="in" />
        <port name="codcomplete" width="1" direction="out" />
        <port name="decodcomplete" width="1" direction="out" />
        <port name="dma" width="1" direction="in" />
        <port name="ext_adr" width="16" direction="in" />
        <port name="ext_in" width="8" direction="out" />
        <port name="ext_out" width="8" direction="in" />
        <port name="ext_rdwr" width="1" direction="in" />
        <port name="m" width="1" direction="in" />
        <port name="nelem" width="16" direction="in" />
        <port name="rwrite2m2" width="16" direction="out" />
        <port name="rwrite2m3" width="16" direction="out" />
        <port name="s" width="1" direction="in" />
        <signal name="bitcnt" width="4" />
        <signal name="br" width="8" />
        <signal name="cnt" width="8" />
        <signal name="cnt_elem" width="16" />
        <signal name="cnt_m1_m3" width="16" />
        <signal name="cnt_m2" width="16" />
        <signal name="m1" width="8" size="65536" />
        <signal name="m2" width="8" size="65536" />
        <signal name="m3" width="8" size="65536" />
        <signal name="mac1" width="16" />
        <signal name="mac2" width="16" />
        <signal name="rbyte" width="8" />
        <signal name="rd" width="8" />
        <signal name="relem" width="16" />
        <signal name="rfilelength" width="16" />
        <signal name="rlengthd" width="8" />
        <signal name="rmask" width="8" />
        <signal name="rmax" width="8" />
        <signal name="rmin" width="8" />
```

```
        <signal name="rt1" width="8" />
        <signal name="rt2" width="8" />
        <signal name="rtemp1" width="16" />
        <signal name="shcnt" width="8" />
        <variable name="m1_address" width="16" />
        <variable name="m2_address" width="16" />
        <variable name="m3_address" width="16" />
    </declarations>
    <required_libraries>
        <vhdl>
            <library name="my_package" />
        </vhdl>
    </required_libraries>
</functional_specifications>
```

Figure 10. Functional Specifications for *Codec*

Functional design at High level (file *Fincmi.vhd* constructed by Synthagate) is presented on Fig. 11. It is not a small design – file contains 761 lines.

Refer to Figure 11 (Chapter 5) in HLS-Figures-and-Tables.pdf

Figure 11. High level synthesis for *Codec*

5.3 RTL Synthesis

Here I strongly advise you to come back to Sections 3.1.3 – 3.1.6 to remember how to construct the connection graph, the list of parallel microoperations, the graph of incompatibility and multiplexers. I will give here the design of three MUXes and direct connections only for more interesting case – for 8-bit connections. Nevertheless, you can construct the others beginning from Functional ASM table in Fig. 12. In this design, we have one Mux for each of the following connections – 1-bit, 4-bit and 7-bit.

```
Y1    y1     0    codcomplete:=1
      y2    16    rwrite2m2:=cnt_m2

Y2    y3     0    codcomplete:=0
      y4    16    relem:=nelem

Y3    y5     0    decodcomplete:=1
      y6    16    rwrite2m3:=cnt_m1_m3

Y4    y7     0    decodcomplete:=0

Y5    y8     0    cnt_m1_m3:=cnt_m1_m3+1

Y6    y9     8    ext_in:=m3[m3_address]
      y10   16    m3_address:=ext_adr

Y7    y10   16    m3_address:=ext_adr
```

Y8	y11	8	m1[m1_address]:=ext_out
	y12	16	m1_address:=ext_adr
Y9	y13	16	m2_address:=ext_adr
Y10	y14	8	ext_in:=m2[m2_address]
	y13	16	m2_address:=ext_adr
Y11	y15	16	rfilelength:=cnt_m1_m3
Y12	y16	0	mac1:=0
	y17	0	shcnt:=0
Y13	y18	0	cnt:=cnt+1
Y14	y19	8	br:=x"ff"
	y20	0	cnt:=0
	y21	0	cnt_m2:=0
	y22	0	mac2:=0
Y15	y23	16	cnt_m1_m3:=tempReg16_1
Y16	y24	4	alu8_1_ctr:="0010"
	y25	8	alu8_1_in1:=rt1
	y26	8	alu8_1_in2:=rmin
	y27	0	cnt_m1_m3:=cnt_m1_m3-1
	y28	8	rt2:=alu8_1_out
Y17	y29	0	cnt_elem:=cnt_elem+1
Y18	y30	8	rt1:=br
Y19	y7	0	decodcomplete:=0
	y22	0	mac2:=0
Y20	y31	8	rt2:=br
Y21	y32	0	cnt_elem:=0
Y22	y33	8	br:=rmin
Y23	y34	0	cnt_m2:=cnt_m2+1
	y35	8	m2[m2_address]:=br
	y36	16	m2_address:=mac2
Y24	y37	0	mac2:=mac2+1
Y25	y38	7	rbyte(7-1):=tempReg8_1(7-1)
	y39	1	rbyte(0):=tempReg8_1(0)
Y26	y40	0	bitcnt:=0
	y41	7	rbyte(7-1):="0000000"
	y42	1	rbyte(0):=0

Y27	y43	8	br:=rbyte
Y28	y44	0	bitcnt:=bitcnt+1
	y45	0	shcnt:=shcnt+1
Y29	y17	0	shcnt:=0
Y30	y46	8	rt2:=tempReg8_1
Y31	y47	1	rbyte(0):=1
Y32	y48	4	alu8_1_ctr:="0011"
	y49	8	alu8_1_in1:=rmask
	y50	8	alu8_1_in2:=rt2
	y51	8	rt1:=alu8_1_out
Y33	y52	8	rmask:=tempReg8_1
Y34	y53	16	mac1:=rtemp1
	y54	8	rmask:=x"01"
	y17	0	shcnt:=0
Y35	y55	8	br:=m1[m1_address]
	y56	0	mac1:=mac1+1
Y36	y57	16	m1_address:=mac1
Y37	y32	0	cnt_elem:=0
	y58	16	rtemp1:=mac1
Y38	y24	4	alu8_1_ctr:="0010"
	y59	8	alu8_1_in1:=rmax
	y26	8	alu8_1_in2:=rmin
	y60	8	rd:=alu8_1_out
Y39	y61	8	rmin:=br
Y40	y62	8	rmax:=br
Y41	y29	0	cnt_elem:=cnt_elem+1
	y62	8	rmax:=br
	y61	8	rmin:=br
Y42	y63	8	br:=m2[m2_address]
	y37	0	mac2:=mac2+1
Y43	y36	16	m2_address:=mac2
Y44	y64	4	alu8_1_ctr:="0001"
	y65	8	alu8_1_in1:=rbyte
	y26	8	alu8_1_in2:=rmin
	y66	8	br:=alu8_1_out
	y17	0	shcnt:=0
Y45	y29	0	cnt_elem:=cnt_elem+1

```
         y41    7     rbyte(7-1):="0000000"
         y42    1     rbyte(0):=0

Y46      y40    0     bitcnt:=0

Y47      y67    8     rlengthd:=br
         y68    8     rmask:=x"80"
         y17    0     shcnt:=0

Y48      y8     0     cnt_m1_m3:=cnt_m1_m3+1
         y69    8     m3[m3_address]:=br
         y70   16     m3_address:=mac1
Y49      y56    0     mac1:=mac1+1

Y50      y71    8     rd:=tempReg8_1
Y51      y20    0     cnt:=0
         y32    0     cnt_elem:=0

Y52      y72    8     br:=cnt
         y73    8     rlengthd:=cnt

Y53      y74    4     alu8_1_ctr:="1100"
         y75    8     alu8_1_in1:=rd
         y76    8     alu8_1_in2:=x"01"
         y77    8     tempReg8_1:=alu8_1_out

Y54      y78    4     alu8_1_ctr:="1010"
         y65    8     alu8_1_in1:=rbyte
         y76    8     alu8_1_in2:=x"01"
         y77    8     tempReg8_1:=alu8_1_out

Y55      y78    4     alu8_1_ctr:="1010"
         y79    8     alu8_1_in1:=rt2
         y76    8     alu8_1_in2:=x"01"
         y77    8     tempReg8_1:=alu8_1_out

Y56      y78    4     alu8_1_ctr:="1010"
         y49    8     alu8_1_in1:=rmask
         y76    8     alu8_1_in2:=x"01"
         y45    0     shcnt:=shcnt+1
         y77    8     tempReg8_1:=alu8_1_out

Y57      y80    4     alu16_1_ctr:="0010"
         y81   16     alu16_1_in1:=cnt_m1_m3
         y82   16     alu16_1_in2:=relem
         y83   16     tempReg16_1:=alu16_1_out
```

Figure 12. Functional ASM Table Funcmi.mrk

The 8-bit connection graph is on Fig. 13, the list of parallel microoperations for 8-bit connections before and after considering direct connections – on Fig. 14.

```
weight : sources                    targets : weight
     5 : alu8_1_out                      br : 1
                                         rd : 1
                                        rt1 : 2
                                        rt2 : 1
                                 tempReg8_1 : 0

     3 : br                 m2[m2_address]  : 0
                            m3[m3_address]  : 0
                                  rlengthd  : 1
                                      rmax  : 0
                                      rmin  : 0
                                       rt1  : 1
                                       rt2  : 1

     2 : cnt                            br  : 1
                                  rlengthd  : 1

     0 : ext_out            m1[m1_address]  : 0

     3 : m1[m1_address]                 br  : 3

     8 : m2[m2_address]                 br  : 7
                                    ext_in  : 1

     1 : m3[m3_address]             ext_in  : 1

     4 : rbyte                  alu8_1_in1  : 3
                                        br  : 1

     1 : rd                     alu8_1_in1  : 1

     3 : rmask                  alu8_1_in1  : 3

     1 : rmax                   alu8_1_in1  : 1

     5 : rmin                   alu8_1_in2  : 3
                                        br  : 2

     1 : rt1                    alu8_1_in1  : 1

     4 : rt2                    alu8_1_in1  : 2
                                alu8_1_in2  : 2

     4 : tempReg8_1                     rd  : 1
                                     rmask  : 1
                                       rt2  : 2

     7 : x"01"                  alu8_1_in2  : 6
                                     rmask  : 1
```

```
1 : x"80"                    rmask : 1

1 : x"ff"                       br : 1
```

Figure 13. 8-bit Connection graph for Codec

```
Parallel Microoperations before considering direct connections:
         Y16       : y25     alu8_1_in1:=rt1
                     y26     alu8_1_in2:=rmin
                     y28     rt2:=alu8_1_out

         Y32       : y49     alu8_1_in1:=rmask
                     y50     alu8_1_in2:=rt2
                     y51     rt1:=alu8_1_out

         Y38       : y26     alu8_1_in2:=rmin
                     y59     alu8_1_in1:=rmax
                     y60     rd:=alu8_1_out
         Y41       : y61     rmin:=br
                     y62     rmax:=br

         Y44       : y26     alu8_1_in2:=rmin
                     y65     alu8_1_in1:=rbyte
                     y66     br:=alu8_1_out

         Y47       : y67     rlengthd:=br
                     y68     rmask:=x"80"

         Y52       : y72     br:=cnt
                     y73     rlengthd:=cnt

         Y53       : y75     alu8_1_in1:=rd
                     y76     alu8_1_in2:=x"01"
                     y77     tempReg8_1:=alu8_1_out

         Y54       : y65     alu8_1_in1:=rbyte
                     y76     alu8_1_in2:=x"01"
                     y77     tempReg8_1:=alu8_1_out

         Y55       : y76     alu8_1_in2:=x"01"
                     y77     tempReg8_1:=alu8_1_out
                     y79     alu8_1_in1:=rt2

         Y56       : y49     alu8_1_in1:=rmask
                     y76     alu8_1_in2:=x"01"
                     y77     tempReg8_1:=alu8_1_out


Parallel Microoperations after considering direct connections:


         Y16       : y25     alu8_1_in1:=rt1
                     y26     alu8_1_in2:=rmin
                     y28     rt2:=alu8_1_out
```

```
Y32        : y49     alu8_1_in1:=rmask
             y50     alu8_1_in2:=rt2
             y51     rt1:=alu8_1_out

Y38        : y26     alu8_1_in2:=rmin
             y59     alu8_1_in1:=rmax
             y60     rd:=alu8_1_out

Y44        : y26     alu8_1_in2:=rmin
             y65     alu8_1_in1:=rbyte
             y66     br:=alu8_1_out

Y47        : y67     rlengthd:=br
             y68     rmask:=x"80"

Y52        : y72     br:=cnt
             y73     rlengthd:=cnt

Y53        : y75     alu8_1_in1:=rd
             y76     alu8_1_in2:=x"01"

Y54        : y65     alu8_1_in1:=rbyte
             y76     alu8_1_in2:=x"01"

Y55        : y76     alu8_1_in2:=x"01"
             y79     alu8_1_in1:=rt2

Y56        : y49     alu8_1_in1:=rmask
             y76     alu8_1_in2:=x"01"
```

Figure 14. Parallel microoperations before and after considering direct connections

After the considering direct connections microinstruction (operator) Y41 and one microoperation in microinstructions Y53 – Y56 were deleted.

The graph of incompatibility (Fig. 15) was constructed from the connection graph (Fig. 13) and the list of parallel microinstructions (Fig. 14). 8-bit MUXes and direct connections are shown in Fig. 16.

```
alu8_1_in1 -> alu8_1_in2, br, rd, rt1, rt2
( rbyte, rd, rmask, rmax, rt1, rt2 )

alu8_1_in2 -> alu8_1_in1, br, rd, rt1, rt2
( rmin, rt2, x"01" )

br -> alu8_1_in1, alu8_1_in2
( alu8_1_out, cnt, m1[m1_address], m2[m2_address], rbyte, rmin, x"ff"
)

rd -> alu8_1_in1, alu8_1_in2
( alu8_1_out, tempReg8_1 )
```

```
rt1 -> alu8_1_in1, alu8_1_in2
( alu8_1_out, br )

rt2 -> alu8_1_in1, alu8_1_in2
( alu8_1_out, br, tempReg8_1 )

rlengthd -> rmask
( br, cnt )

rmask -> rlengthd
( tempReg8_1, x"01", x"80" )

ext_in -> ( m2[m2_address], m3[m3_address] )
```

Figure 15. Graph of Incompatibility for 8-bit connections

```
MUX3
   OUTPUT:
      alu8_1_in1
      rlengthd
    INPUT:
      rbyte                  3    000     in0    alu8_1_in1
      rmask                  3    001     in1    alu8_1_in1
      rt2                    2    010     in2    alu8_1_in1
      rd                     1    100     in4    alu8_1_in1
      cnt                    1    011     in3    rlengthd
      rmax                   1    101     in5    alu8_1_in1
      rt1                    1    110     in6    alu8_1_in1
      br                     1    111     in7    rlengthd

MUX4
   OUTPUT:
      br
      ext_in
      rd
      rmask
      rt1
      rt2
    INPUT:
      m2[m2_address]         8    0000    in0    br
                                                 ext_in
      alu8_1_out             5    0001    in1    br
                                                 rd
                                                 rt1
                                                 rt2
      tempReg8_1             4    0010    in2    rd
                                                 rmask
                                                 rt2
      m1[m1_address]         3    0100    in4    br
      rmin                   2    1000    in8    br
      br                     2    0011    in3    rt1
                                                 rt2
      rbyte                  1    0101    in5    br
```

```
      cnt                     1    0110      in6    br
      m3[m3_address]          1    1001      in9    ext_in
      x"01"                   1    1010      in10   rmask
      x"80"                   1    0111      in7    rmask
      x"ff"                   1    1011      in11   br


MUX5
   OUTPUT:
      alu8_1_in2
    INPUT:
      x"01"                   6    00        in0    alu8_1_in2
      rmin                    3    01        in1    alu8_1_in2
      rt2                     2    10        in2    alu8_1_in2

DIRECT CONNECTIONS:

        SOURCES                         TARGETS

     alu8_1_out                      tempReg8_1

             br                  m2[m2_address]
                                 m3[m3_address]
                                           rmax
                                           rmin

        ext_out                  m1[m1_address]
```

Figure 16. 8-bit MUXes and direct connections

External specifications (174 lines) are in Fig. 17. Data path for this design (Fig. 18) contains 23 components, including Altera's memory. The total number of instantiated components is equal to 50. VHDL code for the Control unit is in Fig. 19. The top design, combining Control unit and Data path is shown in Fig. 20.

```
<external_specifications xmlns="ExtSpec">
    <essential_files>
        <txt path="Funcmi_t.txt" />
        <tab path="Structm.tab" />
        <mrk path="Funcmi_t.mrk" />
        <spec path="Funcmi_t.spec" />
        <mux_files>
            <mux path="funcmi_t1b-mux.xml" bits="1" />
            <mux path="funcmi_t4b-mux.xml" bits="4" />
            <mux path="funcmi_t7b-mux.xml" bits="7" />
            <mux path="funcmi_t8b-mux.xml" bits="8" />
                  <mux path="funcmi_t16b-mux.xml" bits="16" />
        </mux_files>
    </essential_files>
    <settings>
        <bit_range direction="Down" />
```

```
</settings>
<dp_to_out_and_out_to_dp>
    <signal name="clk" in_or_out="in" width="1" />
    <signal name="rst" in_or_out="in" width="1" />
    <signal name="codcomplete" in_or_out="out" width="1" />
    <signal name="decodcomplete" in_or_out="out" width="1" />
    <signal name="ext_adr" in_or_out="in" width="16" />
    <signal name="ext_in" in_or_out="out" width="8" />
    <signal name="rWrite2M2" in_or_out="out" width="16" />
        <signal name="rWrite2M3" in_or_out="out" width="16" />
        <signal name="ext_out" in_or_out="in" width="8" />
    <signal name="nelem" in_or_out="in" width="16" />
</dp_to_out_and_out_to_dp>

  <additional>
        <mo width="1">    clock:=clk  </mo>
  </additional>

  <components>
    <external>

  <!-- Add external components (and their path) that you would
  like to use in your design -->


  <component  path="Components\mem.vhd"     global="clock"    >
        <class name="ramAlt">
              <signal name="%name%_address" />
              <signal     name="%name%[%name%_address]" />
              <signal     name="%name%_wren"                    />
              <signal     name="%name%[%name%_address]"         />
        </class>
        <instances>
              <instance   name="m1"         />
              <instance   name="m2"         />
              <instance   name="m3"         />
        </instances>
              </component>
        </external>
    <automatic>
        <generator type="rsff" global="clk, rst">
            <class>
                <signal name="%name%_reset" />
                <signal name="%name%_set" />
                <signal name="%name%" />
            </class>
            <instances>
                <instance name="codcomplete" />
                <instance name="decodcomplete" />
            </instances>
        </generator>
        <generator type="register" global="clk, rst">
            <class>
                <signal name="%name%" />
```

```
            <signal name="%name%_en" />
            <signal name="%name%" />
        </class>
        <instances>
            <instance name="rmask" />
            <instance name="rmax" />
            <instance name="rmin" />
            <instance name="rt1" />
            <instance name="rt2" />
            <instance name="br" />
            <instance name="rtemp1" />
            <instance name="rbyte" />
            <instance name="rd" />
            <instance name="relem" />
            <instance name="rlengthd" />
            <instance name="rfilelength" />
            <instance name="rwrite2m2" />
            <instance name="rwrite2m3" />
            <instance name="tempreg16_1" />
            <instance name="tempreg8_1" />

        </instances>
    </generator>
    <generator type="counter_ps" global="clk, rst">
        <class>
            <signal name="%name%_en" />
            <signal name="%name%_reset" />
            <signal name="%name%_count" />
            <signal name="%name%" />
            <signal name="%name%" />
        </class>
        <instances>
            <instance name="mac1" />
        </instances>
    </generator>
      <generator type="counter_pm" global="clk, rst">
        <class>
            <signal name="%name%_en" />
            <signal name="%name%_count" />
            <signal name="%name%_rcount" />
            <signal name="%name%" />
            <signal name="%name%" />
        </class>
        <instances>
            <instance name="cnt_m1_m3" />
        </instances>
    </generator>
    <generator type="countero_ps" global="clk, rst">
        <class>
            <signal name="%name%_reset" />
            <signal name="%name%_count" />
            <signal name="%name%" />
        </class>
        <instances>
```

```
            <instance name="shcnt" />
            <instance name="bitcnt" />
            <instance name="cnt" />
                      <instance name="cnt_m2" />
            <instance name="cnt_elem" />
            <instance name="mac2" />
        </instances>
    </generator>
    <generator type="generic_comparator" global="clk, rst">
        <class>
            <signal name="%name%_in1" />
            <signal name="%name%_in2" />
            <signal name="%name%_out" />
        </class>
        <instances>
            <instance name="comp4_12" />
            <instance name="comp8_3" />
            <instance name="comp8_4" />
            <instance name="comp8_6" />
            <instance name="comp8_9" />
            <instance name="comp8_10" />
            <instance name="comp8_11" />
            <instance name="comp8_13" />
            <instance name="comp8_14" />
            <instance name="comp16_1" />
            <instance name="comp16_2" />
            <instance name="comp16_7" />
        </instances>
    </generator>
    <generator type="generic_comparator_alu" global="clk,
                                                      rst">
        <class>
            <signal name="%name%_in1" />
            <signal name="%name%_in2" />
            <signal name="%name%_in3" />
            <signal name="%name%_out" />
        </class>
        <instances>
            <instance name="comp8_8" />
            <instance name="comp16_5" />
        </instances>
    </generator>
          <generator type="alu" global="clk, rst">
        <class>
            <signal name="%name%_in1" />
            <signal name="%name%_in2" />
            <signal name="%name%_ctr" />
            <signal name="%name%_out" />
        </class>
        <instances>
            <instance name="alu8_1" />
            <instance name="alu16_1" />
        </instances>
    </generator>
```

```
        </automatic>
    </components>
</external_specifications>
```

Figure 17. External Specifications in XML

Refer to Figure 18 (Chapter 5) in HLS-Figures-and-Tables.pdf

Figure 18. Data Path

Refer to Figure 19 (Chapter 5) in HLS-Figures-and-Tables.pdf

Figure 19. Control Unit

Refer to Figure 20 (Chapter 5) in HLS-Figures-and-Tables.pdf

Figure 20. Top as a composition of Control Unit and Data Path

The whole design from ASM to RTL took 6.5 seconds. Here the time report from Synthagate is: **HLS Total Time: 00:00:06.4090521**

6 CASE STUDY. DESIGN OF ROBOT

This Chapter was written together with Dr. Benjamin Abramov. Sapper robot was designed as a versatile platform for teaching of High level and Register Transfer Level of digital systems. The robot executes the following missions: in a limited area (3 m on 3m), put the target object (a cube of 10 cm edge). This cube is seen from any point of the mission arena, and the robot can drive up to it from any side. Cube and the robot can be installed anywhere in the arena to meet the above conditions.

After pressing the start button, the robot starts to scan the scene (turning on the spot and sending signals to the distance sensor). In the case of target object detection at a distance no more than 2.5 m, the robot starts moving to it with the speed depending on the distance to the object. Reaching the distance less than 20 cm robot stops (end of mission). If the desired object cannot be found (complete scan with a turn of 360 degrees) the mission will be finished as well.

Don't worry if you didn't understand the behavior of this robot, because you never designed robots. Only follow the design process below beginning from ASM in Fig. 3.

The simplified view of Robot is shown in Fig. 1.

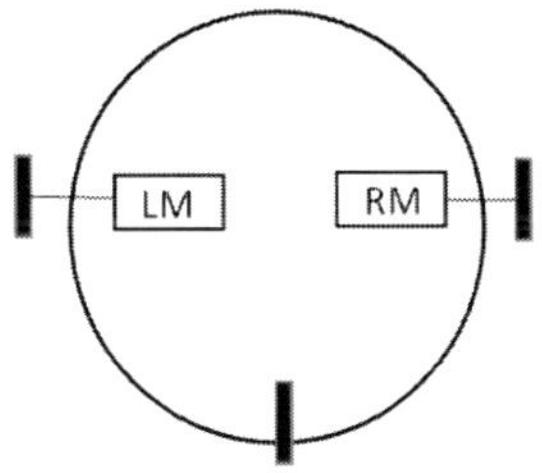

Figure 1. A Sapper Robot – simplified view

Table 1. Control signals of DC motor

PWM	C1	C2	Action
-	0	0	Passive stop. Motion short time continues by inertia
active	0	1	Clockwise rotation
active	1	0	Counter-clockwise rotation
-	1	1	Active stop, motor is blocked

The robot is mounted on a circular base of 30 cm diameter. It has two DC motors, designated as *LM* (left motor) and *RM* (right motor). These two motors drive two independent front wheels. At the rear of the robot, uncontrolled driven wheel (freely rotatable around a vertical axis and establishes in the robot movement direction) is located. Both motors are controlled independently, speed control is performed by the modulated square wave (4 KHz frequency).

The desired speed of the robot can be changed by the control signal duty cycle (Pulse width modulation – *PWM*). Moreover, each motor receives a pair of signals *C1* and *C2* specified in Table 1.

The plane orientation is carried out by two sensors, an ultra-sonic distance sensor and a digital compass. The distance sensor receives a *trigger* signal and returns the *echo* signal. Timing diagrams of those signals are shown in Fig. 2. The digital compass works in a similar mode. The compass is used to determine the azimuth and keeps correct direction during the robot movement.

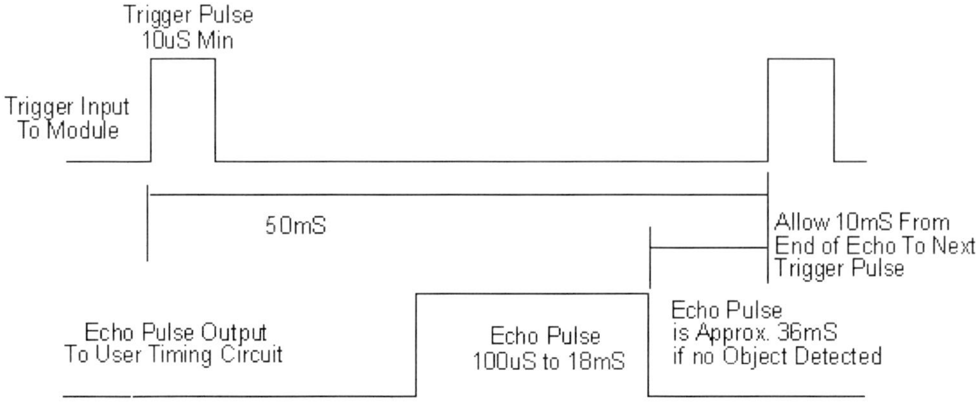

Figure 2. Timing diagram of Ultra-sonic distance sensor

6.1 Algorithmic State Machines for Robot

The main ASM for Robot is shown in Fig. 3.

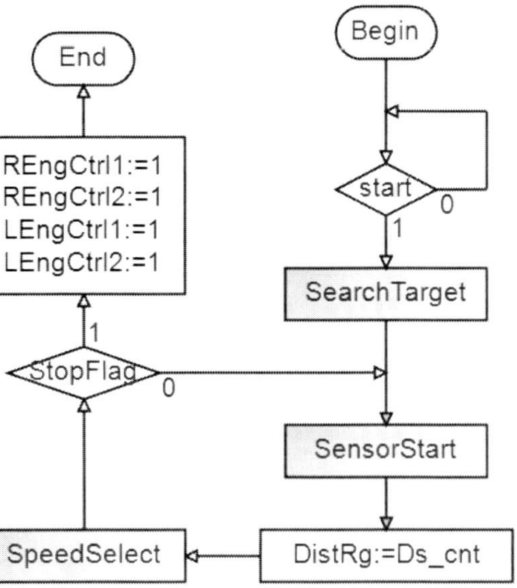

Figure 3. The main ASM of *Robot*

Generalized operators *SearchTarget* and *SensorStart* are presented on Fig. 4, *CompassRead*, *MoveForward* and *SpeedSelect* – on Fig. 5.

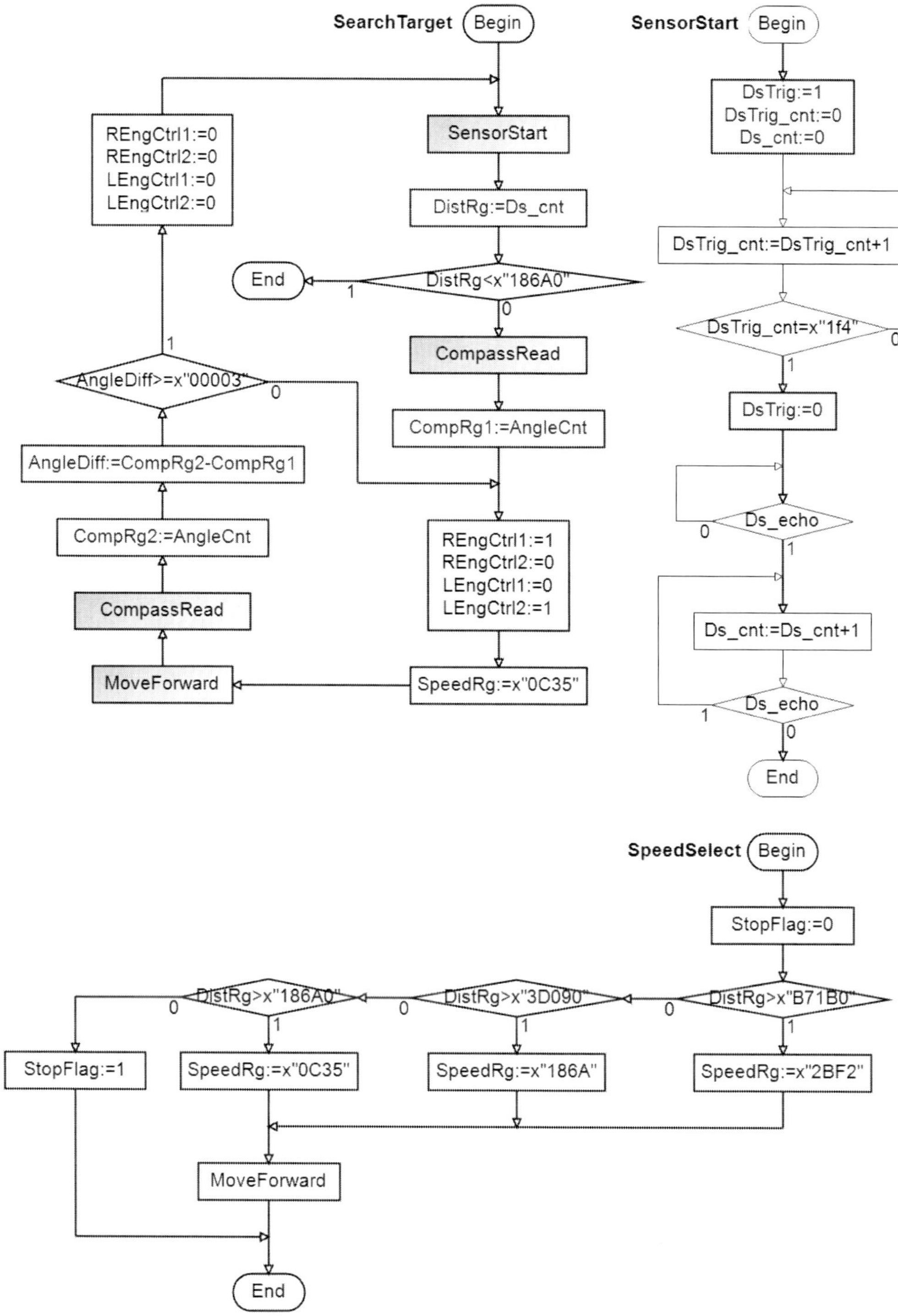

Figure 4. SubASMs of *Robot: SearchTarget, SensorStart* and *SpeedSelect*

The robot begins to work when the signal from the *start* button is equal to one (see the generalized operator *SeachTarget* at the left of Fig. 4). It implements distance readings (*SensorStart on Fig. 4*), compass reading (*CompassRead* on Fig. 5) and the turn on the spot.

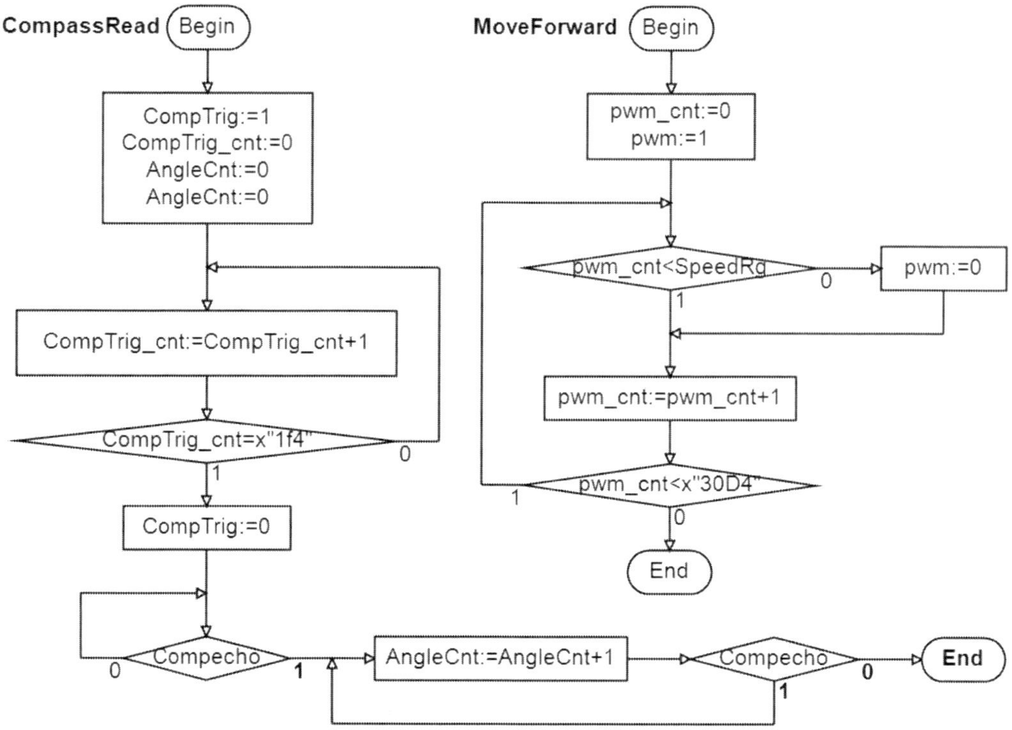

Figure 5. SubASMs of *Robot*: *CompassRead* and *MoveForward*

The procedure *CompassRead (*Fig. 5*)* is working in the similar way. Depending on the distance to the target, the procedure *SpeedSelect* (the same Fig. 5) sets constant values (duty cycle of PWM signal) into registers.

The subASM *SensorSart* controls the distance sensor by sending the *trigger* signal (see Fig. 2) and receiving the *echo* signal. The values of counters and comparators are selected in accordance with timing diagrams (Fig. 2) and the system clock frequency (50 MHz).

The sub-procedure *MoveForward* generates the *PWM* signal depending on the duty cycle chosen by procedure *SpeedSelect.* The period of *PWM* signal (250 us) is defined by a manufacturer.

ASM *Robot* as two-connected list is on Fig. 6. It was constructed after insertion of generalized operators from Fig. 4-5. Its file *Robot.txt* is presented on Fig. 7. ASM *Robot* contains twenty three operators (*Y1 – Y23*), thirty three microoperations (*y1 – y33*) and thirteen logical conditions (*x1, ..., x13*).

Refer to Figure 6 (Chapter 6) in HLS-Figures-and-Tables.pdf

Figure 6. Functional ASM as two-connected list

Refer to Figure 7 (Chapter 6) in HLS-Figures-and-Tables.pdf

Figure 7. List of Microinstructions, microoperations and logical conditions for *Robot*

6.2 High Level Synthesis

The Functional FSM Funcmi.t1 with 34 states is shown in Table 2.

Table 2. Transition table of Functional FSM for Robot

a1	a2	x2	y12y13y14	1
a1	a1	~x2	--	2
a2	a3	1	y16	3
a3	a4	x7	y11	4
a3	a3	~x7	y16	5
a4	a5	x6	y15	6
a4	a4	~x6	--	7
a5	a5	x6	y15	8
a5	a6	~x6	y1	9
a6	a7	x9	y12y13y14	10
a6	a8	~x9	y29y30y31y31	11
a7	a9	1	y16	12
a8	a10	1	y33	13
a9	a11	x7	y11	14
a9	a9	~x7	y16	15
a10	a12	x13	y28	16
a10	a10	~x13	y33	17
a11	a13	x6	y15	18
a11	a11	~x6	--	19
a12	a14	x12	y32	20
a12	a12	~x12	--	21
a13	a13	x6	y15	22
a13	a15	~x6	y1	23
a14	a14	x12	y32	24
a14	a16	~x12	y23	25
a15	a17	1	y6	26
a16	a18	1	y2y19y20y5	27
a17	a19	x5	y9	28
a17	a19	~x5*x4	y10	29
a17	a19	~x5*~x4*x3	y8	30
a17	a20	~x5*~x4*~x3	y7	31
a18	a21	1	y8	32
a19	a22	1	y26y27	33
a20	a1	x1	y2y3y4y5	34

a20	a7	~x1	y12y13y14	35
a21	a23	1	y26y27	36
a22	a24	x11	y25	37
a22	a25	~x11	y24	38
a23	a26	x11	y25	39
a23	a27	~x11	y24	40
a24	a24	x10*x11	y25	41
a24	a25	x10*~x11	y24	42
a24	a1	~x10*x1	y2y3y4y5	43
a24	a7	~x10*~x1	y12y13y14	44
a25	a24	1	y25	45
a26	a26	x10*x11	y25	46
a26	a27	x10*~x11	y24	47
a26	a28	~x10	y29y30y31y31	48
a27	a26	1	y25	49
a28	a29	1	y33	50
a29	a30	x13	y28	51
a29	a29	~x13	y33	52
a30	a31	x12	y32	53
a30	a30	~x12	--	54
a31	a31	x12	y32	55
a31	a32	~x12	y22	56
a32	a33	1	y17	57
a33	a34	x8	y18y19y20y21	58
a33	a18	~x8	y2y19y20y5	59
a34	a2	1	y12y13y14	60

Functional specifications constructed automatically by Synthagate are presented in file *Robot.spec* (Fig. 8). It contains 30 rows.

```
<functional_specifications>
      <declarations>
          <port name="compecho" width="1" direction="in" />
          <port name="comptrig" width="1" direction="out" />
          <port name="ds_echo" width="1" direction="in" />
          <port name="dstrig" width="1" direction="out" />
          <port name="lengctrl1" width="1" direction="out" />
          <port name="lengctrl2" width="1" direction="out" />
          <port name="pwm" width="1" direction="out" />
          <port name="rengctrl1" width="1" direction="out" />
          <port name="rengctrl2" width="1" direction="out" />
          <port name="start" width="1" direction="in" />
          <signal name="anglecnt" width="20" />
          <signal name="anglediff" width="20" />
          <signal name="comprg1" width="20" />
          <signal name="comprg2" width="20" />
          <signal name="comptrig_cnt" width="12" />
          <signal name="distrg" width="20" />
          <signal name="ds_cnt" width="20" />
          <signal name="dstrig_cnt" width="12" />
          <signal name="pwm_cnt" width="16" />
```

```
        <signal name="speedrg" width="16" />
        <signal name="stopflag" width="1" />
    </declarations>
    <required_libraries>
        <vhdl>
            <library name="my_package" />
        </vhdl>
    </required_libraries>
</functional_specifications>
```

Figure 8. Functional Specifications for *Robot*

Functional design at High Level (file *Fincmi.vhd* constructed by Synthagate) is presented on Fig. 9. It is not a very big design – file contains only 435 lines.

Refer to Figure 9 (Chapter 6) in HLS-Figures-and-Tables.pdf

Figure 9. High Level Synthesis for *Robot*

6.3 RTL Synthesis

Here, once again, I strongly advise you to come back to Sections 3.1.3 – 3.1.6 to call to memory how to construct the connection graph, the list of parallel microoperations, the graph of incompatibility, multiplexers and direct connections. As before, I begin from Functional ASM Table (Fig. 10).

Y1	y1	20	distrg:=ds_cnt
Y2	y2	0	lengctrl1:=1
	y3	0	lengctrl2:=1
	y4	0	rengctrl1:=1
	y5	0	rengctrl2:=1
Y3	y6	0	stopflag:=0
Y4	y7	0	stopflag:=1
Y5	y8	16	speedrg:=x"0c35"
Y6	y9	16	speedrg:=x"2bf2"
Y7	y10	16	speedrg:=x"186a"
Y8	y11	0	dstrig:=0
Y9	y12	0	ds_cnt:=0
	y13	0	dstrig:=1
	y14	0	dstrig_cnt:=0
Y10	y15	0	ds_cnt:=ds_cnt+1

Y11	y16	0	dstrig_cnt:=dstrig_cnt+1
Y12	y17	4	alu20_1_ctr:="0010"
	y18	20	alu20_1_in1:=comprg2
	y19	20	alu20_1_in2:=comprg1
	y20	20	anglediff:=alu20_1_out
Y13	y21	0	lengctrl1:=0
	y22	0	lengctrl2:=0
	y23	0	rengctrl1:=0
	y24	0	rengctrl2:=0
Y14	y25	20	comprg2:=anglecnt
Y15	y26	20	comprg1:=anglecnt
Y16	y21	0	lengctrl1:=0
	y3	0	lengctrl2:=1
	y4	0	rengctrl1:=1
	y24	0	rengctrl2:=0
Y17	y27	0	pwm:=0
Y18	y28	0	pwm_cnt:=pwm_cnt+1
Y19	y29	0	pwm:=1
	y30	0	pwm_cnt:=0
Y20	y31	0	comptrig:=0
Y21	y32	0	anglecnt:=0
	y33	0	comptrig:=1
	y34	0	comptrig_cnt:=0
Y22	y35	0	anglecnt:=anglecnt+1
Y23	y36	0	comptrig_cnt:=comptrig_cnt+1

Figure 10. Functional ASM Table

In this design we have here only one 16-bit Mux and direct 4-bit and 20-bit connections (Fig. 11- Fig.13).

SOURCES	TARGETS
"0010"	alu20_1_ctr

Figure 11. 4-bit direct connection in *Robot*

```
MUX0
   OUTPUT:
      speedrg
    INPUT:
```

```
x"0c35"               2    00       in0    speedrg
x"186a"               1    01       in1    speedrg
x"2bf2"               1    10       in2    speedrg
```

Figure 12. 16-bit connections in *Robot*

SOURCES	TARGETS
alu20_1_out	anglediff
anglecnt	comprg1 comprg2
comprg1	alu20_1_in2
comprg2	alu20_1_in1
ds_cnt	distrg

Figure 13. 20-bit direct connections in *Robot*

External specifications (108 lines) are in Fig. 14. Data path for this design (Fig. 15) contains 9 components. The total number of instantiated components is equal to 29. VHDL code for the Control unit is in Fig. 16. The top design, combining Control unit and Data path is shown in Fig. 17.

```
<external_specifications xmlns="ExtSpec">
    <essential_files>
        <txt path="Funcmi_t.txt" />
        <tab path="Structm.tab" />
        <mrk path="Funcmi_t.mrk" />
        <spec path="Funcmi_t.spec" />
        <mux_files>
            <mux path="funcmi_t16b-mux.xml" bits="16" />
            <mux path="funcmi_t20b-mux.xml" bits="20" />
            <mux path="funcmi_t4b-mux.xml" bits="4" />
        </mux_files>
    </essential_files>
    <settings>
        <bit_range direction="Down" />
    </settings>
    <dp_to_out_and_out_to_dp>
        <signal name="clk" in_or_out="in" width="1" />
        <signal name="rst" in_or_out="in" width="1" />
        <signal name="comptrig" in_or_out="out" width="1" />
        <signal name="dstrig" in_or_out="out" width="1" />
        <signal name="lengctrl1" in_or_out="out" width="1" />
        <signal name="lengctrl2" in_or_out="out" width="1" />
        <signal name="pwm" in_or_out="out" width="1" />
        <signal name="rengctrl1" in_or_out="out" width="1" />
        <signal name="rengctrl2" in_or_out="out" width="1" />
    </dp_to_out_and_out_to_dp>
    <components>
```

```
<external>
    <!-- Add external components (and their path) that you
          would like to use in your design -->
</external>
<automatic>
    <generator type="rsff" global="clk, rst">
        <class>
            <signal name="%name%_reset" />
            <signal name="%name%_set" />
            <signal name="%name%" />
        </class>
        <instances>
            <instance name="comptrig" />
            <instance name="dstrig" />
            <instance name="lengctrl1" />
            <instance name="lengctrl2" />
            <instance name="pwm" />
            <instance name="rengctrl1" />
            <instance name="rengctrl2" />
            <instance name="stopflag" />
        </instances>
    </generator>
    <generator type="register" global="clk, rst">
        <class>
            <signal name="%name%" />
            <signal name="%name%_en" />
            <signal name="%name%" />
        </class>
        <instances>
            <instance name="anglediff" />
            <instance name="comprg1" />
            <instance name="comprg2" />
            <instance name="distrg" />
            <instance name="speedrg" />
        </instances>
    </generator>
    <generator type="countero_ps" global="clk, rst">
        <class>
            <signal name="%name%_reset" />
            <signal name="%name%_count" />
            <signal name="%name%" />
        </class>
        <instances>
            <instance name="anglecnt" />
            <instance name="comptrig_cnt" />
            <instance name="ds_cnt" />
            <instance name="dstrig_cnt" />
            <instance name="pwm_cnt" />
        </instances>
    </generator>
    <generator type="generic_comparator" global="clk, rst">
        <class>
            <signal name="%name%_in1" />
            <signal name="%name%_in2" />
```

```
                <signal name="%name%_out" />
            </class>
            <instances>
                <instance name="comp12_4" />
                <instance name="comp12_9" />
                <instance name="comp16_7" />
                <instance name="comp16_8" />
                <instance name="comp20_1" />
                <instance name="comp20_2" />
                <instance name="comp20_3" />
                <instance name="comp20_5" />
                <instance name="comp20_6" />
            </instances>
        </generator>
        <generator type="alu" global="clk, rst">
            <class>
                <signal name="%name%_in1" />
                <signal name="%name%_in2" />
                <signal name="%name%_ctr" />
                <signal name="%name%_out" />
            </class>
            <instances>
                <instance name="alu20_1" />
            </instances>
        </generator>
    </automatic>
  </components>
</external_specifications>
```

Figure 14. External Specifications in XML

Refer to Figure 15 (Chapter 6) in HLS-Figures-and-Tables.pdf

Figure 15. Data Path

Refer to Figure 16 (Chapter 6) in HLS-Figures-and-Tables.pdf

Figure 16. Control Unit

Refer to Figure 17 (Chapter 6) in HLS-Figures-and-Tables.pdf

Figure 17. Top as a composition of Control Unit and Data Path

The whole design from ASM to RTL took 6.5 seconds. Here the time report from Synthagate is: **HLS Total Time: 00:00:04.3080431**

What next?

You can consider this book as a second part of my previous book, "*Finite State Machines and Algorithmic State Machines*" (https://www.synthezza.com/books).

This book contains 189 figures and 23 tables. For your convenience I have prepared a PDF file containing all the images and tables reference in this book. You can download it at www.synthezza.com/hls-figures-and-tables.

Thank you for reading my book. If you found it useful, please post your comments and reviews on Amazon. I read all your reviews, and I appreciate all your feedback. You can also send me comments to samary@synthezza.com. You can get more information and many more examples at www.synthezza.com.

Made in United States
North Haven, CT
05 November 2026

21771707R10113